T0247802

IMITATING CHRIST

IMITATING CHRIST

The Disputed Character of Christian Discipleship

LUKE TIMOTHY JOHNSON

William B. Eerdmans Publishing Company
Grand Rapids, Michigan

Wm. B. Eerdmans Publishing Co.
4035 Park East Court SE, Grand Rapids, Michigan 49546
www.eerdmans.com

Published 2024
Printed in the United States of America

30 29 28 27 26 25 24   1 2 3 4 5 6 7

ISBN 978-0-8028-8310-0

Library of Congress Cataloging-in-Publication Data

Names: Johnson, Luke Timothy, author.
Title: Imitating Christ : the disputed character of Christian discipleship /
    Luke Timothy Johnson.
Description: Grand Rapids, Michigan : William B. Eerdmans Publishing
    Company, 2024. | Includes bibliographical references and index. |
    Summary: "Luke Timothy Johnson explores the history and theology of
    discipleship"—Provided by publisher.
Identifiers: LCCN 2023051526 | ISBN 9780802883100 (hardcover) | ISBN
    9781467466479 (epub)
Subjects: LCSH: Christian life. | Social justice—Religious aspects—Chris-
    tianity. | BISAC: RELIGION / Christian Theology / History | RELIGION /
    Biblical Studies / History & Culture
Classification: LCC BV4501.3 .6343 2024 | DDC 248.4—dc23/eng/20240329
LC record available at https://lccn.loc.gov/2023051526

Contents

Preface

The terms "disciple" and "discipleship" are used so widely and indiscriminately among Christians that the reader of this book deserves some notice concerning its character. This is not a how-to manual for becoming a disciple oneself or helping others pursue that goal. Still less is it a guide to discipling folks within the church.

It is, rather, a historical and theological inquiry into the very nature of Christian discipleship, into the character of following Jesus or imitating Christ. The historical inquiry locates lines of continuity and discontinuity within hortatory literature from the New Testament to the twenty-first century, making the argument that the nineteenth and twentieth centuries—with the development of the social gospel and liberation theology—introduced a deep fissure within Christian understandings of discipleship. The theological inquiry tests the adequacy and cogency of conflicting views against the measure of Scripture.

Such an inquiry is pertinent when what it means to be an authentic Christian—a disciple—is in some quarters noisily disputed and in others quietly distorted. It is especially pertinent when church bodies seem determined to fight every battle except that of forming people into saints.

This study began as two McDonald lectures delivered at the Candler School of Theology in fall 2021, sponsored by the Alonzo McDonald Family Agape Foundation. Alongside the lectures, I worked with some twenty excellent theology students at Candler, reading with them through the spiritual classics of the Christian tradition. My thanks to those students who made such a daunting challenge enjoyable. My thanks also to Dean Jan Love, who invited me to serve as the McDonald chair, and to Associate Dean Jonathan Strom, who coordinated everything. Most especially, I thank Peter McDonald, who like his father, Alonzo, has been generous in supporting theological education that seeks to give glory to God.

As I worked on the shaping of this book, I benefited from conversations with friends, among whom I am happy to include Don Saliers, Christopher Holmes, Elizabeth Arnold, and Jarrett Knight. Finally, I must thank my editor at Eerdmans, James Ernest, for his patient endurance.

INTRODUCTION

Christianity is like its fellow Abrahamic traditions in this respect, that it asks of truly serious believers something more than mere membership, or a formal allegiance to a set of convictions, or even an observance of basic rules. It calls those once saved by God's grace to a further religious and moral engagement, which is broadly designated as discipleship. The disciple is a truly serious Christian, one who is deeply committed to the Christian way.

The English term "disciple" derives from the Latin *discipulus*, used by Saint Jerome's Vulgate to translate the Greek term *mathētēs*. In the New Testament, the term is found only in the narratives of the Four Gospels and the Acts of the Apostles to describe followers of Jesus as "learners" or "students."[1] The portrayal of Jesus as a teacher and of his followers as students finds antecedents in ancient Mediterranean culture. From Socrates forward, Greek and Roman philosophers shared their wisdom and virtue with eager young people whose devotion to their teacher embraced both their words and their manner of life (*anastrophē*).[2] Similarly,

---

1. The term appears some forty times in Mark, seventy-three times in Matthew, thirty-seven times in Luke, seventy-nine times in John, all with reference to followers of Jesus during his ministry, and twenty-eight times in Acts for followers of the resurrected Jesus. The real differences in the respective literary portrayal of the disciples were of no interest to those who read the New Testament seeking guidance for their lives; for a brief sketch of those differences, see Luke Timothy Johnson, *Living Jesus: Learning the Heart of the Gospel* (San Francisco: HarperSanFrancisco, 1998).

2. For the usage in Greco-Roman philosophical schools, see K. H. Rengstorf, "μαθητής," in *Theological Dictionary of the New Testament*, 10 vols., ed. Gerhard Kittel and Gerhard Friedrich, trans. Geoffrey W. Bromiley (Grand Rapids: Eerdmans, 1964–1976), 4:415–25.

1

the Jewish *talmidim* who sat at the feat of a rabbi memorized the sage's interpretations of law as well as the way he kept it (*halakah*).[3] The notion of imitation (*mimēsis*) is consequently ingredient to the ancient understanding of discipleship: such learning is not confined to words alone but involves a certain transformation in character. The philosopher and the sage present a model to their followers. Their manner of life states not simply "learn these things" but also "walk in the way I walk."[4] Matthew captures it perfectly when he has Jesus declare,

> Come to me, all who labor and are heavy laden, and I will give you rest. Take my yoke upon you, and learn from me, for I am gentle and lowly in heart, and you will find rest for your souls. For my yoke is easy and my burden is light. (Matt 11:28–30)

Now, it might be thought that in a tradition as ancient and intricately developed as Christianity, the nature of discipleship might be obvious or, at the very least, agreed upon by those who turn their thought to the subject. What is the telos of those who regard themselves as called by Christ and who choose to devote themselves to that vocation? For some nineteen centuries, in fact, there was such broad agreement among Christians.

But over the past two centuries, the understanding of discipleship has, among many Christians, changed dramatically, to the point that the meaning of following Jesus—something utterly basic—is a matter of disputation and even division among adherents of the world's largest religion. The causes and the shape of that disputation is the theme of this study.

My title comes from the fifteenth-century devotional classic composed in Latin by Thomas à Kempis (1380–1471) called *De imitatione Christi* (literally, "On the Imitation of Christ"), best known in English as *The Imitation of Christ*. The author was a member of a semimonastic religious order in

---

3. An introduction to rabbinic usage is found in Rengstorf, "μαθητής," *Theological Dictionary of the New Testament*, 4:426–441. The cultural context for the Markan portrayal of Jesus is well examined by Vernon K. Robbins, *Jesus the Teacher: A Socio-Rhetorical Interpretation of Mark* (Philadelphia: Fortress, 1984).

4. See, for example, the way the philosopher Epictetus presents himself as an example for his students (*Discourses* 3.22.45–49); see Luke Timothy Johnson, *Among the Gentiles: Greco-Roman Religion and Christianity*, Anchor (Yale) Bible Reference Library (New Haven: Yale University Press, 2009), 75–78.

the Netherlands called the Brethren of the Common Life, an order committed to the ideals of the late medieval spiritual movement called the *Devotio Moderna*. Thomas was an ordained priest and served a variety of roles, including novice master and prior. He was best known to his contemporaries as a superb copyist of manuscripts.[5] He wrote a number of short works, but none of them had the impact of this small volume that is arranged in four books.[6] Manuscript copies spread quickly but were soon surpassed by versions in print. Before 1650, the book had been printed over seven hundred times, and before 1700 was translated into thirteen languages. It now exists in some two thousand distinct editions.

Next to the Bible, the *Imitation* is arguably the most widely read and admired work of Christian spirituality. Saint Thomas More said it was one of three books that everyone ought to own.[7] Saint Ignatius of Loyola (1491–1556) read it daily.[8] John Wesley (1703–1791) considered it an admirable summary of the Christian life.[9] For Saint Thérèse of Lisieux, the *Imitation* was an early spiritual influence.[10] In the twentieth century, Thomas Merton and Dag Hammarskjöld were influenced by it.[11]

5. For biography, see "Thomas à Kempis," *The Catholic Encyclopedia*, https://new advent.org.

6. Books 1 and 2 ("Helpful Counsels of the Spiritual Life" and "Directives for the Interior Life") are mainly in the form of maxims. Books 3 and 4 ("On Interior Consolation" and "On the Blessed Sacrament") present dialogues between Jesus and the disciple.

7. See his *Confutatio* (against Tyndale, 1532), "Preface to the Christian Reader." See E. E. Reynolds, *Saint Thomas More* (New York: Kennedy, 1953), 236–37.

8. At Manresa, according to the memory of his followers, Ignatius kept only a New Testament and a copy of the *Imitation* in his room. They recall that "each day, after his meal, he would read a chapter in sequence. He would often also open at random and savor some verses." See H. Pinard de la Boullaye, SJ, *Saint Ignace de Loyola: Directeur d'Ames*, Les maitres de la spiritualité chrétienne (Aubier: Éditions Montaigne, 1946), vii.

9. Wesley recalls, "In the year 1726, I met with Kempis' *Christian Pattern*. The nature and extent of inward religion, the religion of the heart, now appeared to me in a stronger light than ever it had done before" (*A Plain Account of Christian Perfection*, section 3 [1777]). In 1735, Wesley himself published an *Extract of the Christian's Pattern: Or a Treatise on the Imitation of Christ of Thomas à Kempis*.

10. Thérèse began reading the *Imitation* when she was fourteen years old: "It was the only book which helped me for I had not yet discovered the treasures which are hidden in Sacred Scripture. I carried this little book around with me at all times" (*The Story of a Soul*, ch. 5).

11. For Merton, reading the *Imitation* was one of the precipitants of his conver-

Dietrich Bonhoeffer had the *Imitation* among his books in Tegel prison before his execution by the Nazis.[12] The list of admirers could be extended indefinitely.

The *Imitation* found such popularity because it communicated in a simple but powerful fashion what might be called the classic or perennial understanding of Christian discipleship, namely, that the goal of the dedicated Christian—the disciple—is the transformation of the self in the image of Christ. The *Imitation* makes no pretense of being original but offers itself simply and straightforwardly as a distillation of traditional Christian wisdom. It is animated throughout by certain core convictions: that the risen Christ is powerfully present among believers—above all in the Eucharist—and is both the source of salvation and the model for imitation; that the image of Christ to be imitated is presented in the words of Scripture, above all in the Gospels and the writings of Paul; that the judgment of God on the human heart is unerring; that human life is short and cannot be compared to eternity; that suffering with Christ in this life leads to a future life of blessedness with God; that humility, obedience, and charity are the dispositions that above all lead to perfection.

A taste of the *Imitation*'s approach can be gained by a handful of citations from book 1, indeed from its very first words:[13]

> Of the imitation of Christ and of contempt for the world and all its vanities. "He that followeth me shall not walk in darkness," saith the Lord. These are the words of Christ, and they teach us how far we must imitate His life and character, if we seek true illumination, and deliverance from all blindness of heart. Let it be our most earnest study, therefore, to dwell upon the life of Jesus Christ. (1.1.1)

---

sion. See *The Seven Storey Mountain* (New York: Harcourt & Brace, 1946), 216, 220. Hammarskjöld cites the *Imitation* twice in his *Markings* (New York: Knopf, 1964), 125, 132, and had it with him before his death in a plane crash. See Henry P. Van Dusen, *Dag Hammerskjold: The Statesman and His Faith* (New York: Harper & Row, 1964), 184–85.

12. See Eberhard Bethge, *Dietrich Bonhoeffer: A Biography*, trans. Eric Mosbacher et al., rev. and ed. Victoria J. Barnett (Minneapolis: Fortress, 2000), 943.

13. There are countless translations of the *Imitatio*. I use the robust version of William Benham (1831–1910), because, unlike some more recent versions, it does not soften Thomas's language. It can be accessed digitally at http://www.gutenberg.org.

Thomas writes, we understand, for those who, like himself, have committed themselves to this study that is the following of Christ:

> But there are many who, though they frequently hear the Gospel, yet feel but little longing after it, because they have not the mind of Christ. He, therefore, that will fully and with true wisdom understand the words of Christ, let him strive to conform his whole life to that mind of Christ. (1.1.2)

Notice that the understanding of the words of Christ demands a process of transformation into the mind of Christ through the "conforming of his whole life." In comparison with this endeavor, everything else is nugatory:

> I had rather feel contrition than be skillful in the definition thereof. If thou knewest the whole Bible, and the sayings of all the philosophers, what should all these profit thee without the love and grace of God? Vanity of vanities, all is vanity, save to love God, and Him only to serve. This is the highest wisdom, to cast the world behind us, and to reach forward to the heavenly kingdom. (1.1.3)

> He only is truly great who hath great charity. He is truly great who deemeth himself small, and counteth all height of honour as nothing. He is the truly wise man, who counteth all earthly things as dung that he may win Christ. And he is the truly learned man, who doeth the will of God, and forsaketh his own will. (1.3.6)

Thomas à Kempis perfectly expressed the traditional understanding of Christian discipleship as the transformation of the self in the image of Christ, an ideal stated poignantly by the French writer Leon Bloy (1846–1917), who declared, "The only real sadness, the only real failure, the only great tragedy in life, is not to become a saint."[14]

14. *La Femme Pauvre* (1897). Throughout this book, I use the term "saint" not in the sense of being canonized by the Vatican but in the sense of becoming a certain kind of transformed (holy) person. Thus Paul uses the language of saint or holy ones as a way of designating members of the church (for example, Rom 16:2; 1 Cor 6:1–2; 2 Cor 1:1; 9:12; Eph 1:15; Phil 4:21; Col 1:2) but also makes clear that God "calls" his readers to a

Yet one of the most prominent Roman Catholic theologians of the twentieth century, Hans Urs von Balthasar, harshly criticizes the *Imitation*. He says that it

> abstracts from the colourful multiplicity of the Bible . . . disregards the world, in all its richness, as a field for Christian activity . . . a subdued and melancholy resignation runs through the book . . . the individual is unaware that his love of God can only be fulfilled if it expands into love of neighbor and into the apostolate. All that remains is a flight from the world.[15]

Although Balthasar is himself profoundly traditional in many ways and is by no means antagonistic to Christianity's mystical and spiritual dimensions,[16] his critique of the *Imitation* (perhaps unintentionally) gives voice to what has emerged in the past two centuries as the second and competing vision of discipleship, which begins with a rejection of the first vision. For Balthasar, the *Imitation* is too little scriptural, too world-negating, too resigned, too individualistic, too contemplative, and too little actively engaged with the world.

Genuine discipleship, based on this critique, should be more world-affirming, more scriptural, more communal, and definitely more active: following Jesus means changing the world for the better; seeking the kingdom of God is working for a radically improved society. As one of the most influential shapers of this vision states, "Church and the State are alike but partial organizations of humanity for special ends. Together they serve what is greater than either: humanity. Their common aim is to transform humanity into the kingdom of God."[17]

---

process that leads to "sanctification"/"holiness" (see 1 Cor 1:2; 1 Thess 4:3; 5:23; 2 Thess 2:13; Rom 6:19, 22; Eph 5:6).

15. Hans Urs von Balthasar, *The Glory of the Lord: A Theological Aesthetics*, 7 vols., trans. E. Leiva-Merikakis (San Francisco: Ignatius, 1983–1991), 5:103–4.

16. See especially Karen Kilby, *Balthasar: A (Very) Critical Introduction* (Grand Rapids: Eerdmans, 2012).

17. As I will show later, Walter Rauschenbusch's *Christianity and the Social Crisis* (1907) is one of the decisive stages in the development of this vision of discipleship. The quotation (like all ascribed to him in this book) is drawn from the centenary edition edited by Paul Rauschenbusch that includes essays by contemporary thinkers: *Christianity and the Social Crisis in the 21st Century* (New York: HarperCollins, 2007), 308.

This second vision of discipleship, which emphasizes the transformation of the world or, more precisely, the transformation of society, has become ever more dominant among first-world Christians, above all those in the so-called first world who are the most affluent and the best educated. Within this population, indeed, the second vision threatens to displace the older, classical view entirely.

Remarkably, little serious attention seems to have been given to this quite astonishing development.[18] I speak of "disputed understandings of discipleship," but actual disputation among interested parties is largely absent. A massive tectonic shift in Christian self-understanding on this most basic of issues, namely, what is the character of discipleship, appears to have taken place without significant notice. Or perhaps better, when noticed, it is mainly celebrated, with little awareness of what might have been lost as well as gained in the shift.

My study is in part an intellectual history: how, after eighteen hundred years, did the universal understanding of discipleship as the transformation of the self change so dramatically over the course of two centuries among so many Christians? What factors, internal and external, were at work in this seismic change? But it is also in part a theological inquiry: what are the strengths and weaknesses of each conception of discipleship—and for that matter, what are the criteria for assessing strength and weaknesses? I will ask about the way each vision reads Scripture, about its theological premises and characteristic practices. What is at issue—or what should be at issue—is not which version is most popular in the present age, or most appeals to contemporary proclivities, but which corresponds more adequately to the truth of the gospel (Gal 2:5, 14).

Any serious inquiry ought to be driven in equal parts by intellectual curiosity and personal passion. Intellectual curiosity pursues a genuine puzzle that demands investigation; personal passion arises from the stake that the inquirer has in that pursuit. If there is only passion, then

---

18. I addressed the question in an inchoate fashion in *Faith's Freedom: A Classic Spirituality for Contemporary Christians* (Minneapolis: Fortress, 1990), but I am not aware of other efforts. In that effort, I proposed a classic understanding of discipleship located between gnostic and liberation understandings. In this book, I hope to advance a more subtle analysis. As I note in the first chapter, however, I leave aside consideration of the various manifestations of a gnostic spirituality, even though versions of it continue to appear. See my essay "A New Gnosticism: An Old Threat Made New," in *A Catholic Consciousness: Scripture, Theology, and the Church* (New York: Paulist, 2021), 195–206.

the danger is one of special pleading; but without passion there may be lack of genuine engagement. If there is only intellectual curiosity, then the danger is otiose abstraction; but without intellectual legitimacy, no real contribution can be made to human understanding. The topic of what constitutes genuine discipleship is one that should stir passion among those calling themselves Christian, and the fact that there is such profound disagreement among them concerning discipleship is a historical and theological problem of some significance.

My personal stake in the present inquiry is clear enough. I am a Roman Catholic who has lived his life for seventy-nine years with the firm and constant conviction that the point of being a Christian is to become a certain kind of person, a saint, and that any other standard for the success or failure of a human life is superficial by comparison. Becoming a saint, in my understanding, is not simply a matter of moral effort (the way we often think about human perfection) but above all a matter of responding to the word of God disclosed both in Scripture and in the specific circumstances of life. The saint is the person who progressively puts on the mind of Christ, by faithful obedience to the call of God, and self-emptying service to others in the grinding processes of quotidian existence. I continue to hold to this conviction and measure my life by this standard.[19]

But over a professional career of some fifty years as a professor of New Testament, I have also taught thousands of students preparing for ministry in Protestant churches, for ten years at Yale Divinity School and for twenty-four years at the Candler School of Theology.[20] Increasingly, I had the sense that my students and I were talking past each other. We did not share the same instinctive sense of sacrament and church. And when we talked about discipleship, we seemed to be operating within

19. The reader will certainly understand that the application of such measurement consistently indicates that my actual state of transformation is not far advanced! I should also note that the exciting reforms of the Second Vatican Council gave a sharper edge to the "service to others" dimension of discipleship without fundamentally challenging the vision of discipleship as transformation of persons in Christ.

20. In addition to these long-term placements, my interactions with ministerial students included shorter gigs at Columbia School of Theology, Virginia Theological Seminary, Boston College Institute of Religion, and Notre Dame University, as well as hundreds of other encounters and conversations generated by lectures. See *The Mind in Another Place: My Life as a Scholar* (Grand Rapids: Eerdmans, 2022).

quite different spheres. Whereas my default understanding of discipleship was becoming a saint, this language was utterly strange to them. They thought of discipleship in terms of changing the oppressive systems of society, and this understanding was abetted by the steady diet of liberation discourse they were fed in theology and ethics classes. When students at Yale and Candler became aware of spirituality, they were eager to experience it, but (as in the classes taught by Henri Nouwen at Yale Divinity School) it was a boutique add-on rather than the heart of their theological education.

For a time, I thought that the source of my cognitive dissonance was the simple disjunction between me being Catholic and them being Protestant. Catholics had saints, Protestants social progress. But then I saw that a great deal of liberation theology was Catholic in origin, and, even more puzzling, my reading in Reformation and post-Reformation literature clearly indicated that the traditional understanding of discipleship as personal transformation continued in Protestantism well through the eighteenth century. Something other than denominational difference was at work.

When I had the opportunity to work at the question of discipleship directly with a group of fine ministerial students at Candler last year, my sense of cognitive dissonance was confirmed. Not only were the students completely unaware of the rich tradition of Christian devotional literature, but when they read it, they were puzzled, perplexed, and even dismayed: How could those ancient writers have written the way they did, think the way they did, have those premises so alien from their own, commit their lives to practices of which they had scarcely heard? Prayer without ceasing, the practice of the presence of God, physical asceticism, self-sacrifice—these little accorded with a view of discipleship as a moderately normal life whose most demanding expression was the evangelizing of others. My students were sincerely committed believers—they were, after all, seeking to become leaders of other believers—yet they were unaware of the largest part of the Christian tradition; moreover, they lacked any sense that their default understanding of discipleship was both recent and superficial.

My study begins with historical exposition: How did the first vision of discipleship find support in Scripture and liturgy? What were its various modalities or expressions across the centuries? What were the intellectual and social factors involved in the eclipse of that first vision and the dominance of the second? Then, I turn to a theological analysis of the respective visions: how and how well does each read Scripture? What are the theological premises of each, and what is their coherence and cogency? How theologically convincing are the characteristic practices of each? Is the kingdom of God more likely to be realized by prayer or by politics? Finally, I ask whether and in what way the two visions can learn from each other: is a richer and more harmonious vision of discipleship possible?

The materials for the study are literary. I look at writings composed by Christians for the instruction or exhortation of other Christians. Such devotional literature is the obvious source for discerning the understanding of discipleship in diverse periods and circumstances, for the point of instruction and exhortation is precisely to become more fully a follower of Jesus. No pretense of sociological adequacy can thereby be claimed. The writings that exhibit a martyr piety tell us nothing about the attitudes or actions of most pre-Constantinian Christians. But they do tell us a great deal about those who identified true discipleship precisely with the willingness to suffer and die in imitation of Jesus. The literature concerning discipleship, both ancient and modern, is directed to those whose consciousness of God's call and whose desire to live out that call is exceptional.

This hortatory literature is broadly European and American, for two basic reasons. The first and most obvious is that the so-called first world is where the disjunction in the understanding of discipleship has taken place. The second is that the bulk of literature under consideration is European and American. Yes, Origen and Augustine and the desert fathers and mothers were located in North Africa, and yes, John Climacus and the Hesychasts were broadly Byzantine, but their writings in Greek fed the Latin West and became an integral part of the tradition that shaped Thomas à Kempis and Luther alike. Even more pertinently, it was the intellectual and political upheavals in Europe and America that abetted the rejection of the older vision of discipleship and abetted the propagation of the newer.

1

Discipleship as Transformation of Self

The classical vision of discipleship is based squarely on the careful reading of Scripture, above all the New Testament. The charge made by some that pre-Reformation Christians were somehow "not biblical" is a canard. *The Imitation of Christ*, for example, is saturated with scriptural language, which is not surprising, given the fact that à Kempis was reputed to have copied the whole Bible through four times! Indeed, never has "the world imagined by Scripture" been so fully inhabited as by believers from the first through the sixteenth centuries.[1] For such believers, there was no gap between the world portrayed by Scripture and the empirical world. Their story was played out in the same imaginative (real) universe as had the story of Abraham and the story of Jesus. Precisely the degree to which believers saw themselves as still within the world of Scripture is one of the most difficult things for secularized present-day Christians to grasp. But if they fail to grasp this, then they miss everything.

Ancient believers found the story of Jesus—and by implication their own story—especially in the Four Gospels and the Letters of Paul (including Hebrews) and Peter. In the Gospels, especially the Synoptics, believers made the obvious identification between those called disciples in the narratives and themselves. Like Peter, James, and John, they also were called to "follow Jesus." Such identification was not a form of fantasy, because for them Jesus was not a figure of the past alone but was the risen Christ, powerfully present to them now through the Holy Spirit

1. For my language here, see Luke Timothy Johnson, "Imagining the World That Scripture Imagines," in *The Future of Catholic Biblical Scholarship: A Constructive Conversation* (with William S. Kurz) (Grand Rapids: Eerdmans, 2002), 119–42.

and calling them to follow him just as urgently as he had the ones who walked with him in Galilee.

THE NEW TESTAMENT WITNESS

In the Synoptic Gospels, believers could read how Jesus demanded of his disciples that they follow him (Matt 4:19; 8:19; 9:9; 10:38; 16:24; 19:21), and it was clear to those first readers that such following demanded a form of imitation, specifically an imitation of Jesus's self-sacrificial death. The Son of Man, he told his arrogant would-be students, did not come to be served but to serve and to give his life as a ransom for many (Mark 10:45). The Gospels show Jesus's manner of service, from his healings and exorcisms (Mark 2:1–3:6) to the multiplication of loaves for the hungry multitude (Mark 6:30–44), and the sharing of his own body and blood for the life of the world (Mark 14:22–25). They make unmistakably clear that the end of Jesus's earthly road of radical obedience and service was death on the cross (Mark 8:31; 9:30–31; 10:32–34; 15:1–39).

If believers after his death and resurrection heard the same call to follow him in their dramatically changed circumstances, then they needed to empty themselves through the same sort of radical obedience to God and self-donation to others. Luke's Gospel makes the demands of such discipleship starkly clear. Followers of Jesus must be willing to leave family and home (Luke 9:57–61) and their ordinary occupations (5:12, 27). They must live by the stringent teaching of the Sermon on the Mount/ Plain that is directed specifically at Jesus's "students" (Matt 5–7; Luke 6:20–49). They are to travel in Jesus's name without staff, bag, bread, or money (9:3). They are to abandon all things (14:33), trusting the promise that such abandonment will secure them a place in God's kingdom (12:28–34; 18:22–30) and that God will sustain them in tribulation (21:12–19). If they are in positions of leadership, they are to exercise power as a form of humble service, imitating the one who tells them, "I am among you as one who serves" (22:24–27).

Luke's distinctive twist to one of Jesus's demands sums it up: "And he said to all, 'If any man would come after me, let him deny himself and take up his cross daily and follow me. For whoever would save his life will lose it; and whoever loses his life for my sake will save it'" (9:23–24). The addition of the Greek phrase *kath' hēmeran* ("daily") makes the statement an invitation to readers after the resurrection to transpose cross-carrying of their own into more quotidian circumstances.[2] Another connection to the lives of readers is made by Jesus's complementing the demand to leave all things with the command to share possessions with others. Thus, he tells the rich ruler, "One thing you still lack. Sell all that you have and distribute to the poor, and you will have treasure in heaven; and come, follow me" (18:22; see also 12:33; 16:1–31; 19:1–10). Such sharing, Jesus declares, is available even to the poorest of the poor (21:1–4).[3]

The Gospel of John supplemented the Synoptics' picture of discipleship without fundamentally disagreeing with them; its emphasis on discipleship as a form of mutual presence with Jesus (see John 1:35–53; 14:1–31) had a particularly strong influence on Christian mystical traditions. John does not include the many sayings of Jesus concerning the demands of discipleship, but those demands are obvious: the disciples are called from their ordinary life (1:35–41) and, despite their closeness to Jesus, can misapprehend or even betray him (6:1–71; 13:1–11, 26–27; 18:15–27) precisely because what he demands seems paradoxical or impossible. As the good shepherd, Jesus lays down his life for his sheep (10:1–18). He is the seed that must die in order to bear fruit (12:23–24), and (in language close to the Synoptics), Jesus declares, "He who loves his life loses it, and he who hates his life in this world will keep it for eternal life. If anyone serves me, he must follow me; and where I am, there shall my servant be also; if anyone serves me, the Father will honor him" (12:25–26). In the epilogue to the gospel, Jesus's demand that Peter demonstrate his love for him by feeding his sheep (21:15–17) combines these elements of devotion to Jesus and the service of others, which will

2. The phrase is well attested in the manuscript tradition.

3. When reading the Acts of the Apostles, early believers would have found a portrayal of Jesus's disciples after the resurrection as consistent with that in the gospel: they bore witness to the resurrection boldly (4:23–31), shared all their possessions in common (2:41–47; 4:32–37), tended to the needs of the poor and afflicted (6:1–7), displayed servant leadership (20:28–35), obediently followed the lead of the Holy Spirit (10–15), and patiently endured the suffering that came to them as a consequence of their following Jesus: Paul and Barnabas strengthen new disciples, "exhorting them to continue in the faith, and saying that through many tribulations we must enter the kingdom of God." On the consistency of Luke-Acts, see Luke Timothy Johnson, *Prophetic Jesus, Prophetic Church: The Challenge of Luke-Acts to Contemporary Christians* (Grand Rapids: Eerdmans, 2011).

lead to Peter suffering a death like that of Jesus (21:18–19). Thus, Jesus commands him twice, "you follow me" (21:19–22).

Two aspects of discipleship are particularly stressed in John's Gospel. The first is that the disciples who follow Jesus along his path to the Father will share in his own divine life (17:20–26): Jesus declares, "Where I am going you cannot follow me now; but you shall follow afterward" (13:36). When Peter rashly states his readiness to lay down his life for Jesus, he is rebuked by the prediction that he will betray Jesus three times (13:38). Jesus is nevertheless going to the Father to prepare a place for them, "that where I am you may be also" (14:3). When Thomas protests that they do not know the way to go, Jesus responds, "I am the way, and the truth, and the life; no one comes to the Father, but by me" (14:6). The hope of a heavenly reward in the Synoptics becomes in John the hope for life in the presence of Jesus and the Father.

The second Johannine emphasis is Jesus's insistence on mutual love (*agapē*) among his followers. The supremacy of love of God and love of neighbor enunciated by Jesus in the Synoptics (Matt 22:35–40; Mark 12:28–31; Luke 10:25–28) is now expressed in terms of the love of Jesus and his followers, a love that is measured by that which Jesus showed them: "A new commandment I give to you, that you love one another; even as I have loved you, that you also love one another. By this all men will know that you are my disciples, if you have love for one another" (13:34–35). Again, "This is my commandment, that you love one another as I have loved you. Greater love has no man than this, that a man lay down his life for his friends . . . this I command you, to love one another" (15:12–17). Keeping Jesus's commandments is the way in which the disciples' love for him is demonstrated (14:15); mutual love among disciples is therefore also love for Jesus.

The letters of the apostle Paul, in turn, were read as deeply harmonious with the Four Gospels, for while the term "disciple" never occurs in his compositions, they everywhere assume the same fundamental pattern of following Jesus as is found in the Gospels, even if Paul's discourse is considerably more complex. Thus, when Paul tells the Corinthians to "imitate me as I imitate Christ" (1 Cor 11:1), he evokes the entire structure of ancient pedagogy.[4] He seeks to provide a model for his readers of what

4. See Devin L. White, *Teacher of the Nations: Ancient Educational Traditions and*

he calls "the mind of Christ" (1 Cor 2:16), a disposition—and mode of behavior—that was willing to forgo individual rights, as genuine as those might be, for the sake of serving others. This is the argument he develops through 1 Corinthians 8–11, which climaxes in 11:1. He begins that argument by drawing a sharp contrast between a "knowledge" (*gnōsis*) that expresses itself in arrogance and a "love" (*agapē*) that expresses itself in service to the weak (8:1–2), precisely in imitation of Christ: "And so by your knowledge this weak man is destroyed, the brother for whom Christ died. Thus, sinning against your brethren and wounding their conscience when it is weak, you sin against Christ" (8:11–12).

In 1 Corinthians 13:1–13, Paul shows his readers a "still more excellent way," which is the way of love (*agapē*). Love is greater than speaking in tongues, which Paul sees as an interesting but private gift, and greater than prophecy, which Paul extols because love "builds" the church (14:1–3). It is even greater than the most dramatic form of self-renunciation: "If I give away all I have, and if I deliver my body to be burned, but have not love, I gain nothing" (13:3). The superiority of love lies in its transcending of the selfish solipsism that characterizes "childish" thinking and behavior (see 1 Cor 3:1–4; 13:11) and in awareness of and care for the other that characterizes the mature adult: "Brethren, do not be children in your thinking; be babes in evil, but in thinking be mature" (14:20). Thus,

> Love is patient and kind; love is not jealous or boastful; it is not arrogant or rude. Love does not insist on its own way; it is not irritable or resentful. It does not rejoice at wrong, but rejoices in the right. Love bears all things, believes all things, hopes all things, endures all things. (1 Cor 13:4–7)

In Paul's letters, the love of God that had been poured into the hearts of believers through the gift of the Holy Spirit—the Spirit that came from the exalted Lord Jesus whom Paul terms as "life-giving Spirit" (1 Cor 15:45)—moved within them to serve the needs of others even more than their own (Phil 2:1–4). They were freed from sin and death by Christ in order to become slaves of each other (Gal 5:13) in imitation of

---

Paul's Argument in 1 Corinthians 1–4, Beihefte zur Zeitschrift für die neutestamentliche Wissenschaft 227 (Berlin: de Gruyter, 2017).

the one who humbled himself in obedience to take the form of a slave (Phil 2:5–11). Instead of doing "the works of the flesh" that are antisocial and community-destroying vices, they are to act out of the moral dispositions—the fruits—given by the Holy Spirit: "if we live by the Spirit," Paul declares, "we ought to walk according to the Spirit" (Gal 5:16–25).

Such walking means concretely, "bearing one another's burdens" in order to fulfill "the law [*nomos*] that is Christ" (Gal 6:2). Paul's language of law is deliberately provocative. He has already stated that the reason they have been made free is in order that "through love you might be slaves for each other, for the whole law [*nomos*] is fulfilled in one word, 'You shall love your neighbor as yourself'" (Gal 13:14; compare Rom 13:8–10), but as in John's Gospel, the love of neighbor is measured by the love shown by Christ. Christ is the pattern to which believers "conform" (*stoichein*) themselves.

Such love is not simply attitudinal; it finds expression in specific and embodied forms of mutual support, such as the collection that Paul raises from his gentile communities for the support of "the saints in Jerusalem" (Gal 2:10; Rom 15:22–33; 1 Cor 16:1–4; 2 Cor 8–9). In seeking to convince his Corinthian community to join in that effort, Paul invokes the example of Christ: "For you know the grace (*charis* = "gift") of our Lord Jesus Christ, that though he was rich, yet for your sake he became poor, so that by his poverty you might become rich" (2 Cor 8:9).

Paul shares the synoptic paradigm of present suffering leading to future reward. In Romans, for example, he declares,

> We rejoice in our suffering, knowing that suffering produces endurance, and endurance produces character, and character produces hope, and hope does not disappoint us because God's love has been poured into our hearts through the Holy Spirit which has been given to us. (Rom 5:3–5)

Later, he speaks of believers as "children of God, heirs of God and fellow heirs with Christ, *provided we suffer with him in order that we may also be glorified with him*" (8:17; emphasis added). Likewise, in 2 Corinthians 4:17, he says that "this slight momentary affliction is preparing for us an eternal weight of glory beyond all comparison" (compare 2 Tim 2:11–13).

But Paul also considerably complicates the notion of "imitating Christ" by his insistence that discipleship is not merely a matter of the

human will—a moral choice—although it is certainly also that. Paul
sees such moral dispositions as faith, hope, and love as made possible by
the presence and power of the Holy Spirit. The Spirit in fact empowers an
internal change within humans, a renewal of the corrupted human mind
(see Rom 12:1–2) that begins with a sacramental participation in the
death of Jesus and issues in a "new life" according to God (Rom 6:1–11).
The Spirit brings about the creation of a new humanity (Rom 5:12–21;
Gal 3:28; Col 3:11) shaped in the image of Jesus (1 Cor 15:49; 2 Cor 3:18; 4:4;
Col 1:15; 3:10), the firstborn of many children (Rom 8:29). Paul thereby
posits a mystical identification between Christ and those who are "in
Christ," played out especially in his own story (see Gal 2:19–21; 6:14–15;
2 Cor 3:17–4:6; Col 1:24) but also in the lives of believers: as Paul has been
"crucified to the world" (Gal 6:14), so have those "who belong to Christ
crucified the flesh with its passions and desires" (5:24).

It is Paul who most insistently speaks of this change brought about
by God, in terms of sanctification or holiness.[5] Those called by God into
the *ekklēsia* are "holy ones" or "saints" (*hagioi*) in distinction from "the
world" (*kosmos*) because they participate in the energy field that is God's
Holy Spirit (see, for example, 1 Cor 6:1–3). It is the power of the Holy
Spirit that makes humans holy (1 Cor 3:16). But Paul also sees the human
response to God's gift as a process of becoming more holy (see Rom 15:16;
Eph 1:4; 5:3; Col 1:22; 3:12; 1 Tim 2:15; 2 Tim 1:9). Paul greets his readers
in Corinth as "sanctified in Christ Jesus, called to be saints" (1 Cor 1:2).
He tells the Thessalonians, "God has not called us for uncleanness but
in holiness" (1 Thess 4:7), and states flatly, "this is the will of God, your
sanctification" (4:3). Those who have been baptized "now yield [their]
members to righteousness for sanctification" (Rom 6:19). Perhaps most
dramatically, Paul tells the Corinthians, "Since we have these promises,
beloved, let us cleanse ourselves of every defilement of body and spirit,
and make holiness perfect in the fear of God" (2 Cor 7:1).

The Holy Spirit empowers an "imitation of Christ" that is internal and
indeed ontological;[6] it is a transformation of the self that begins in the

---

5. The Greek cognates of *hagios* ("holy") are translated into English by cognates of
"holy" and of "saint." Thus, "holy one" = "saint," "holiness" = "sanctity," "becoming holy"
= "sanctification."

6. See Luke Timothy Johnson, "Life-Giving Spirit: The Ontological Implications of

empirical and finds its term in the eschaton, when like the exalted Christ, they shall have a "spiritual body" (*soma pneumatikon* [1 Cor 15:44]): "just as we have borne the image of the man of dust, we shall also bear the image of the man of heaven" (1 Cor 15:49).[7] Paul says of himself that he has counted all his human privileges as refuse,

> That I might gain Christ and be found in him, not having a righteous-ness of my own, based on law, but that which is through faith in Christ [or, "Christ's faith"],[8] the righteousness from God that depends on faith, that I may know him and the power of his resurrection, and may share in his sufferings, becoming like him in his death, that if possible I may attain the resurrection from the dead. (Phil 3:10)

And of his readers in Philippi, he declares,

> Our commonwealth is in heaven, and from it we await a savior, the Lord Jesus Christ, who will change our lowly body to be like his glo-rious body, by the power which enables him to subject all things to himself. (Phil 3:20)

Despite some doubts about its authorship, the Letter to the Hebrews was generally considered one of Paul's letters and was treated as such.[9] Its powerful rhetoric contributed two important elements to the classical understanding of discipleship. The first was its construction of the world: reading Scripture much like the Jewish philosopher Philo, the author of Hebrews understood the Bible's language about "heaven" and "earth" in Platonic terms as the distinction between the inferior material (or em-

---

Resurrection in 1 Corinthians," in *Interpreting Paul*, vol. 2 of *The Canonical Paul* (Grand Rapids: Eerdmans, 2021), 69–85.

7. The best work on this is now Frederick David Carr, *Being and Becoming: Human Transformation in the Letters of Paul* (Waco, TX: Baylor University Press, 2022).

8. For the exegetical (and theological) issues attached to Paul's use of the phrase *pistis Christou*, see Luke Timothy Johnson, "Romans 3:21–26 and the Faith of Jesus: The Soteriological Significance of Christ's Obedience," *Interpreting Paul*, 13–26.

9. A discussion of Hebrews' authorship and symbolic world is found in the intro-duction to Luke Timothy Johnson, *Hebrews: A Commentary*, New Testament Library (Louisville: Westminster John Knox, 2006), 1–60.

pirical) realm of human mortality and the superior spiritual realm of the divine presence. Christ's death and resurrection/exaltation/enthrone-ment, then, meant his moving "through the veil" of mortal existence into the presence of God, where he serves as an eternal priest on behalf of his brothers and sisters (Heb 10:19–22). The second was the vision of disciple-ship itself: Jesus was "the pioneer and perfector" of faith (12:2) who led his followers on pilgrimage to God's promise, which was not the empirical land of Israel but the "heavenly homeland" (11:16). The task of disciples, therefore, is not to imitate those ancestors who "fell away" because of their lack of faith (3:1–19) but to imitate those ancestors who as aliens and so-journers on earth sought the sabbath rest of God in heaven (4:1–13; 11:1–39) and, above all, Jesus, "who for the joy that was set before him endured the cross, despising the shame, and is seated at the right hand of the throne of God" (12:2–3). The path of such imitation is obedient faith in God: just as Jesus as God's Son "learned obedience through what he suffered and being made perfect became the source of eternal salvation of all who obey him" (5:8–9), so were his followers to be faithfully obedient, enduring their sufferings "for the sake of an education" as sons.[10]

A final New Testament witness critical to the formation of the clas-sical vision of discipleship is the First Letter of Peter, in which the im-itation of Christ is made explicit and is applied to the very *manner* in which Jesus suffered—a manner that itself fulfills the messianic reading of Isaiah 53:5–12 (compare Acts 8:26–40). Exhorting servants to endure even suffering that comes upon them unjustly, he says,

> For to this you have been called, because Christ also suffered for you, *leaving you an example, that you should follow in his steps.* He com-mitted no sin; no guile was found on his lips. When he was reviled, he did not revile in return; when he suffered, he did not threaten; but he trusted to him who judges justly. He himself bore our sins in his body on the tree, that we might die to sin and live to righteousness. By his wounds you have been healed. For you were straying like sheep, but have now returned to the Shepherd and Guardian of your souls. (1 Pet 2:21–25; emphasis added)[11]

---

10. For this translation, see Johnson, *Hebrews*, 319–23.

11. It can be stated briefly that both 2 Peter and the book of Revelation, each in its

From pondering such New Testament witnesses, then, Christians could think of discipleship in terms of a personal transformation that, in imitation of Jesus who first suffered and then entered glory, would lead them along the same path through their mortal existence and in circumstances dramatically different from those experienced by Jesus himself. The medium of such transformation was the Holy Spirit, which came to them from Jesus, who through his exaltation to God's presence became "life-giving Spirit," and which empowered them to new dispositions and behaviors. The process of transformation showed itself in an ever-growing faithful obedience to God and loving self-donation to others. The means of such transformation—from the side of human effort or discipline—were prayer, self-denial, service of the weak and poor, and the patient endurance of the suffering endemic to bodily existence.

The Effect of Sacramental Life

The traditional understanding of discipleship was not drawn from the reading of the New Testament alone. It was inscribed and reinscribed in the hearts of believers through the sacramental life of the church. The church was regarded as most real when believers—even if only two or three—gathered "in the name of Jesus" (Matt 18:20) to form "the body of Christ" (1 Cor 12:1–31) wherein the Holy Spirit could shape a "holy" people (Tit 2:11–14), different in disposition and behavior from "the world" (Rom 12:1–2; 1 Cor 6:1–2) around it. The assembly of believers, as Paul states in Philippians 1:27–28, is to "stand firm in one spirit, with one mind striving side by side for the faith of the gospel, and not

---

fashion, aligns with the understanding of discipleship as the endurance of present suffering for the sake of a future share in God's life. Peter prays that his readers "escape from the corruption that is in the world because of passion, and become partakers of the divine nature" (1:4), and that they "be in lives of holiness and godliness, waiting for and hastening the coming of the day of God" (3:11–12). In Revelation, Jesus is the faithful witness (*martys*), the firstborn of the dead, who freed from sins by his blood (1:5); and under the altar in heaven are the souls of those who had been slain for "the word of God and the witness they had borne" (6:9). The burden of this prophetic book is stated in 14:12: "Here is a call for the endurance of the saints, those who keep the commandments of God and their faith in Jesus," in the expectation of a new heaven and new earth where "the Lord God will be their light" (21:1–22:5).

be frightened in anything by your opponents." They are, he continues, to be "blameless and innocent, children of God without blemish in the midst of a crooked and perverse generation, among whom you shine as lights in the world" (Phil 2:15).[12]

The church is to be the place where the reconciling work of Jesus Christ—uniting in one new humanity Jew and Greek, male and female—stands as a witness to the world of what is possible (Eph 1:15–3:11), even, or especially, when the world itself fights against that witness (see Eph 6:10–20; 2 Cor 10:1–5). The church, in a word, best serves the world by *being* church. The task of the church is precisely to be other than the world (the basic meaning of "holy" after all), a community of saints "called to be holy" (1 Cor 1:2): as Paul tells the Corinthians, "Do you not know that you are God's temple, and that God's Spirit dwells in you? If anyone destroys God's temple, God will destroy him. For God's temple is holy, and that temple you are" (1 Cor 3:16–17; compare 2 Cor 6:14–7:1).[13]

The ritual actions—the liturgy—of the church formed and reinforced the understanding of discipleship as an imitation of Christ that was not mechanical but participatory, as we see already in the New Testament passages that speak of baptism and the Eucharist.

In Romans 6:1–11, Paul says of himself and his readers who were baptized "into Christ Jesus" that they were "buried therefore with him into his death, so that as Christ was raised from the dead by the glory of the Father, we too might walk in newness of life" (6:4). The identification of believer with Christ is real:

> If we have been united with him in a death like his, we shall certainly be united with him in a resurrection like his. We know that our old self was crucified with him so that the sinful body might be destroyed, and we might no longer be enslaved to sin. . . . [I]f we have died with Christ, we believe that we shall also live with him. . . .

---

12. One of many places in Paul where the words of Jesus find an echo: "you are the light of the world. . . . [L]et your light shine before men, that they may see your good works and give glory to your Father who is in heaven" (Matt 5:14–16).

13. The pronouns and verbs are all plural; Paul is addressing the church as such. For the temple imagery and its entailments, see now Michael K. W. Suh, *Power and Peril: Paul's Use of Temple Discourse in 1 Corinthians*, Beihefte zur Zeitschrift für die neutestamentliche Wissenschaft 239 (Berlin: de Gruyter, 2020).

[Y]ou must consider yourselves dead to sin and alive to God in Christ Jesus. (Rom 6:5–11)

From this mystical and sacramental immersion into the death and resurrection of Jesus follows the moral imperative to "yield [themselves] to God as men who have been brought from death to life, and [their] members to God as instruments of righteousness" (6:13). The goal? Complete transformation of the self: "Now that you have been set free from sin and become slaves of God, the return you get is sanctification [holiness] and its end, eternal life" (6:22; see also 1 Cor 12:12–13; Gal 3:29; and especially Col 2:20–3:11; Tit 3:3–7).[14]

The ritual meal, or Eucharist, also established and celebrated mystical connections between the risen Jesus and his followers. In his warning to the Corinthians not to partake of cultic meals at the shrines of idols, Paul draws an analogy between such meals and those celebrated by the community:

The cup of blessing which we bless, is it not a participation [*koinōnia*] in the blood of Christ? The bread which we break, is it not a participation [*koinōnia*] in the body of Christ? Because there is one bread, we who are many are one body, for we all partake [*metechomen*] of the one bread. . . . What do I imply, then? That food offered to idols is anything or that an idol is anything? No, I imply that what pagans sacrifice they offer to demons and not to God. I do not want you to be partners [*koinōnoi*] with demons. You cannot drink the cup of the Lord and the cup of demons. (1 Cor 10:16–21)[15]

This passage precedes the one in which Paul recalls the words of Jesus before his arrest, when he broke bread and declared, "this is my body which is for you," and also gave the cup, saying, "this is the new covenant

14. This strong understanding of baptism continues as the liturgy becomes more developed, as, for example, in Cyril of Jerusalem's *Mystagogical Catecheses*, preached at the climax of the Lenten period of catechumenate instruction; see T. L. Regule, "The *Mystagogical Catecheses* of Cyril of Jerusalem: Forming the Identity of a Christian," *Liturgy* 35 (2020): 42–47.

15. Paul follows the LXX translation of the MT's "the gods of the heathen are idols" as "the gods of the heathen are demons [*daimonia*]" in Ps 95:6 LXX.

in my blood," and exhorted his followers, "do this, as often as you drink it, in remembrance of me" (*emēn anamnēsin* [11:24–25]). It is clear from the earlier passage that "remembrance" cannot mean a simple imitative memorial but must involve some form of real participation (*koinōnia*) in the body and blood of the one who died for them. The two passages together indicate how the eucharistic meal pulled together the paradoxical parts of the imitation of Christ: on one side, the presence of the risen Jesus (*ho kyrios*) among them means that "whoever eats the bread or drinks the cup of the Lord in an unworthy manner will be guilty of profaning the body and blood of the Lord" (11:27). On the other side, the meal proclaims the most important part of the Jesus story: "you proclaim the Lord's death until he comes" (11:26).

The sacraments of baptism and Eucharist as interpreted by Paul represent a somatic and spiritual intensification of the vision of discipleship as depicted in Scripture. Following Jesus, the sacraments make clear, involves a deep and mystical identification of the believer with Christ, both the living Lord powerfully present in the church through the Holy Spirit, and the Lord who in his mortal existence gave his life for others. Disciples are empowered by the Spirit to pass through suffering and death to a future share in that "glory" of which in their mortal existence they have only a pledge (see 2 Cor 1:22; 4:17; Col 1:27; Rom 8:18).

The development of the liturgy over the following centuries extends this vision over space and (especially) time in two great cycles of celebration. The first was the seasonal cycle that moved worshipers through an imaginative reliving of the scriptural story, dominated by the forty penitential days of Lent, whose climax was Holy Week, when the events of Jesus's last days were recalled in exquisite detail. Holy Week itself culminated in the Sacred Triduum of Good Friday, Holy Saturday, and Sunday, the day of resurrection. All during Lent, those seeking to become disciples were instructed, and entrusted, bit by bit, with the arcana of discipleship; during the Easter Vigil the catechumens were ritually received into the body of Christ through baptism and anointing. Such ritual imprinting had an obvious and profound effect on the shaping of Christian consciousness: being a disciple meant following Jesus through suffering and death in this mortal existence in the hope of sharing his resurrection life in the future.

A second great cycle of celebration (later in development than the first) was the sanctoral, which celebrated those disciples who became perfect or holy by following Jesus precisely on the path that he had walked. All the earliest saints thus celebrated pointed to the paschal pattern of discipleship. The martyrs gave their life in witness to God as had the first witness, Jesus. The confessors did not literally shed their blood, but they testified to the truth in the face of opposition and suffering. The virgins bore witness to the resurrection by eschewing biological generation in view of the resurrection life, anticipating the future with God when all will "be like angels" (Matt 22:30). Thus, disciples through the example of such as these had reinforced the sense of being part of a great communion of saints that came to be understood as being made up of the church triumphant in heaven, the church militant on earth, and the church penitent in purgatory. The saints celebrated liturgically were now where disciples longed to be.

Premises and Practices

Premises

I use the term "premise" here for the convictions on which practices are based. To take the most obvious example, everything in the traditional understanding of discipleship is based on the premise that the biblical story is true. Scripture is God's word and makes humans "wise unto salvation" (2 Tim 3:15). The word "truth" here attaches not to historical accuracy or to every detail of every passage but to the grand sweep of Scripture's account of the world's origin, its peril, its salvation, and its future. Above all, Scripture speaks truth concerning the human condition, concerning the identity and work of Jesus Christ, and concerning the path of discipleship. On these matters of faith and morals, Scripture does not deceive.

It is certainly the case, however, that the traditional reading of Scripture was selective. The New Testament was given ultimate significance, while negotiating the Old Testament—apart from those parts of the story already appropriated by the New Testament—was secondary (and more difficult). Within the New Testament, furthermore, the accounts and interpretations of Jesus's suffering, death, and resurrection were the most decisive. The words and deeds of Jesus during his ministry were, to be sure, treasured and applied to the disciple's life,[16] but it was what God accom-

---

16. See, for example, 1 Clem. 13 and 46; Justin, *1 Apology* 1.12–17.

plished in the paschal mystery that established the paradigm for discipleship, a paradigm that was reinforced by the liturgical life of the church. The sense of church, in turn, was strong. Discipleship was first of all communal,[17] for God's interest was in gathering a holy people. Disciples formed a community and, like those who first followed Jesus, learned how to imitate Jesus together. The common learning was quite literal in that the reading of Scripture and instruction in discipleship happened above all in liturgical reading and preaching. The common life was expressed through worship, through the exercise of spiritual gifts, through the sacraments, and through the sharing of possessions. The meaning of church was communicated most powerfully through metaphors: it was a pilgrim people moving toward a heavenly homeland (Hebrews); it was God's household/temple to be built up and made holy; it was the very body of Christ whose members exercised mutual love (Paul). The church was in the world a place of salvation from the (corrupt) world and was called to be holy, that is, distinct attitudinally and behaviorally, from the corruption of the world.[18] Salvation finds its logical term in sanctification, and both are communal as well as individual.

The eschatological premise for traditional discipleship was at once complex and simple. It was complex because the New Testament offered diverse and not altogether consistent visions of the end time, some more cosmic and future (the coming of the Son of Man) and some more individual and immediate (dying and being "with the Lord"). With the parousia indefinitely delayed, the second version became dominant. Paul's statement that "the frame of this world is passing away" (7:31) was understood more in existential than in temporal terms. Here is where

17. This deeply somatic and communal sense of traditional discipleship distinguishes itself from the sort of piety found in Gnosticism, which continued the Greco-Roman mode of religiosity that "transcended the world" not least by eschewing the physical altogether and emphasizing individual progress toward perfection. See Luke Timothy Johnson, *Among the Gentiles: Greco-Roman Religion and Christianity*, Anchor (Yale) Bible Reference Library (New Haven: Yale University Press, 2009), 79–92, 214–33, 268–71, with notes, and *Faith's Freedom: A Classic Spirituality for Contemporary Christians* (Minneapolis: Fortress, 1990), passim.

18. The term "world" (*kosmos*) in this sort of disjunctive statement refers not to God's creation (Acts 17:24; Rom 1:20; Eph 1:4) but to the social, economic, political, and religious sphere of activity shaped by human ambition and sin (see Acts 17:31; John 15:19; 18:36; Rom 3:6; 12:2; 1 Cor 1:20–21; 2:12; 3:19; 5:10; 6:2; Gal 6:14; Eph 2:2; Phil 2:15; Col 2:20, and especially Jas 4:4).

Hebrews was particularly important, with its sharp vertical contrast between the material and the spiritual, the earthly and the heavenly, and its vision of humans moving after Christ from the temporal to the eternal. Thus, eschatology was conceived of as both individual ("we will all stand before God's judgment seat . . . each of us will give an account of ourselves before God" [Rom 14:10, 12]) and as communal: "you have come to mount Zion, to the city of the living God, the heavenly Jerusalem, to an innumerable company of angels, to the assembly and church of the firstborn that are written in heaven, and to God the judge of all, and to the spirits of the righteous made perfect" (Heb 12:22–23).

Both the witness of Scripture and their own experience encouraged believers to perceive mortal existence as at once brief and portentous. On one side, the shortness of human life and its transitory character made any effort to make it absolute or all-important risible. On the other side, precisely the fragility of human existence made every human decision of ultimate importance. The classic form of eschatology consisted in "the four last things," which were death, judgment, and heaven or hell. The choices made in the brief compass of mortal life had, in this view, eternal consequences. The vision of the final judgment in Matthew 25:31–46, which pictures Jesus separating sheep from goats and sending each to an eternal bliss or damnation was transferred to the kind of judgment and destiny awaiting each person at death. Given the transitory nature of all human accomplishment and the perishability of all material things, human life seemed not less but more significant. Repentance, or getting right with God, was clearly the "one thing necessary" for disciples, rather than "being busy about many things" (Luke 10:41–42).[19]

Scripture and experience also testified to the truth that human life was inevitably one of suffering. Human existence was, in the Vulgate translation of Psalm 83:7 LXX, a *valle lacrimarum*, a "valley of tears." The patient endurance of suffering was therefore an essential element in discipleship. Some suffering was natural in the sense that it was a concomitant of somatic existence: the vagaries of childbirth, sickness, injury, pain, the loss of power in aging, and death itself; all these were simply the human lot after the sin of Adam (Rom 15:12–21), a matter

---

19. See the emphasis on repentance throughout 1 Clement as well as 2 Clem. 8, 16; for the certainty of judgment after death, see 2 Clem. 17–18 and Did. 16.

of "bearing the image of the man of dust" (1 Cor 15:45). The salvation brought by Christ did not rescue people from mortal pain and death but transformed them, making them the very avenue of sanctification: Jesus said, "By your patient endurance you will gain your souls (*psychai* = "lives").[20]

Other forms of suffering came, not from the simple fact of being mortal bodies but from the singular kind of commitment made by disciples. In the first place, the kind of obedient faith demanded of the disciple, that he or she follow Jesus by constantly placing God's will before his/her own, itself demands a kind of suffering and death, for such an absurd leap requires overcoming interior resistance, putting to death the claims and demands of the self. Thus, Hebrews speaks of Christ himself becoming perfect son "learning obedience from the things he suffered" (Heb 5:10) and speaks of disciples as "enduring for the sake of an education" (12:7, my translation).

But disciples could expect suffering to arise as well from the outside, because a life of total dedication to God, a life witnessing to the paradoxical work of God in the dying and rising Messiah Jesus, stands as a challenge to the world's lesser powers that seek to hurt God by doing harm to humans. These are the authorities and powers that stand behind and animate the social systems that run on envy, greed, and the lust for power, and resist any threat to their control over humans.[21] It is in this connection that the tradition employs the language of the demonic. The demons (*ta daimonia*) are the agents of Satan, the ruler of the counter-kingdom inimical toward God.

Paul, we have seen, associates demons with the practices of gentile worship (1 Cor 10:21–22), and he speaks of Satan as a powerful and deceptive seducer seeking the harm of believers (Rom 16:20; 1 Cor 5:5; 7:5; 2 Cor 2:11; 11:14; 12:7; 1 Thess 2:18; 2 Thess 2:9; 1 Tim 1:20; 5:15). In the Gospels, similarly, the demons sponsor the mental and physical afflictions

20. Ignatius tells the Ephesians, "Let us be zealous to be imitators of the Lord" (Ign. *Eph.* 10), and Polycarp, "Let us become imitators of his endurance" (Ign. *Pol.* 8), and the Magnesians, "for this cause [i.e., the resurrection] we endure patiently, that we may be found disciples of Jesus Christ, our only teacher" (Ign. *Magn.* 4).

21. Heinrich Schlier, *Principalities and Powers in the New Testament*, Quaestiones Disputatae (Freiburg: Herder, 1961); Walter Wink, *Naming the Powers: The Language of Power in the New Testament* (Philadelphia: Fortress, 1984).

of those possessed. When Jesus liberates such people from the power of demons and "unclean spirits" (Matt 4:24; 8:16; Mark 1:32, 34; Luke 4:14; 8:27), he threatens to overthrow Satan's kingdom (Matt 12:26; Mark 23–26; Luke 10:18; 11:18), which Satan himself offered to him (Matt 4:1–11; Mark 1:12–13; Luke 4:1–13). In the Gospels of Luke and John, Satan was at work when Jesus was caught in the hands of Jewish and Roman authorities (Luke 22:3, 31; John 13:27). In Acts, Satan continues to be an active enemy of the church (Acts 5:3; 26:18), so that the casting out of "unclean spirits" accompanied the proclamation of the good news (Acts 8:7; 16:16–18; 19:12–16). In the early church, when catechumens were asked at baptism whether they renounced Satan and all his works, a positive response implied the willingness to resist the powers thought to be at work in gentile religion, which in turn represented the power of the state.[22]

Practices

The characteristic practices of discipleship were consonant with its vision of God and the world. The degree to which such practices were communal needs to be emphasized: in the first place, worship, with its reading, preaching, singing, and teaching, was very much a *leitourgia*, a public work of the Christian *ekklēsia*, not least because before printing, Scripture had to be proclaimed and interpreted from a single community manuscript, but also because convictions concerning the sacramental body of Christ—being participants in one body, sharing the one cup—combined with convictions concerning ministry within the church, that is, gathering together with one bishop.[23]

But in addition to worshiping God with one voice, the church expressed love toward neighbors in a concerted and concrete fashion. Two New Testament compositions stress the emptiness of faith that is not demonstrated in the practical care of those in need. The most famous, perhaps, is the Letter of James's outrage at the dishonor shown to a poor

22. See Cyril of Jerusalem, *Mystagogical Catecheses* 19.4–8. For the intimate linkage between Greco-Roman religion and the fabric of society, see Johnson, *Among the Gentiles*, 32–49, 93–110.

23. See Did. 14–15; Ign. *Magn.* 3, 7; Ign. *Trall.* 2; Ign. *Smyrn.* 6, 8; Ign. *Eph.* 4–5, 13, and above all, 20.

man in the assembly (2:1–6), and at the replacement of specific help to the starving and naked with good wishes; "faith without deeds," he declares, "is dead" (Jas 2:14–26). Equally emphatic is the First Letter of John: "If anyone has material possessions and sees a brother or sister in need but has no pity on them, how can the love of God be in that person? Dear children, let us not love with words or speech, but with actions and in truth" (1 John 3:17–18).

In his letter to his delegate Titus, Paul declares that God sought a people "zealous for good deeds" (2:11), and in his conclusion, he tells Titus to encourage such "good deeds" in his churches. And there is abundant evidence in the New Testament itself for such practical zeal. Thus, we see that Acts portrays the first community as sharing all of its possessions, "so that there was none needy among them" (Acts 2:41–47; 4:32–37), and we see Paul exhorting his gentile churches to cooperate in a massive financial collection for the "poor among the saints" in Jerusalem (Gal 2:10; 1 Cor 16:1–4; 2 Cor 8–9; Rom 15:25–32). In Acts 6:1–7, we see widows in the community being fed from the community resources, and in 1 Timothy 5:3–16, we find a thoughtful response to the burden such care for widows places on the church when households do not help support their elderly. In the concluding chapter of Hebrews, the author exhorts his readers to practice hospitality (13:1), to visit those in prison (13:2), and to share their possessions (13:16). When Paul states in 1 Corinthians 13:3 that without love (*agapē*), even giving away all his possessions to the poor or handing over his body to be burned is nothing, he does not in the least suggest that *agapē* should not be expressed by the donation of one's goods or the giving of one's body for others![24]

The individual practices of traditional discipleship are prayer, fasting, and almsgiving. Each is addressed by Jesus as forms of practicing piety in Matthew's Sermon on the Mount, which from Augustine to Luther was read as something of a handbook on discipleship (Matt 6:1).[25] Prayer is

24. For the continuation of such communal expressions of mercy among the Apostolic Fathers, see 1 Clem. 11–12, 30, 35, 38, 49; 2 Clem. 17; Ign. *Smyrn.* 6; Ign. *Pol.* 4; Did. 1, 4; Pol. *Phil.* 2, 4–6.

25. Augustine and Luther are among many who have devoted commentaries to the sermon. See Luke Timothy Johnson, "The Sermon on the Mount," in *The Oxford Companion to Christian Thought*, ed. A. Hastings, A. Mason, and H. Pyper (Oxford: Oxford University Press, 2000), 654–56.

not to be a matter of public display or of empty phrases but something done in secret—to be seen by the one who sees in secret—and simply. Jesus's own prayer to his father is the perfect model, combining doxology and petition—so long as it is understood that asking God for forgiveness is useless if disciples do not offer forgiveness to others (Matt 6:7–15). Prayer is to be persistent, in the trust that "your father in heaven will give good things to those who ask him" (7:7–12; compare Luke 18:1–14). The Gospels showed Jesus frequently at prayer and instructing his followers to pray.[26] The Lord's Prayer became central to Christian piety both within and outside the liturgy (see also Luke 11:1–12).[27]

So did the praying and chanting of the Psalms (see Eph 5:19; Col 3:16). The Psalms were taken not only as pointing to Jesus—as their frequent citation throughout the New Testament attests—but were regarded as the very prayers of Jesus himself,[28] so that reading the Psalms in common or when alone meant in a very real sense praying with Jesus. Because the Psalms themselves address God in prayer, they are the ideal vehicle for others to "lift the mind and heart to God." And because the Psalms imagine the world as one in which God is present and powerfully active within creation at every moment, they distinctively enable those who pray them to "imagine the world that Scripture imagines."[29] With the passage of time, as I shall later show, prayer became ever more central a feature of discipleship, as Christians sought ways to fulfill Paul's exhortation to "pray without ceasing" (1 Thess 5:17; see also Rom 12:12; Eph 6:18; Phil 4:6; Col 4:2) in modes of contemplation that brought to consciousness the presence of God. On the example and teaching of Jesus himself, prayer was regarded as distinctively powerful (Matt 21:22; Mark 9:29; 11:24; Jas 5:15–16) and to be preferred to lesser activities (see 1 Cor 7:5; 1 Tim 5:15–16).

26. See Matt 14:23; 19:13; 26:39, 41; Luke 3:21; 5:16; 6:12; 9:18, 28–29; 11:1–2; 22:32, 41–44; John 17:9.

27. See the version of the Lord's Prayer in Did. 8.

28. Not least at his crucifixion: in Matthew and Mark, Jesus is reported as praying Ps 22 at the moment of his death; in Luke, he prays Ps 31, and in John it is Ps 69. See especially Augustine's *Commentary on the Psalms*.

29. See Luke Timothy Johnson, *Miracles: God's Presence and Power in Creation*, Resources for the Use of Scripture in the Church (Louisville: Westminster John Knox, 2018), 81–86, 269–70.

Like prayer, fasting was a practice of Jewish piety closely aligned with prayer. Leviticus 23:26–32 calls for the people to "afflict" themselves on the Day of Atonement as a personal commitment to repentance, and the prophets call for fasting as a sign of recommitment to the covenant (see Joel 1:13–14; 2:12–15; Zech 7:1–5). Depriving oneself of food, even for a day, is a means of directing attention to the true source of life. Isaiah condemns a mere show of fasting that is not accompanied by a genuine turn to the social demands of the law (Isa 58:1–9). By the time of Jesus, regular fasting was practiced by those dedicated to the Lord; thus, the disciples of the Pharisees fast, and the disciples of John fast (Matt 9:14–15; Mark 2:18–19; Luke 5:33–34); the Jewish enemies of Paul fast (Acts 23:12). The prophet Anna spent her life in fasting and prayer (Luke 2:37), and the arrogant Pharisee boasts to God, "I fast twice a week" (Luke 18:12). Jesus himself fasted extravagantly during his forty days in the wilderness, leaving him hungry and prey to the temptations put to him by the devil (Matt 4:1–11; Luke 4:1–12). But because he was the bridegroom present to his followers, he did not demand fasting of them while he was with them (Matt 9:15; Mark 2:19; Luke 5:33); indeed, they "ate and drank" as he did (Luke 5:33).

But as Jesus predicted, his disciples fasted after his death and resurrection, in close combination with prayer. Thus, Paul fasted after his encounter with the risen Lord (Acts 9:9); Peter was hungry in prayer when he saw his vision of clean and unclean animals (Acts 10:9); the church at Antioch prayed and fasted before sending Paul and Barnabas on mission (13:2–3); Paul and Barnabas appoint elders in Iconium and Lystra, committing them to the Lord "with prayer and fasting" (14:23).

In the Sermon on the Mount, Matthew has Jesus instruct his disciples on the manner of their fasting (Matt 6:16–18). As with prayer, they are not to put themselves on display so as to receive human honor; instead, he tells them, "When you fast, anoint your head and wash your face, that your fasting may not be seen by men but by your father who is in secret; and your father who sees in secret will reward you." The more discipleship is defined in terms of repentance—that is, of turning from self and world to God—the more prominent the role of fasting (and prayer) will become. The liturgical institution of a forty-day fast during Lent, of a weekly fast on Fridays, and of a eucharistic fast made this practice not simply a gesture of individual commitment but of communal habit.

If the practices of prayer and fasting express loving the Lord with all the mind and heart, then the practice of almsgiving (*eleēmosynē*) expresses loving the neighbor as the self. And like the other practices addressed by Jesus, almsgiving was a long-established practice in Judaism, which eschewed the utopian dream of "all possessions in common" favored by Greeks and instead used their possessions to "do justice" (*zedakah*) through alleviating the specific suffering of others.[30] In the gospel narrative, Jesus's demand to leave all things to follow him has as its corollary the giving of alms to the poor (Luke 12:32; 16:1–31; 19:8; 21:1–4). He tells the rich ruler who had kept all the commandments, "One thing you still lack. Sell all that you have and distribute to the poor, and you will have treasure in heaven; and come, follow me" (Luke 18:22; Matt 19:16–30; Mark 10:17–31). Matthew has almsgiving the first practice addressed by Jesus in the Sermon on the Mount. As with the instructions concerning prayer and fasting, Jesus forbids giving alms for the sake of human attention and praise—that praise is "reward now"—and enjoins giving them in secret and hiding the action even from oneself: "do not let your left hand know what your right hand is doing." In this way, "the Father who sees in secret will reward you" (Matt 6:2–4).

Toward the conclusion of the sermon, Jesus distinguishes between those who perform many impressive religious deeds (prophesying, casting out demons) in his name, and those who "do the will of my Father who is in heaven." Those who do God's will "shall enter the kingdom of heaven," but to those who fail doing God's will, Jesus will declare, "I never knew you; depart from me, you evildoers" (Matt 7:21–23).

This shocking discrimination is elaborated in Matthew's scene of the last judgment, a passage that was of supreme importance for the classic vision of discipleship (Matt 25:31–46). The basis for separating sheep from goats—sending the sheep to "the kingdom prepared for [them] from the foundation of the world" (25:34), that is, "eternal life" (25:46), and the goats to "the eternal fire prepared for the devil and his angels" (25:41), that is, "eternal punishment" (25:46)—is whether they served Jesus without knowing it, when they served or failed to serve the little ones among whom they lived. The modes of serving fill out what is

30. See Luke Timothy Johnson, *Sharing Possessions: What Faith Demands*, 2nd ed. (Grand Rapids: Eerdmans, 2011), 109–34.

meant by almsgiving; it embraces all the practical ways of sharing possessions, time, energy, and care as they are needed by others: giving food to the hungry, drink to the thirsty, hospitality to the stranger, clothing to the naked, and visiting the sick and those in prison (25:35–36). Jesus declares, "As you did it to one of the least of these my brethren, you did it to me" (25:40). In this single passage, we find the traditional vision's eschatological hope, mystical identification between the risen Jesus and humans, and moral code. The measure of righteousness is not doctrinal correctness but concrete and specific love for the neighbor.

Conclusion

This, I submit, is the vision of discipleship as the transformation of the self in the image of Christ, the classic understanding of the imitation of Christ, centered in the sharing of the suffering of Christ in the hope of sharing in his resurrection life. It is a vision that is intensely focused on the love of God and the love of neighbor. It is not individualistic but is grounded in the communal life of the church. It is not selfish or solipsistic but is self-denying and self-giving, not according to the measure of a utopian scheme but according to the measure of Christ and the specific needs of other people.

With certain changes in emphasis, largely determined by changes in the worldly condition of disciples, this vision was shared, generation after generation, until very recently. I seek to identify elements of both continuity and discontinuity in my argument's next stage.

2

Discipleship before the Reformation

As the world in which Christians lived changed—sometimes dramatically—so did the precise ways in which the most dedicated believers expressed their commitment to Christ. It is the argument of the present chapter that despite such modifications in emphasis, the character of discipleship remained remarkably steady—in terms especially of its premises and practices—from the time of the apostles to the time of the Protestant Reformation. In the following chapter, I will show that, mutatis mutandis, the same continuity is found from the time of the Reformation until the Enlightenment of the eighteenth century. This consistency is the more remarkable, given the dramatic alterations of the social circumstances in which Christians lived.

I remind the reader that this survey of teachings about discipleship is necessarily partial, based as it is on the literature that has been preserved. We have precious little evidence for how ordinary believers lived out their commitment. We gain some hints from sermons, which tell us at least what preachers saw as inadequacies in dedication—as when John Chrysostom rants against wealthy ostentation, or when Augustine worries about his congregants attending *refrigeria*[1]—but these hints also are particular and partial and fall far short of providing the stuff for a social history. As in the compositions of the New Testament itself, then, we have for the most part the evidence provided by the most ardently committed of believers—they *are* disciples—who write for the sake of those equally or almost as equally committed to Jesus as they are. But if such

1. These were memorial celebrations at the tombs of the dead. See F. Van der Meer, *Augustine the Bishop* (New York: Sheed & Ward, 1961).

writings do not tell us what Christians actually did, they are splendid evidence for what Christians thought they *should* be doing. In a word, this literature serves our purpose precisely by its idealistic character: it expresses the vision of discipleship held by the writer, and the vision the writer supposes his or her reader to hold as well.

MARTYR PIETY

By the time he wrote the Acts of the Apostles around the year 85 CE, the evangelist Luke already knew of the violent deaths suffered by Stephen, James, and Paul—all at the hands of religious and political authorities (Acts 7:54–60; 12:1; 20:21–24). He knows about at least some of the multiple imprisonments Paul suffered as a servant of Christ (Acts 16:19–24; 21:31–36; 23:31–35; 28:17–22; compare 2 Cor 11:23–27). Indeed, he portrays the execution of Stephen and the imminent arrest of Paul in terms that unmistakably echo the suffering and death of Jesus.[2] Already in Acts, the link between being a "witness" (*martyr*; see Acts 1:8) and a violent death is established.

The epilogue to John's Gospel, written sometime around 90 CE, likewise knows of Peter's death by execution (see John 21:18–19). The book of Revelation speaks of the many followers of Jesus who had borne witness in their blood (6:9–10; 12:11; 16:6; 17:6; 18:24; 19:2). Writing to the Corinthian church from Rome around 95, the author of 1 Clement speaks of "the noble examples" of Peter and Paul, telling his readers to "set before [their] eyes the good apostles," the "most righteous pillars of the church [who] were persecuted, and contended even unto death" (1 Clem. 5).

By the end of the first century, in short, it was clear that being a disciple was a hazardous proposition, and that to the degree believers publicly renounced the gods of the state, to the same degree a variety of afflictions could follow. Even the Letter to the Hebrews, which notes that its readers had not yet suffered death because of their resistance to sin (12:4), nevertheless noted how they had already experienced insult and persecution, imprisonment, and the expropriation of their property (10:32–34). The First Letter of Peter, in turn, tells readers,

2. See Luke Timothy Johnson, *The Acts of the Apostles*, Sacra Pagina 5 (Collegeville, MN: Liturgical Press, 1992), 138–44, 368–72.

> Do not be surprised at the fiery ordeal which comes upon you to prove you, as though something strange were happening to you. But rejoice insofar as you share Christ's sufferings, that you may also rejoice and be glad when his glory is revealed. If you are reproached for the name of Christ, you are blessed, because the Spirit of glory and of God rests upon you. Let none of you suffer as a murderer, or a thief, or a wrongdoer or a mischief-maker; yet if one suffers as a Christian [*hōs Christianos*], let him not be ashamed, but under that name let him glorify God. (1 Pet 4:12–16)

Bearing witness to Jesus in any public fashion would, it appears, bring with it the affliction that the witness Jesus himself bore (Rev 1:5).

The persecution and execution of Christians, first from the side of Jewish leaders, then (and more persistently) from the side of Roman authorities, who regarded the denial of the state gods and the ultimate lordship of the empire to be subversive of good order, were sporadic over the first three centuries of Christianity's existence but very real.[3] From the side of the state, the early second-century correspondence between Pliny the Younger and the emperor Trajan (*Letters of Pliny* 10.96) is of particular importance. From the Christian side, there are first the apocryphal acts of the apostles (dating from the second to third century) that end with a violent (even if transfigured) death of the apostle at the hands of the state.[4] Extant also are the *Acta* of contemporary martyrs, which make clear that the death of Christ's witness is in some real way an imitation of the witness of Jesus.[5]

3. For an overview, see W. H. C. Frend, *Martyrdom and Persecution in the Early Church: A Study of Conflict from the Maccabees to Donatus* (Oxford: Blackwell, 1965); Candida R. Moss, *Ancient Christian Martyrdom: Diverse Practices, Theologies, and Traditions* (New Haven: Yale University Press, 2012), and especially for the motif of imitating Jesus, Moss, *The Other Christs: Imitating Jesus in Ancient Ideologies of Martyrdom* (New York: Oxford University Press, 2010).

4. See Acts of Thomas 169–170; Acts of Andrew 51–55; Acts of Peter 34–41; and that section of the Acts of Paul called Martyrdom of Paul 1–7. The outlier is Acts of John, which lacks the martyrdom of the apostle (113–115).

5. See, for example, "The Martyrdom of the Holy Martyrs, Justin, Chariton, Charites, Paeton and Liberianus, Who Suffered at Rome," in *The Ante-Nicene Fathers*, ed. Alexander Roberts and James Donaldson, 10 vols. (1885–1887; repr., Peabody, MA: Hendrickson, 1994), 1:305–6; Herbert Musurillo, *The Acts of the Christian Martyrs* (Oxford: Oxford

Especially impressive in this regard is the Letter of the Christians in Vienne and Lyons to the Churches in Asia and Phrygia,[6] written and sent shortly after the (demon-inspired) persecution under Marcus Aurelius (177). The letter provides a vivid sense of what can be called a "martyr piety." Death is not chosen, but it is endured as a consequence of resisting the absolute claims of the state and standing in witness to Christ as Lord. Christians die because of their zeal for Christ (5.1.6), and their death is an imitation of Christ. The martyr Vettius "chose to lay down even his own life for the defense of the brethren. For he was and is a true disciple of Christ, and he follows the lamb wherever he goes" (5.1.10). In the case of Sanctus, "Christ suffering in him manifested great glory." In the suffering of Ponthinus, "Christ might triumph . . . as though he was Christ himself" (5.1.29–30). As an account purportedly written shortly after the events, we can suppose the use of such language to be spontaneous rather than a matter of literary calculation.

Another letter said to be composed shortly after the event (ca. 155–156) was sent from the church in Smyrna to the church in Philomelium and to churches everywhere, recounting the Martyrdom of Polycarp. The bishop's arrest and death are described intentionally in terms that recall the death of Jesus, "to show us from above a martyrdom in accordance with the gospel" (1.1; see also 19.1), and "that we too might become his imitators" (1.2). Polycarp's death put an end to a persecution in which many were killed: by "the grace of Christ," they were able to contend with the beasts (3.1), which was at the same time combat with the devil (2.4), because they "looked to the good things that are preserved for those who endure" (2.2–3).

Polycarp enters the arena to be a "partner with Christ" (*Christou koinōnos* [6.2]). When set on fire, his prayer continues the theme of participation: "I bless thee, that thou hast granted me this day and hour, that I may share, among the number of the martyrs, in the cup of thy Christ, for the resurrection to everlasting life, both of soul and body in the immortality of the Holy Spirit" (14.2). His burning flesh seemed to those witnessing "as bread that is baked, or as gold and silver being refined in

---

University Press, 1972), contains the Acts of the Scillitan Martyrs (in North Africa) as well as the Passion of Felicity and Perpetua, 86–89 and 106–31.

6. The letter is preserved by Eusebius, *Ecclesiastical History* 5.1.1–5.2.2.

a furnace."[7] The authorities did not want to release Polycarp's body to his followers, "lest they leave the crucified one and begin to worship this man" (17.2), and in fact some of the saint's associates wanted "to have fellowship [*koinōnia*] with his holy flesh" (17.1). The narrator clarifies the proper form of piety: "for Him [viz. Jesus] we worship as the Son of God, but the martyrs we love as disciples and imitators of the Lord . . . grant that we too might be their companions and fellow-disciples" (*koinōnous kai symmathētas* [17.3]).

By far the most vivid firsthand evidence for martyrdom as the logical telos of discipleship is found in the seven letters by Ignatius, bishop of Antioch, written to churches on his journey to Rome as a captive during the reign of the emperor Trajan (98–117). His letters take up a number of topics—false teaching, the authority of bishops, the importance of unity—but as Ignatius faces almost certain death because of his belief, his mind and heart focus on the moment when he will become, as he puts it, "a true disciple" (Ign. *Eph.* 1.2; Ign. *Rom.* 4.2) and "attain to God" (Ign. *Eph.* 12.2; Ign. *Magn.* 14.1; Ign. *Rom.* 8.3) or "attain to Jesus Christ" (Ign. *Rom.* 5.3).[8]

The power in which Christians participate draws them to the same destiny and the same reward as Jesus. Ignatius declares that his spirit is "devoted to the cross" (Ign. *Eph.* 18.1), and that by his own death he hopes to "be worthy to show the honor of God" (Ign. *Eph.* 21.2). The reality of Christ's own suffering and reward—rather than being a mere appearance as some maintain—is of ultimate importance because Ignatius has literally staked his very life on its truth. If Christ's sufferings are not real, he asks, "why am I a prisoner and why do I fight the beasts?" (Ign. *Trall.* 10.1). And he makes the connection explicit: "For this reason also we suffer, that we may be found disciples [*mathētai*] of Jesus Christ our only teacher" (Ign. *Magn.* 9.1).

Ignatius is most explicit concerning his desire to imitate Christ ("to set the world towards God, that I may rise to Him") in his letter to the Ro-

---

7. The images of "cup" and "bread" clearly evoke the sacramental participation in the body and blood of Christ in the Eucharist (see ch. 1). I am using the translation of Kirsopp Lake, *The Apostolic Fathers*, Loeb Classical Library (Cambridge: Harvard University Press, 1915), 2:312–43.

8. Citations from Ignatius are likewise taken from Lake, *Apostolic Fathers*, 1:172–277.

man church, for that congregation is most able to either hinder or help him on his way. He asks them not to prevent his act of witness: "suffer me to be eaten by the beasts, through whom I can attain to God." Using a metaphor that echoes the eucharistic meal, he declares, "I am God's wheat, and I am ground by the teeth of the wild beasts that I may be found the pure bread of Christ" (Ign. *Rom.* 4.1). Instead, he wants his Roman readers to speed the process along: "Rather, entice the wild beasts that they may become my tomb, and leave no trace of my body, that when I fall asleep I be not burdensome to any. Then I shall truly be a disciple of Jesus Christ, when the world shall not see even my body" (4.2). It would be difficult to find a more startling identification drawn between the death and resurrection of Jesus and the anticipated martyrdom of his saint. Ignatius therefore sees his progress toward martyrdom as "beginning to be a disciple" (5.3) and is committed to reaching that goal: "suffer me to follow the example of the passion of my God" (*epistrepsate moi mimēten einai tou pathous tou theou mou* [6.3]).

Origen of Alexandria (184–254) is a final witness to the martyr piety of the second and third centuries. His father, Leonides, was executed under Septimus Severus in 202, but Origen was deflected from following him in martyrdom by the obligation of caring for his family and the Alexandrian catechetical school whose head he had become. Although not technically a martyr, he himself died as a consequence of the tortures he underwent in the persecution of Decius in 253. Earlier, he wrote *Exhortation to Martyrdom* to his friends Ambrose and Protocteus during the persecution of Maximin Thrax in 235. Origen is the first great Scripture scholar in Christianity and arguably its first and greatest theologian, so the *Exhortation* is carefully reasoned and replete with scriptural citations; but the personal passion of the author also shines through.[9]

Origen emphasizes that the impression of Christ's death being a loss is mistaken; it is, rather, the source of benefits (2) greater than can be imagined (3, 34, 47). Like Ignatius, he sees martyrdom as the means of being fully united with God (3)—by leaving the body, one lives with the Lord (4). Martyrdom is the expression of the fullest possible love toward God (6), in which the gift of the entire self to God (11) results in

---

9. I use the translation of John J. O'Meara in Origen, *Prayer, Exhortation to Martyrdom*, Ancient Christian Writers 19 (New York: Newman, 1954).

the fullness of life (12). Such benefits accrue not only to the one dying. The martyr's death also benefits others (30), not only through providing an example that edifies (41) but in the same manner that Christ's death brought benefits to all (50). Origen sees martyrdom as a contest—just as the life of faith is a contest for virtue (5)—but one that involves battling the demons that are at work in idolatry, the idolatrous state, and the human desire for safety (18, 32, 34, 40, 45):

> Thus, we can see what piety and the love of God, which is stronger than all other loves, can achieve against the most cruel sufferings and the severest tortures. This love of God does not tolerate the co-existence of human weakness but drives it away as an enemy alien from the whole soul. And this weakness becomes powerless in the case of one who can say, "the Lord is my strength and my praise," and, "I can do all things in Him who strengthens me, Christ Jesus, our Lord." (27)

Paradoxically, the death that appears in the eyes of the world as shameful is in fact a sharing in the triumph of Christ:

> We must also sense no shame whatever at suffering what God's enemies consider to be shameful. . . . [N]ow you appear, as it were, in triumphal procession, taking up the cross of Jesus and following him as he goes before you to appear before magistrates and kings, that by making the journey with you, he may give you a mouth of wisdom. (36)[10]

Is martyr piety a distortion of the vision of discipleship found in the New Testament? Far from it. In the most exigent circumstances imaginable—the threat of violent death—these Christians focused on the central truth of the New Testament concerning the death and resurrection of Jesus and laid claim to the promise of eternal life extended to those who took up their own cross and followed Jesus even to the same kind

---

10. The reversal of imperial propaganda ("triumphal procession") would have struck the original readers much more powerfully than it can present-day readers. Note as well how Origen both quotes Paul and merges the following of Christ to trial before imperial magistrates with the promissory language of Luke 21:12–19.

of violent and unjust death. As Origen suggests, the contest that is the life of faith in all circumstances becomes, in martyrdom, a face-to-face battle with the demonic forces that demands obeisance to human power rather than God's authority. Following Christ has little meaning if it does not also entail following him to death in witness to the truth.

Desert Discipleship

The most sudden and cataclysmic alteration in Christian circumstances occurred in the fourth century with Constantine's conversion and subsequent patronage of the faith that had suffered so severely (and recently) under imperial suppression and persecution. At one stroke, the danger of violent death was removed, and with it, the disappearance of martyrdom as the natural expression of discipleship. By imperial decision, Christians were moved from places of hiding to a posture of public display, from a situation in which their property could be expropriated by the state to one in which the emperor bestowed property on them, from occupying a marginal, indeed repudiated, social status to a central role in society. The cross of Christ went from the cause of shame and torture to the symbol of imperial victory emblazoned on the banners that imperial troops carried into battle.[11] It is not in the least surprising that most Christians not only adapted themselves quickly to their new status as the favored (and eventually exclusive) imperial religion and celebrated their triumph as miraculous.[12]

But not all believers regarded this new privileged position positively. Even before the peace of Constantine, in fact, some believers, especially

11. For the complexities of the progression into "the Constantinian era," see Robin Lane Fox, *Pagans and Christians* (New York: Knopf, 1987); Jaroslav Pelikan, *The Excellent Empire: The Fall of Rome and the Triumph of the Church* (San Francisco: HarperSanFrancisco, 1987); Ramsay MacMullen, *Christianizing the Roman Empire, AD 100–400* (New Haven: Yale University Press, 1984). For the privileges showered on the church, see Eusebius, *Life of Constantine*.

12. See Luke Timothy Johnson, *Among the Gentiles: Greco-Roman Religion and Christianity*, Anchor (Yale) Bible Reference Library (New Haven: Yale University Press, 2009), 253–60, and notes, 387–92. For expressions of triumphalism, see Firmicius Maternus, *On the Error of Pagan Religions*, Lactantius, *The Divine Institutes* and *The Death of the Persecutors*.

in Egypt, Syria, and Palestine, sought a more demanding form of discipleship by fleeing cities and inhabiting the desert places of the wilderness. The prototypical figure is Anthony of Egypt (ca. 251–356), whose life was encomiastically depicted in 360 by Athanasius of Alexandria. His *Life of Anthony* was explicitly written to provide an example to other solitaries (*Life* 93–94), and the little book had a tremendous influence on them.[13]

This first anchorite—the term comes from the Greek *anachōrein* ("to dwell apart")—fled to the desert as a literal response to Jesus's call in the Gospel to sell all one's possessions and follow him, words that Anthony heard read at worship (*Life* 2–4). Bestowing what he had owned on his relatives, Anthony sought a total commitment to the Lord. In the wilderness, stripped of worldly comforts, he did battle with demons through fasting and prayer. The evil spirits that formerly were seen to be at work in pagan worship (and the pagan state that supported such worship) now were revealed as the insidious powers at work in human vice. Only serious fasting and prayer could reveal how profound and persistent are the attractions of gluttony, sloth, and lust. The contest waged against such demons could legitimately be termed a "white martyrdom": if blood was not shed, life was nevertheless spent utterly in the quest for God.

The desert disciples also sought to fulfill Paul's command in 1 Thessalonians 5:17 to "pray without ceasing."[14] The favorite form of such constant prayer was the Psalms. Some of the desert disciples were reputed to have recited the entire Psalter in a single day. Such prayer could accompany work at simple tasks such as weaving. Paradoxically, a life of such self-renunciation proved to be highly attractive, drawing men and women from every social class. Athanasius notes, "And so, from then on, there were monasteries in the mountains and the desert was made a city by monks, who left their own people and registered themselves for citizenship in the heavens" (*Life* 14).

---

13. I use the translation of Robert C. Gregg in Athanasius, *The Life of Anthony*, Classics of Western Spirituality (New York: Paulist, 1980). For overall orientation, see William Harmless, SJ, *Desert Christians: An Introduction to the Literature of Early Monasticism* (New York: Oxford University Press, 2004), and Derwas J. Chitty, *The Desert a City: An Introduction to the Study of Egyptian and Palestinian Monasticism under the Christian Empire* (Crestwood, NY: St. Vladimir's Seminary Press, 1999).

14. Sayings of the Fathers 12.2, 10.

Anthony himself sought solitude in ever more remote areas but found himself, almost in the manner of present-day celebrities, hounded by admirers and imitators (*Life* 47–50).[15] A distinctive feature of desert discipleship turned out to be the individual guidance provided to novices by those more experienced in the battle against Satan (the beginning of Christian "spiritual direction").[16]

The desert fathers and mothers who expressed through asceticism and prayer the witness to Christ that was formerly available through martyrdom therefore found themselves in a complex social network of communication and exchange, in which the constant feature was the search for greater wisdom, greater fidelity to the gospel.[17] The declarations and wise sayings found in the *Apophthegmata Patrum* (Sayings of the Fathers) were gathered and published by believers who had traveled great distances from the cities to learn directly from those who seemed to have triumphed over the world, the flesh, and the devil, and many joined their ranks.[18] In the early fifth century, a bishop named Palladius, who had himself spent years as a solitary, set off at the age of fifty-six to visit male and female anchorites "in the Egyptian desert and Libya, in the Thebaid and Syene . . . the Tabennesiotes, and those in Mesopotamia, and Palestine, and Syria, and in the West, those in Rome and Campania, and points near by."[19] In each location, he gathered accounts of the ascetical practices and miracles associated with diverse anchorites, proposing them as examples to be imitated by others.

Palladius's narrative concerning Melania, a wealthy matron who visited various monks, was imprisoned, and then became the patron

15. See Peter Brown, "The Rise and Function of the Holy Man in Late Antiquity," in *Society and the Holy in Late Antiquity* (Berkeley: University of California Press, 1982), 103–52.

16. See Luke Timothy Johnson, "Mentoring in the Roman Catholic Tradition," in *Mentoring: Biblical, Theological, and Practical Perspectives*, ed. D. Thompson and D. C. Murchison (Grand Rapids: Eerdmans, 2018), 136–47.

17. For a positive appreciation of desert discipleship, see Roberta C. Bondi, *To Love as God Loves: Conversations with the Early Church* (Philadelphia: Fortress, 1987).

18. For samples, see Helen Waddell, *The Desert Fathers* (Ann Arbor: University of Michigan Press, 1957).

19. See the prologue in Palladius, *The Lausiac History*, trans. Robert T. Meyer, Ancient Christian Writers 34 (New York: Newman, 1964). A similar account of anchorites in Syria is provided by Theodoret of Cyr (393–466) in *A History of the Monks of Syria*, trans. R. M. Price, Cistercian Studies 88 (Kalamazoo, MI: Cistercian, 1985).

of women religious, is instructive, for it shows how after Constantine, even believers who occupied high places in the empire longed for a more radical form of discipleship than was available in their newly comfortable circumstances (47). Palladius himself was a pupil of the learned archdeacon Evagrius of Pontus (345–399), whose youth in Constantinople had been both sophisticated and worldly, and who likewise sought salvation among the monks, first in Jerusalem and then in the Egyptian desert, where he gathered the sayings that form the basis of his ascetical works, the *Praktikos* and *Chapters on Prayer*.[20] A deeply learned teacher in the tradition of Origen of Alexandria, Evagrius brought the sensibility of contemplation to the practice of prayer, an element that was of great importance in subsequent monastic and mystical manifestations of discipleship.[21]

The importance of this desert moment in the shaping of the subsequent Christian understanding and practice of discipleship is clear. The anchorites defined their entire life as a participation in the passion of Christ. Their asceticism stood in witness to the hope of resurrection. A celibate life in solitude and poverty dedicated to prayer and fasting is either utter foolishness (and fanaticism) or a powerful witness to the gospel promise of eternal life.[22]

The desert monks contributed something more: the sages discerned the workings of the Spirit (or the unclean spirits) within the hearts of those they trained and in the process brought genuine psychological insight into the "journey of the soul."[23] The subtleties of self-deception and grandiosity among would-be disciples are identified and analyzed. When John Cassian (360–435), a great admirer of his Egyptian teachers, organized their wisdom into his *Institutes and Conferences*, he in effect constructed something like a Christian version of Plutarch's *Moralia*,

20. In Socrates's *Ecclesiastical History* 4.23 is found an admiring portrait of Evagrius as the disciple of two desert monks named Macarius, and substantial quotations from his work.

21. Contemplative prayer appears briefly in Sayings of the Fathers 18–19.

22. It would be a mistake to think of their life as completely solipsistic or self-preoccupied. They had great concern for patience (Sayings of the Fathers 7.5, 32, 36, 38; 19.19), for humility (8.9, 19; 15.1, 7, 28), for hospitality (13.7), for obedience (14.5), and for love of the neighbor as well as of God (17.1–2).

23. See the sayings on "discretion" (10.16, 33, 53).

with a distinctively evangelical understanding of the vices that opposed
the life of the Spirit and of the virtues that expressed the genuine work
of the Spirit—and all with impressive psychological sophistication.[24]
Cassian, in turn, was required reading for monks in both Eastern and
Western monasticism.

MONASTIC DISCIPLESHIP

That the eremitical life in the desert was inherently unstable is clear
even from the writings that praise it: motives for following such a charismatic life could be mixed, character could remain underdeveloped, and
the dangers of self-delusion were amplified by a solitary life. It was in
response to such concerns that the first form of coenobitic monasticism
was established by Saint Pachomius (290–346), a former Roman soldier who was converted in 313 and who founded a monastery at Taben-
nisi around 320. By the time of his death, he had under his authority
some nine monasteries for men and two for women, with thousands
of members.[25]

The *Pachomian Rule* regulated a semieremitical form of monasticism,
in which "the solitary life" was carried out in association with others.[26]
Most of the monk's time was spent alone, in prayer and the working
of small crafts. Times in common were devoted to meals and common
prayer (including the Eucharist) and instruction by elders. The *Conferences* of Cassian reflect this social arrangement, as do his *Institutes*. The
Pachomian version of monasticism was taken over and altered by Basil
the Great, whose *Rules* ("lesser" and "greater") influenced Benedict but

24. On the vices, for example, see conference 5 ("On Principal Faults"), conference 6
("On the Death of Saints"), conference 7 ("On Inconstancy of Mind"), and conferences
9 and 10 ("On Prayer"). Cassian's *Institutes*, books 5–12, also provide a full analysis of
the vices that monks must combat.

25. "Coenobite" and "coenobitic" derives from the Greek *koinos bios* ("common life").
The Greek utopian antecedents (see Plato's *Republic* and Iamblichus's *Life of Pythago-
ras*) as well as Jewish experiments in this mode (see Philo's description of the Essenes,
and the sectarian community at Qumran) are obvious.

26. When Athanasius wrote *The Life of Anthony*, Pachomian monasticism was
already widespread in Egypt and undoubtedly formed much of the readership for
that work.

also became the frame for the semieremitical monasticism practiced in the East up to the present. Pachomius and his successors restored a critical balance to the monastic life by insisting that discipleship was not merely a matter of solitary searching but above all a matter of instantiating *church*. Discipleship means, in one degree or another, learning Christ and imitating Christ in the presence of—or at least in communication with—other learners.

Deservedly considered the patriarch of Western monasticism, however, is Benedict of Nursia (ca. 480–550),[27] who founded coenobitical communities in Italy at Subiaco and Monte Cassino, and whose *Rule for Monks* (ca. 540) quickly became the most significant frame for the practice of discipleship over the next thousand years. Written in lapidary Latin replete with citations of and allusions to Scripture, it is widely and properly regarded as one of the most impressive constitutions ever composed, providing a version of monastic discipleship possible to very ordinary people. In contrast to the impression given by desert ascetics whose feats of physical and mental exertion were daunting, Benedict constructed a way of life that any believer with good will could pursue. He modestly calls the monastery "a school of the Lord's service," thereby precisely invoking all the ancient associations of "discipleship." Benedict's sister Scholastica served as abbess over female Benedictines who also lived by the *Rule of Saint Benedict*.

Although Benedict's genius was legislation rather than rhetoric, the prologue to the *Rule of Saint Benedict* shows itself profoundly steeped in scriptural imagination. The disciple is summoned to "hearken to the words of the master" and return to God by obedience after having turned from God by disobedience.[28] Obedience (to the rule and the abbot) is central to this form of discipleship. Disobedience is a manifestation of pride, while obedience is the expression of humility (ch. 5). Benedict imagines the return to God as (paradoxically) an ascent up a ladder of

27. The few details about his life (well adorned with scripturally allusive legend) are found in Gregory the Great, *Dialogues* 2.

28. The designation "master" (*magister*) here may be an echo of another ("earlier"?) rule, called by scholars the *Rule of the Master*. Its precise relationship to the *Rule of Saint Benedict* is debated. What is not debatable is that Benedict's version was the one that carried the day.

increased degrees of humility (ch. 7). He concludes the prologue in a fashion that epitomizes the classical vision of discipleship:

> Through the continual practice of monastic observance and the life of faith, our hearts are opened wide, and the way of God's commandments is run in a sweetness of love that is beyond words. Let us then never withdraw from discipleship to him, but persevering in his teachings in the monastery until death, let us share in the sufferings of Christ through patience, and so deserve also a share in his kingdom.[29]

Benedict admires hermits and thinks that some who have passed through his "school of service" might be fit for that life. But his school is for "beginners" and is demanding enough to require a lifetime to learn. His rule does not demand severe physical asceticism; in matters of clothing, food, and drink, the monks are probably more comfortable, because more secure, than the majority of peasants in the sixth century. The chief asceticism demanded by Benedict came from the distinctive Benedictine vow of *stabilitas*, namely, the asceticism of a common life that was truly common. A life together that avoided murmuring (*murmuratio* = complaining and gossiping) and cultivated charity in all circumstances is an asceticism based in the daily grind of living face-to-face over the course of a lifetime.

In addition to vows of obedience and stability, Benedictine monks have another distinctive vow: *conversatio morum* promises to change or transform one's life in the context of the monastic regimen. Benedictines do not vow poverty, even though "a monk shall call nothing his own" (ch. 33); rather they have a community of possessions in which everything is at the disposition of the abbot, a practice that is explicitly linked to that of the earliest church. Monks "do not retain disposition even over their own bodies or wills." The commitment to celibacy, finally, does not require a vow because it is the natural concomitant of a single-gender community.[30]

---

29. I am using the translation by Abbot Parry, OSB (Hertfordshire: Fowler Wright Books, 1990), 4.

30. Nevertheless, celibacy was widely understood as one of the evangelical virtues

Benedict organizes his school around the broad categories of prayer (*ora*) and work (*labora*). Work involves all of the tasks required for life in common (cooking, washing, tailoring, baking, receiving guests) as well as the tasks of supporting the community through farming and herding (ch. 48). Work is as essential as prayer, and the cellarer of the monastery should regard the material resources of the community "as though they were the sacred vessels of the altar" (ch. 31). Younger monasteries, or those in straitened circumstances, will need all the monks to do manual labor (ch. 63). In larger or more well-established communities, some can be choir monks whose main work involves study and the production of manuscripts, while lay brothers do the bulk of the heavy manual labor.

The link between work and prayer is suggested by Benedict's term *Opus Dei* ("the work of God") for the common prayer of the monastery. The rule gives careful attention to the disposition of reciting (chanting) the Psalms in the divine office every day, so that in a week, the entire Psalter—and a little more—is prayed (chs. 8–18). Benedict chides the lazy monks of his day for requiring an entire week to accomplish what the desert fathers did in a single day (ch. 18)! Based on the psalmist's statement, "seven times a day have I praised you" (Ps 119:164), the office is divided into seven daylight hours of prayer (lauds, prime, terce, sext, none, vespers, compline), and following the psalm's verse, "At midnight I got up to give you praise" (119:62), the monks rise in the night to pray matins (ch. 16). The prayer life of Benedictines included the celebration of the Eucharist, and the form of contemplation called *lectio divina*, a ruminative and reflective reading of Scripture or the fathers:

> Is not every page of the Old or New Testament, every word of the Divine Author, a most direct rule for our human life? Does not every book of the Catholic Fathers proclaim that we should make our way by the most direct path to our creator? (ch. 73)

The spirituality of the Benedictine line is not complicated. It emphasizes obedience as the expression of faith, humility, and silence. Silence

---

together with obedience and poverty, based on Jesus's statement concerning eunuchs in Matt 19:11–12.

is not only a prerequisite for hearing God's word but is also essential for the practice of charity in a community where people are joined together for life. Benedict saw his school as preparatory for the life of a hermit, but for most who lived within it, his rule was so rigorously evangelical as to demand a lifetime of transformation (*conversatio morum*). As Benedictine monasteries became more prosperous—as they were bound to do with energetic people working hard and pooling their resources—his school took on a more explicitly educational dimension: over the next millennium, Benedictine monasteries formed the basis both for Christian discipleship and for scholarship, a linkage nicely captured by the phrase "the love of learning and the desire for God."[31]

The piety of Benedictines was by no means turned totally inward. Benedict devotes a substantial chapter to the reception of guests (ch. 53), noting that in such guests, "Christ is received." He states, "Special care is to be shown in the reception of the poor and of pilgrims, for in them especially Christ is received." The echo of Matt 25 is unmistakable, and hospitality has remained the signal mark of this form of monasticism down to the present day. For almost a thousand years, monasteries were the center of ecclesial life and the place where technology and culture were sustained and developed. Monks were also the first and most important missionaries throughout Europe.

The monastic form of discipleship, moreover, proved impressively resilient. The various reforms of Benedictine life—at Cluny in 910, at Citeaux in 1098 (the Cistercians), at Grand Chartreuse in 1084 (the Carthusians), and at Camaldoli in 1012 (the Camaldolese)—did not reject Benedict's vision but intensified it by being more ascetically demanding. And the religious orders that arose during the medieval period shared the ideal of a vowed commitment to Christ and a communal life marked by prayer and fasting; the mendicant orders (Dominicans [1216] and Franciscans [1210]) included both male and female members and were—at least in the ideal—far more radical in their poverty than were monks. Their distinctiveness lay in their joining these practices to a specific form of active ministry (preaching or teaching or caring for the outcast). Forms of religious association proliferated in semimonastic

---

31. See Jean LeClercq, *The Love of Learning and the Desire for God: A Study of Monastic Culture* (New York: Fordham University Press, 1961).

orders like the Beguines, or the Brethren of the Common Life (Thomas à Kempis's community), or in Cathedral Chapters and the Canons Regular that were connected to them. Laypeople participated as they could despite their worldly occupations in such associations through becoming an oblate or a member of a third order. Still other men and women recovered the solitary asceticism of the desert by becoming anchorites or anchoresses—devoting themselves totally to prayer and fasting, and dependent on the charity of others for their survival.

The monastic life in the medieval church was not an isolated phenomenon but was an ethos that pervaded all of society, providing the basic frame for Christian discipleship and the basis for the rich forms of mysticism that flourished between the tenth and fifteenth centuries. The most salient feature of this mysticism, indeed, is its firm grounding in the ecclesial practices at the center of all Christian life: praying the Psalms, participating in the Eucharist, sharing possessions, fasting, meditating on the passion of Christ. Christian mysticism was not an exception to this ethos; it was its concentrated expression. The diminishment of the self (mortification) had as its goal the enlargement of the presence of God and the more perfect imitation of Christ. Within the evangelical paradigm of death and resurrection, the "mortification of the flesh" liberated the spirit to participate proleptically in "the life of the angels."[32]

MEDIEVAL MYSTICISM

Mystical prayer flourished within this complex network and Christian associations. The contemplative element already present among the desert disciples expanded and deepened within this stable environment.[33] Even Benedict of Nursia, whose *Rule* could not be more down-to-earth, was said by his biographer to have beheld the whole world in a single

32. Mortification (putting to death) of the flesh only began with physical asceticism and involved the suppression of all impulses toward vice—clearly a lifetime task. The "flesh" here, in other words, is thoroughly Pauline in meaning (see Gal 5:13–21). The "angelic life" (*bios angelikos*) was early on applied to monastic observance, troping Jesus's response to the Sadducees that in the resurrection, there would not be marriage because the children of the resurrection are like angels (Luke 20:27–38).

33. For an overview, see Bernard McGinn, *The Presence of God: A History of Western Christian Mysticism*, 4 vols. (New York: Crossroad, 1991–1995).

ray of the sun while at his nighttime prayer.[34] Mystical writings within
the broadly Benedictine tradition tended to be grounded in the reading
of Scripture, seeking the deeper implications for the soul beneath the
literal (historical) sense of the text. Thus, already in the sixth century,
Gregory the Great, himself a Benedictine monk, composed the *Moralia
on Job*, which probed the moral and allegorical dimensions of the text.
The *Moralia* was read by monks at matins for centuries. Thus, Bernard
of Clairvaux (1090–1153) preached eighty-six sermons to his fellow Cistercians on the Song of Songs. Having experienced the warming love
of God in his own life (sermon 74), he uncovers layer after layer of the
meaning of divine love as it was expressed allegorically in the ancient
erotic poem. Similarly, the Cistercian William of Saint-Thierry (1085–
1148) wrote *Exposition on the Epistle to the Romans*, which moved the
reader from scriptural interpretation to contemplative prayer, and the
Augustinian canon Richard of Saint Victor (d. 1173) developed an entire
psychology and epistemology of contemplative prayer in *The Twelve Pa-
triarchs (Benjamin Minor)* and *The Mystical Ark (Benjamin Major)*. The
female Benedictine Hildegard of Bingen (1098–1179) was unusual only
to the extent that her scriptural readings (as in *Scivias*) were fueled by
personal visions, and her mystical life was aligned with a wide-ranging
scientific curiosity and impressive administrative ability.

Perhaps the greatest—and most widely diffused—example of monastic contemplative practice is the anonymous fourteenth-century
Cloud of Unknowing, which, while emphasizing the classical monastic
virtues of humility and charity, proposes in a simple and charming manner that does not in the least disguise the author's deep immersion in
the mystical tradition, as represented by authors such as Dionysius the
Areopagite, to instruct a disciple in the path of prayer. Intensely practical, it eschews speculative knowing and advocates a work of prayer in
which the desirous will shoots "darts of love" toward God through the
cloud of unknowing.[35]

34. Gregory the Great, *Dialogues* 2.35.
35. Dionysius the Areopagite is the pseudonym of a late fifth- and early sixth-
century writer in Greek whose employment of a Neoplatonic philosophical framework
in compositions such as *The Celestial Hierarchy* and *Mystical Theology* was of considerable importance in asserting the apophatic dimension of theology (every positive
statement made about God must be countered by a negative statement—God is not

Mystics and teachers of mysticism were found among the mendicant orders as well. Francis of Assisi (1181–1226) was committed to a radical form of evangelical poverty—the first friars survived by begging—and to an active ministry among the poorest of the poor. He was himself a mystic (and stigmatic),[36] and with Clare of Assisi (1193–1274) combined simplicity with a passionate love for Christ. Franciscan spirituality finds its greatest exponent in Bonaventure (1221–1274): *The Soul's Journey into God* is a masterpiece of theological compression that links Francis's ecstatic spirituality to medieval, Eastern, and even Islamic elements, and his *Tree of Life* continues Francis's emphasis on the humanity of Jesus with a set of meditations on Jesus's life. The Dominicans followed their intellectual bent—this was the order that produced the thirteenth-century systematic theologians Albert the Great and Thomas Aquinas—in such teachers as Meister Eckhardt (1260–1328), who made extensive use of apophatic theology, Johannes Tauler (1300–1361), whose sermons delivered to a lay association called "the friends of God" were much admired by Martin Luther, and Henry Suso (1300–1366), who also worked with "the friends of God."

The number of female mystics in the medieval church is striking, especially when contrasted to Judaism and Islam, where the mystical strands of Kabbalism and Sufism were almost entirely male.[37] In addition to the Benedictine Nun Hildegard of Bingen, there are the two great reformer-mystics. Birgitta of Sweden (1303–1373) began the Order of the Holy Savior (the Birggittines) after the death of her husband and fought for the reform of the clergy and the unification of the papacy. The visions that she had over the last thirty years of her life she recorded in *The Heavenly Book of Revelations*. Catherine of Siena (1347–1380) was a third-order

---

approached through positive knowing so much as by prayerful unknowing). Another work from the Eastern monastic tradition composed by John Climacus (sixth to seventh century), *The Ladder of Divine Ascent*, also affected the Western mystical tradition. The *Ladder* provided a systematic analysis of the approach to God through virtue (remember the *Rule of Saint Benedict*, ch. 7), leading to contemplative prayer, at the highest reaches of which is found the simple repetition of the Jesus prayer ("Lord Jesus Christ, have mercy on me a sinner" [see *Ladder* 27–30]).

36. The *stigmata* are the wounds of the crucified Christ (hands, feet, side) that have been experienced by certain saints, from Francis to Padre Pio in the twentieth century.

37. In Sufism, the great mystic and teacher Rabi'a Basri is the obvious exception.

Dominican whose three hundred extant letters testify to her efforts to reform the church, and whose *Dialogue of Divine Providence* was impressive enough to have her eventually declared a "Doctor ("Teacher") of the Church."[38] Mystics were found also among the Beguines, the lay associations of committed female disciples. Mechtild of Magdeburg (1208–1282/94) was such a Beguine before spending her last years in a Cistercian monastery. She had her first visionary experience at twelve, and in her forties began recording her visions at the command of her Dominican confessor, completing the seven books of *The Flowing Light of the Godhead*, in which the genres and subgenres of courtly literature are exploited, transposing the language of erotic love into that of mystical rapture. Similarly, a thirteenth-century Beguine known only as Hadewijch left a substantial collection of writings (letters, poetry, accounts of visions) having considerable literary merit, with eroticism once more serving to express the passion of the divine-human relationship.

It is important to stress that this great outpouring of mysticism was not eccentric or individualistic, much less rebellious. Medieval mystics did not seek something other than the canon and creed; they sought only the deepest meanings of the canon and creed. The mystics I have named, for example, all lived within communities and associations that prayed the Psalms together, that celebrated the sacraments together (above all the Eucharist), that walked together through the cycles of the liturgical year, following Jesus. Given the premise that God is most real and most present and most powerful, moreover, prayer appears as correspondingly the most powerful expression of love, not only toward God but also for others. The communion of saints was not in the medieval period an abstract or, still less, an otiose theological proposition. It was the reality within which disciples lived. They appealed to the saints who had already entered God's realm (above all the Virgin Mary) for assistance both for themselves and for others. Their prayer for believers who had died, in turn, was regarded as the best and highest assistance that they could render them. Just as at the material level, churches, cathedral chapters, monasteries, religious orders, and lay associations were all linked in pat-

38. The designation is one that the Catholic Church has accorded such great theologians as Augustine, Basil, and Thomas Aquinas. Teresa of Ávila has also been so designated, and much more recently, Thérèse of Lisieux.

terns of mutual support and assistance, so at the spiritual level, the body of Christ and the communion of saints symbolically undergirded these complex interactions.

Two further dimensions of this life of contemplative prayer in diverse social settings can be observed. First, it is noteworthy how the prayer of the mystics tended to focus on the presence of Christ in the Eucharist and the passion (suffering) of Christ. Within a highly routinized pattern of life shaped by ascetical practices, the same understanding of imitating Christ that we saw in martyr piety continues. Now, meditation on the suffering of Jesus by one practicing the mortification of the flesh enables a true participation (fellowship) in that suffering—in the hope of a share in the blessed resurrection. Second, those committed to serious contemplative prayer did so under the direction of a confessor or spiritual guide—someone who had already progressed in the same way and knew its pitfalls and dangers. The antecedent here was the practice of the desert disciples.

These aspects are illustrated by mystics who lived as anchorites or anchoresses, that is, lived basically as hermits whose minimal material needs were met by those for whom the anchorite devoted his or her life in prayer.[39] The anonymous composition *Ancrene Wisse* was written as a guide for anchoresses: it takes a moderate approach to the external "rule of life" and emphasizes the inner rule of the heart; devotion should manifest love for God and love for Christ. Richard Rolle (1300–1349) left the academic life of Oxford at the age of nineteen and spent the rest of his life as a hermit. His many writings include a reflection on his own mystical life—that centered intensely and with personal warmth on the passion of Jesus (see *Incendium Amoris*)—and advice directed to anchoresses (*Form of Perfection*). Walter Hilton (1343–1396) was likewise university educated but spent his life as an Augustinian canon. He wrote *The Scale of Perfection* for an anchoress. Like John Climacus's *Ladder of Divine Ascent*, it provides a systematic discussion of the contemplative life, with a concentration on mortification and practice of prayer. It is filled with powerful feeling and an intense devotion to Jesus.

The complex social fabric of the late medieval period is illustrated by

---

39. See Eric Colledge, *The Medieval Mystics of England* (New York: Scribner's Sons, 1961).

The Book of Margery Kempe, the first English language autobiography, in which an illiterate but deeply religious laywoman (the mother of many children) dictates her religious adventures—including a pilgrimage to Jerusalem and a visit to the regional anchoress, Julian of Norwich—to her confessor, who puts them in writing. An anchoress, we learn, is as holy a site as is Jerusalem. Julian herself (1342–1423) is, apart from the brief mention by Margery Kempe, known only from her *Showings* (or *Revelations*), which have engrossed spiritual seekers even to the present (Thomas Merton was a devoted reader). The first and shorter version of her experience was composed shortly after the visions of the passion of Christ she received while, at the age of thirty, she was deathly ill. The longer version was composed some years after the event. Her deep and personal identification with the passion of Christ is a familiar theme—even though less noteworthy to present-day readers! But more startling are the insights found in some of the showings, such as the vision of all things in a hazelnut, or the assurance that "all things will be very well," and the language of "mother" used of God and of Jesus.[40]

Julian was an older contemporary of Thomas à Kempis,[41] whose *Imitation of Christ* was, as I noted in the introduction, written while he was a member of the Brethren of the Common Life. He would have recognized and praised what he read (had he the chance) in her *Showings*, as she would have been glad in what she read (had she the chance) in his *Imitatio*. They were both part of the great tradition that was, with all its variations, the classical construal of discipleship.

Thomas à Kempis died only twelve years before the birth of Martin Luther (1471/1483). Would the great Reformation brought about in the sixteenth century fundamentally alter the vision of earlier centuries? It is to that question I turn in the next chapter.

---

40. See Caroline Walker Bynum, *Jesus as Mother: Studies in the Spirituality of the High Middle Ages* (Berkeley: University of California Press, 1982).

41. Julian's dates are 1343–1416, and those of Thomas à Kempis are 1380–1471.

3

Post-Reformation Discipleship

The Protestant Reformation of the sixteenth century was not entirely unanticipated.[1] The fourteenth-century mystics Birgitta of Sweden and Catherine of Siena had agitated for the reform of the clergy and the papacy. In 1440, the Renaissance scholar Lorenzo Valla challenged the authenticity of the Donation of Constantine, the document on which the papacy had rested its claims to political authority.[2] The lawyer Marsilius of Padua posed an even more fundamental challenge to the legitimacy of papal power (*Defensor Pacis*, 1324). The Dominican friar Savonarola called for a return to Scripture in the original languages and a moral reform of the church and for his efforts was burned as a heretic in 1498. The scholars John Wycliffe in England (1330–1373) and Jan Hus in Bohemia (1372–1415) similarly called for a "return to Scripture" and a rethinking of the sacraments.[3] But such challenges were insufficiently massive to force substantial change in the institutional church. Nor, so far as I know, did any of these challenges touch on the character of discipleship as the imitation of Jesus.

In contrast, the protest and call to reform generated by leaders like Martin Luther (1483–1546) and Andreas Karlstadt (1486–1541) in Germany, John Calvin (1509–1564) and Ulrich Zwingli (1484–1531) in Swit-

---

1. For historical surveys of the period, see Diarmaid MacCulloch, *The Reformation: A History* (New York: Penguin Books, 2005), and Carlos M. N. Eire, *Reformations: The Early Modern World* (New Haven: Yale University Press, 2018).

2. In *Religious Profession*, he also attacked the ideals of the religious life as lived by monks and mendicants.

3. The Lollards associated with Wycliff, for example, considered the presence of Christ in the Eucharist as consubstantial rather than transsubstantial.

zerland, John Knox (1514–1572) in Scotland, William Tyndale (1494–1536) and Thomas Cromwell (1485–1540) in England, and Menno Simons (1496–1561) and John of Leiden (1509–1536) in the Netherlands—to name only a few—were both massive and substantial and fundamentally changed the shape of the Christian world in the West.

In one sense, the Reformation was overdetermined, with a variety of nonreligious factors contributing to the paroxysm of the early sixteenth century: the technology of printing that enabled the rapid spread of ideas; world exploration that opened eyes to peoples and cultures not included in the Bible; the intellectual impetus of the Renaissance, with its return to sources; and the development of European languages that began to dislodge the hegemony of medieval Latin. The Reformation both helped stimulate and was stimulated by all these cultural phenomena.

The Reformation was diverse from the beginning, leading some to speak of "reformations." But Reformed movements were always much clearer about what they rejected than what they affirmed, so that the positive programs advanced by diverse reformers differed considerably, ranging from Anglicanism at one extreme, which retained many elements of Catholicism but had the English king at its head, through Lutheranism, which was daring theologically but socially conservative, and Calvinism, which scoured the decks much more vigorously and erected an alternative society, to the Anabaptists, who combined religious reform and social subversion.

But all reformers agreed on certain things. The entire monastic tradition was rejected, and in many cases, monasteries were pillaged. The authority of the pope and with it the entire hierarchical system under the pope were dismantled. Sacramental and liturgical forms were whittled down, with the Eucharist reduced to a memorial meal—no more real presence, no more sacrifice of the mass—and all the paraphernalia of late medieval piety (pilgrimages, indulgences, relics, sacramentals of every sort) were dismissed as superstitious claptrap.[4] Jettisoning the

---

4. There was considerable disagreement, however, on exactly what sort of presence of Christ did occur in the celebration of the Lord's Supper, as the debate between Zwingli and Luther on this point indicates. Such disagreement on the Eucharist also had antecedents in the eleventh-century controversies connected to Berengar of Tours.

Sacramentals are those aspects of paraliturgical practice that are regarded as holy

real presence of Christ in the Eucharist naturally meant abandoning the forms of devotion to the Eucharist found in Julian and Mechtild and Thomas à Kempis. Since Scripture alone was the absolute measure of faith, the logic-chopping of the university doctors that so complicated theology were to give way to the simple and perspicuous teaching of the Bible. Perhaps most radically, discipleship was not to be the privilege of those who had made vows and lived in religious communities but an obligation of all believers by virtue of their baptism.[5]

Since medieval Catholicism was such a religious and political unity,[6] religious challenges also inevitably had political consequences. Most obviously, the dominance of the Holy Roman Empire and papal authority was shattered. The Holy Roman emperor became just another king, and the pope was just another bishop, as Europe divided and subdivided into discrete nations with distinct languages and versions of Christianity. Some nations remained steadfastly Catholic (notably Spain and France); others converted to diverse expressions of reform (the Netherlands, Germany, Switzerland, England, and Scotland), so that the axiom *cuius regio eius religio* ("whoever is king, his is the religion") obtained, leading to centuries of internecine war and international colonial competition.

The question we are pursuing, however, is this: amid all these seismic changes in religious form and expression, did the fundamental understanding of Christian discipleship also change? Did the charge against monks and mendicants—that they did not live up to their evangelical ideals but were dissolute and corrupt—mean that the reformers also disagreed with those ideals? Did they think that discipleship ought to mean something else entirely than the sort of imitation of Christ advocated by earlier Christians? Was discipleship portrayed as the amelioration of society rather than the perfection of the human person? Did the Reformation, in a word, represent an absolute rupture in Christian

---

and sanctifying but not at the level of the seven sacraments. For example, from 1524, Zwingli forbade the use of images, processions of the clergy, and the carrying of palms or relics in Holy Week.

5. The entire program is laid out with great vigor by Luther in his 1520 tractate, "An Open Letter to the Christian Nobility," found in *Three Treatises* (Philadelphia: Fortress, 1960), 9–111.

6. The Avignon Papacy (1309–1376) and the subsequent Western Schism (1378–1417), when rival popes vied for power, do not counter but rather confirm the point.

consciousness, or were there genuine lines of continuity? As in the last chapter, I seek to answer this question by looking at works of devotion or religious exhortation written from the Protestant side in the sixteenth through the eighteenth century.[7]

CATHOLIC CONTINUITY

Before pursuing that question, however, it is important to avoid giving the impression that the Catholic tradition (now Roman Catholic in Protestant eyes) disappeared. Just the opposite. The Counter-Reformation, as it is sometimes called, represented not only a polemical stance against Protestants but an internal reform within the Catholic communion. But this reform was moral rather than theological. Religious orders returned to their ascetical roots, and new orders arose in response to the new situation. Where they were allowed, monasteries and convents flourished, and the Catholic mystical tradition continued, even as more active religious orders worked to energize and educate Catholic laypeople.

No new order, for example, was more active in its ministry of education than the Society of Jesus (the Jesuits). But Ignatius of Loyola (1497–1541), as I noted in the introduction, was a devoted reader of *The Imitation of Christ* and had mystical experiences of his own. His *Spiritual Exercises* provided a template of a spirituality based firmly on the following of Christ to the members of the society from his own day to the present. Building on the foundation provided by *The Spiritual Alphabet* of the Franciscan Francisco de Osuna (1497–1541), in turn, Teresa of Ávila (1515–1582) and John of the Cross (1542–1591) shaped an understanding of contemplative prayer that was both profound and intricate, even as they reformed the Carmelite Order.[8] In a far simpler and more accessible fashion, Nicolas Herman (Brother Lawrence, 1614–1691), a lay brother in a Parisian Carmelite monastery, became a significant influence through *The Practice of the Presence of God*.

7. Because of the rapid proliferation both of denominations and their founders/ teachers, my review must be even more severely selective.

8. For Teresa (another female doctor of the church), see her *Life*, *The Way of Perfection*, and *The Interior Castle*; for John, see *The Ascent of Mount Carmel*, *The Spiritual Canticle*, and *The Dark Night of the Soul*.

Perhaps the greatest change within the Catholic tradition was the extension of discipleship instruction to those outside of monasteries and religious orders. The classic and widely disseminated work by Francis de Sales (1567–1622),[9] *An Introduction to the Devout Life*, was directed to committed laypeople of his Archdiocese of Geneva, adapting traditional notions of mortification (fasting, prayer, almsgiving) to the circumstances of educated, worldly, and even wealthy disciples. Similarly, Alphonsus Liguori (1696–1787) added to his technical work on moral theology accessible compositions on Mary, the way of perfection, the stations of the cross, and many other small treatments of specifically Catholic spirituality for lay readers. Finally, there is *The Spiritual Combat* by Lorenzo Scupoli (1530–1610), which rivaled even *The Imitation of Christ* in popularity and provided a systematic treatment of asceticism and prayer that was absolutely continuous with the *Conferences* of John Cassian, providing instruction in discipleship to Catholics for centuries.

This brief review should make clear that at least among Catholics, the first and classic vision of discipleship still held: the goal of the disciple is to be transformed according to the mind of Christ, to share in his sufferings in this mortal life in the hope of sharing as well in his eternal glory. But do we find (mutatis mutandis) the same among Protestant teachers? Remember that my concern is not for theological subtleties (justification/salvation/sanctification; the nuances of predestination) except as these might directly affect teaching on discipleship. The best access to their vision of discipleship, once more, is not through theological treatises but, whenever possible, the teaching that they directed to disciples themselves, now most often as the instruction of congregants by pastors.

LUTHER AND LUTHERAN PIETY

However great Martin Luther's impact on the future, it is accurate to say that he is deeply immersed in his medieval past. An Augustinian monk from the age of twenty-two to the age of thirty-seven (1505–1520), his

9. The printing press was an equal opportunity technology, and the post-Reformation proliferation of publications on both Catholic and Protestant sides is daunting.

angry rejection of what he regarded as the corruptions and perversions of the true faith in late medieval Catholicism was based on the tradition of authentic discipleship that had preceded him and in which he was deeply steeped. His Catholic piety can be seen, for example, in his devotion to Mary (see his commentary on the Magnificat) and in his conviction that discipleship required prayer and discipline as the expression rather than the replacement of faith.

His early treatise "The Freedom of a Christian" (addressed in 1520 to Pope Leo X), for example, states clearly, "It is appropriate for all Christians to let their only work and exercise be *forming the word and Christ in themselves*, constantly practicing and strengthening such faith, because no other work can make a Christian" (7; emphasis added). And because the soul that anticipates the next life remains now in the body, Luther considers forms of asceticism to be appropriate:

> One still remains in this bodily life on earth and must rule one's own life and relate with people. Now works begin to play a role, and one must not be idle. The body must be compelled and exercised by fasting, waking, working, and every form of discipline in moderation, so that it can obey and match the form and faith of the internal person and not hinder and resist them, as it is its nature to do when not compelled . . . an individual can derive the measure and insight for chastising the body, fasting, keeping vigil, working as necessary to subdue the obstinate willfulness of the body. (20–21)

Concerning the deeds that arise from faith, he declares, "If a work is not oriented toward serving others or toward suffering under another's will (so long as one is not forced to act against God's will), then it is not a good, Christian work" (29).[10] Luther teaches "Peter, the Master Barber," a simple way to pray, emphasizing the repetitive recitation of the Lord's Prayer, the Ten Commandments, and the creed, stressing that, whereas "praying constantly" may include other good deeds, prayer itself remains paramount in the life of discipleship:

10. I use the translation in *Luther's Spirituality*, ed. Philip D. W. Krey and Peter D. S. Krey, Classics of Western Spirituality (New York: Paulist, 2007).

One must see to it, however, that we do not gradually lose the habit of true prayer and begin to imagine that a great many works are necessary for our salvation and that doing them is ultimately better than prayer, and then interpret them to be necessary when they are not. In the end, as a result, we will become lax and lazy, cold, tired, and weary of prayer. For the devil, all around us, is not lazy or lax, and our flesh is still all too alive and ready to sin and inclined against the spirit of prayer.[11]

Luther did not in the least deviate from the traditional understanding of suffering as an essential component of following Christ. In a sermon preached at passion time in 1530,[12] he defends his teaching against the "false fanatics" who accuse him of teaching nothing but faith alone and ignoring the role of good works and suffering:

We note in the first place not only that Christ by his suffering saved us from the devil, death, and sin, but also that His suffering is an example we are to follow in our suffering. God has appointed not only that we should believe in the crucified Christ, but also be crucified with Him, as He clearly shows many places in the Gospels: "He who does not take his cross and follow me is not worthy of me" (Matt 10:38).

Such suffering is endured with an eye to a future reward promised by God: "Even though I suffer long, what is that compared with the great treasure that God has given to me—that I shall live eternally with Him, both now and in the world to come?" The promise is good because the suffering is not self-imposed but comes from fidelity to God: "We suffer because we hold the Word of God, preach it, learn it, practice it. Since this is the cause of our suffering, we have the same promise and the same cause for suffering which all the saints have always had." Nothing could be more traditional than Luther's conviction concerning the reason for such suffering by disciples:

11. "A Simple Way to Pray, for Master Peter the Barber," in *Luther's Spirituality*, 218.

12. "Sermon on Cross and Suffering," in *The Martin Luther Treasury*, ed. Erwin Paul Rudolph (Wheaton, IL: Victor Books, 1979), 81–86.

We want also to consider why our Lord God sends us such suffering. The reason is that in this way He wants to make us conformed to the image of His dear Son, so that we might become like Him here in suffering, and there, in that life to come, in honor and glory; as He says, "Was it not necessary that the Christ should suffer and enter into glory?" (Luke 14:26). God cannot accomplish this except through suffering and affliction.

The same traditional sense of discipleship continues in Lutheran teachers of the sixteenth and seventeenth centuries. Johan Arndt (1555–1621) wrote *True Christianity* between 1605 and 1610, a work that is regarded as seminal to Lutheran Pietism. His object, he says, was to "show to plain readers wherein true Christianity consists, namely in the exhibition of a true, living, and active faith which manifests itself in genuine godliness and the fruits of righteousness. . . . I further desired to show that true repentance proceeds from the inmost center of the heart; that the mind, heart, and affections must be changed; that we must be conformed to Christ and His holy gospel; and that we must be renewed by the Word of God, and become new creatures." Being a true Christian, he says, means that "we live in Christ and that he lives in us" (introduction 1).[13]

Arndt acknowledges that he follows in the path of such predecessors as Bernard, Tauler, and Thomas à Kempis but promises to avoid all taint of papish perversion in his instruction (introduction 8). When Arndt speaks of the kind of discipleship that bears the cross, for example, he distinguishes it from the errors of the monastic life:

This yoke of Christ is the real cross, which when a man bears he truly dies to the world. It is not to retire into monasteries and cloisters, nor to adopt a set of rules and orders for the regulation of life; for while the heart remains disordered and the love corrupt; while the man is puffed up with spiritual pride and a pharisaical contempt of others; while he is devoted to lust, envy, hypocrisy, secret hatred and malice; he does not die to the world but altogether lives to it. This is not the Christian yoke nor is it the cross of Christ; for these consist

13. I am using the text provided digitally by the Project Gutenberg, https://www.gutenberg.org.

in mortifying the flesh, with its sinful propensities; in turning away
from the world to God; in an inward and constant sorrow for our sins;
in a daily dying to the world, and living to Christ by faith; in following
his steps in sincere lowliness and humility; and in confiding only in
the grace of God in Christ Jesus. (1.4.6)

In a word, Arndt rejects the monastic life but not the ideals to which
monks pledged themselves. Outside of monastic walls, discipleship remains a commitment to personal transformation through the grace of
God, demanding the denial of the self and the bearing of the cross.

Similarly, Johann Gerhardt (1582–1637) begins his *Sacred Meditations* (1606) with citations from Justin, Ignatius, and Augustine, before
quoting with favor the opening lines of *The Imitation of Christ*. He says
further that "following in the footsteps of Augustine, Bernard, Anselm,
Tauler, and others, I often sprinkle their words through this handbook."
He thinks that theology should not be a matter merely of knowledge or
theory but above all of practice. "I am writing," he says, "homilies not
precise disputations . . . you will not find discussion of thorny questions
here, but, rather, fervent exhortations to a holy life."[14] He declares, "We
are either advancing or retreating in the way of the Lord; therefore examine your life every single day to see whether you are going forward or
backward in your zeal for piety . . . while you live, die daily to yourself and
your vices, so that when you die, you may live unto God."[15] And again,
"The holy life of Christ is the most perfect model of virtue; indeed, every
action of Christ is for our instruction. Many wish to attain to Christ but
draw back from following him; they want to enjoy Christ but not to imitate him. . . . if one's life does not conform to the life of Christ, it is proven
that the person neither clings to Christ nor has the Spirit of Christ."[16]

The traditional vision of discipleship is communicated to lay readers
also by Heinrich Mueller (1631–1675), whose *Spiritual Hours of Refresh-*

14. Johann Gerhardt, foreword to his *Sacred Meditations*. I am drawing from Eric
Lund, ed., *Seventeenth Century Lutheran Meditations and Hymns*, Classics of Western
Spirituality (New York: Paulist, 2011).

15. "Meditation 28: General Rules for a Godly Life," *Seventeenth Century Lutheran
Meditations*, 112.

16. "Meditation 30: Imitation of the Holy Life of Christ," *Seventeenth Century Lutheran Meditations*, 117–19.

ment (1664–1666) was written in an easy and conversational style. The sense of striving for sanctity can be found in paragraph 77, "The Characteristics of a True Christian":

> Oh, how far we still are from perfection! How short the time is! How many hindrances there are! The Devil, the world, and the flesh are always active. How often shall we be struck down as soon as we begin? . . . The Christian life is a steady climb. I have already ninety-nine good thoughts and good works together, but one is still lacking: the entire forgetting of myself. Therefore, I must seek as long as I live to begin again to deny myself.[17]

Mueller follows with paragraph 78, "The Growth of a Christian":

> Where virtue does not advance, it declines. The seed of goodness within us is like a faint spark that is easily extinguished . . . therefore, we must always see to it that we become more perfect. We are like spiritual pilgrims who are always going forward and coming nearer the goal . . . if your faith and holiness always remain as a spark, you have reason to fear that sometime all will be extinguished in a moment. I always like to remember the words of Bernard [of Clairvaux]; "It is not possible to become pious without desiring to become pious, and where you begin and do not want to become pious, you will not be pious."[18]

CALVIN AND REFORMED DISCIPLESHIP

Taking on John Calvin (1509–1564) and the Reformed tradition associated with Calvinism is daunting. For the first time in my survey, I am led to wonder whether my affirmations concerning the first vision of discipleship are as universal before the time of the Enlightenment as I have stated. From one perspective, exhortations to true discipleship strike the same themes: the brevity of life, the certainty of judgment, love toward God and neighbor, and the importance of prayer, of enduring suffering,

---

17. *Seventeenth Century Lutheran Meditations*, 212.
18. *Seventeenth Century Lutheran Meditations*, 213.

and of hoping for eternal bliss. From another perspective, every theme appears slightly modified because of the theological framework and ecclesiastical polity established by Calvin.

Trained in the law, Calvin was a brilliant and learned interpreter of Scripture, which he read as the exclusive source of truth about God.[19] He was also a fierce polemicist who not only pilloried Catholic practices but attacked as well those who deviated from his own theological positions. On the basis of his reading of Scripture and the application of a rigorous (one might even say, unrelenting) logic to Scripture, Calvin developed a distinctive covenantal theology, within which an emphasis was placed on the sovereignty of God—seen above all in the election of some and the rejection of others,[20] and the utter incapacity of humans (because of their thoroughgoing depravity) to will or do the righteous works without God's grace (*Institutes* 2.1.1–2.6.4). Within the Reformed tradition, the emphasis on election and predestination inevitably involved concern for who might be saved (i.e., go to heaven) and who would not.

The senses of sanctification and of perfection that were congenial even to Lutheran pastors shift within this theological framework. Only Christ is holy, and it is his sanctification that is imputed to believers together with his righteousness (*Institutes* 3.11.2 and 3.16.1). Faith in Christ makes humans righteous in God's eyes (by imputation), but the gift of the Holy Spirit does not then initiate a process of moral and ontological transformation of the human person. The cultivation of virtue is a necessary manifestation of faith, but it does not fundamentally change the believer, who is righteous solely and always by God's imputing to one the righteousness and holiness of Christ (*Institutes* 3.11.16–23).

Calvin also brought civil government within his theological framework, defining the legitimacy of civil magistracy in terms of its efficacy in "defending the sound doctrine of piety and the position of the church" (*Institutes* 4.20.2). The issue of how Christian discipleship was related to citizenship in the state, and how the legitimacy of the state had to do with its protection of the right version of Christianity, would subse-

19. Calvin's commentaries on Scripture are still worth reading for their exegetical clarity and sensitivity to rhetoric, so long as one can bracket the frequent rants against contemporary opponents that also occur with some frequency.

20. See *Institutes of the Christian Religion* (1559 ed.) 3.21.1–3.24.10.

quently color the Reformed tradition through the following generations in England and in North America. Within the safe atmosphere of the Genevan theocracy, though, refugee scholars from England produced the Geneva Bible in 1560, a translation that rendered scripturally the ecclesial convictions of Reformed theology. The translation of *ekklēsia* was not "church" but "congregation"; *presbyteroi* were not "priests" but "elders," and *episkopoi* were "overseers" rather than "bishops." The Geneva Bible antedated the King James Bible by fifty years and enjoyed wide readership among reform-minded readers in England.

A second reason why the Reformed tradition challenges easy analysis is its fissiparous character. Splintering began with the work of James Arminius (1560–1609) in the Netherlands, who softened some of Calvin's harsher teachings. In response, the Synod of Dort (1608) established the five essential points by which they defined "Calvinism": (1) total depravity; (2) unconditional election; (3) limited atonement; (4) irresistible grace; (5) perseverance of the saints.[21] Undoubtedly, the strongly cognitive and polemical element (who is saved after all, and who is not) that was so pronounced in the founder abetted the frequent dividing and subdividing within the subsequent Reformed tradition, which, whether in severe or softer forms, affected all Reformed groups (Presbyterian, Puritan, Congregational, and even some Baptist denominations) and manifested many variations even within denominations.[22]

Despite such significant differences from the Catholic, Lutheran, and (as we shall see) Anglican traditions, it is nevertheless accurate to state that Calvin and the Reformed teachers who followed him in the sixteenth and seventeenth centuries fell within the classic understanding of discipleship.[23] As I have already noted, in addition to the *Institutes*, Calvin wrote commentaries on virtually the entire Bible—commentaries marked by considerable learning, literary and rhetorical sensitivity,

21. For an unabashed celebration of these, see the pamphlet by W. J. Seaton, *The Five Points of Calvinism* (Edinburgh: Banner of Truth Trust, 1970).

22. A sense of the variety just in the United States can be gained from Roger E. Olson et al., *Handbook of Denominations in the United States*, 14th ed. (Nashville: Abingdon, 2018).

23. Given his condemnation of vows, rejection of celibacy, and moderation of fasting, Calvin's focus was on prayer and almsgiving as expressions of discipleship within a worldly—that is, nonmonastic—context.

and theological engagement—as well as sermons in which he sought the instruction and edification of his hearers. The commentaries and sermons are filled with exhortations to the faithful following of Christ. Even in book 3 of the 1559 edition of the *Institutes*, Calvin devotes attention to the shape of discipleship. It is noteworthy that he considers, in turn, self-denial (3.7), bearing the cross (3.8), the future life (3.9), and the use of the present life (3.10). The topics are familiar, even if Calvin's treatment of each is distinctive. Under self-denial, for example, Calvin emphasizes obedience to God's will (3.7.1–3) and service to others (3.7.4–10) rather than physical asceticism:

> Now, in seeking to benefit one's neighbor, how difficult it is to do one's duty! Unless you give up all thought of self and, so to speak, get out of yourself, you will accomplish nothing here. For how can you perform those works that Paul teaches to be works of love, unless you renounce yourself, and give yourself wholly to others? . . . the lawful use of all benefits consists in a liberal and kindly sharing of them with others. No surer rule and no more valid exhortation to keep it could be devised than when we are taught that all the gifts we possess have been bestowed by God and entrusted to us on condition that they be distributed for our neighbor's benefit.[24]

Calvin's understanding of carrying the cross as an aspect of self-denial, however, is thoroughly traditional:

> Why should we exempt ourselves, therefore, from a condition to which Christ our head had to submit, especially since He submitted to it *for our sake to show us an example of patience in Himself*? [emphasis added] Therefore, the apostle teaches that God has destined all His children to the end that they be conformed to Christ (Rom 8:29). Hence also in harsh and difficult conditions, regarded as adverse and evil, a great comfort comes to us: we share Christ's sufferings in order that as He has passed from a labyrinth of all evils

---

24. *Institutes* 3.7.5. I use the translation in John Calvin, *Writings on Pastoral Care and Piety*, ed. Elsie Anne McKee, Classics of Western Spirituality (New York: Paulist, 2002), 275.

into heavenly glory, we may in like manner be led through various tribulations to the same glory.[25]

Also continuous with the entire prior tradition of spirituality is his meditation on present life in view of future joy:

> For if heaven is our homeland, what else is the earth but our place of exile? If departure from the world is entry into life, what else is the world but a sepulcher? What else is it for us to remain in life but to be immersed in death? If to be freed from the body is to be released into perfect freedom, what else is the body but a prison? If to enjoy the presence of God is the summit of happiness, is not to be without this, misery? But until we leave the world "we are away from the Lord" (2 Cor 5:6). Therefore, if the earthly life be compared with the heavenly, it is doubtless to be despised and trampled underfoot.[26]

Calvin, to be sure, modifies this contrast by his emphasis on the positive use of the gifts of this earthly existence (3.10). But despite the distinctive (and important) variations to the classic model of discipleship Calvin introduces, his overall understanding clearly still fits within it: the (inevitable) sufferings of the present life are a preparation for future glory in the presence of God.

If we turn to Puritan preachers of seventeenth- and eighteenth-century New England, we find in their thoroughly Reformed sermons and exhortations some of the same features exhibited by Calvin, above all a mode of rigorous (almost scholastic) presentation within a universe defined exclusively by Holy Scripture. Every sermon and discourse exhibits such a web of citation and allusion as to demand (and suppose) serious biblical literacy among listeners. The combination of logic and scriptural proof was, on one hand, a strength of Puritan discourse but, on the other hand, would also prove to be a weakness, as the threat of Enlightenment reason grew more real. Despite the quaintness of some of their language, and the narrowness of their focus, however, Puritan preachers like Thomas Hooker (1586–1647), Joseph Cotton (1584–1652),

---

25. *Institutes* 3.8.1; translation in Calvin, *Writings*, 279.
26. *Institutes* 3.9.4; translation in Calvin, *Writings*, 285.

Samuel Willard (1640–1707)—along with many others—advocated a form of discipleship that was thoroughly within the classic vision.[27]

In a sermon delivered at Hartford, for example, Thomas Hooker speaks at length on the importance of meditation in the disciple's life, concluding,

> Hence it is Meditation laies siege unto the soul, and cuts off carnal pretences that a wretched self-deceiving hypocrite would relieve himself by. . . . It provokes a man (by a kind of over-bearing power) to the practice of that thing with which he is so affected; A serious and settled Meditation of any thing, is as the setting open of the Flood-gates, which carries the soul with a kind of force and violence, to the performance of what he so bestows his mind upon; as a mighty stream let out turns the mill. . . . [R]ight consideration brings a right Reformation with it.[28]

A similar use of water imagery appears in Joseph Cotton's reflection on "wading in grace," in a manner that almost recalls the water imagery in Teresa of Ávila's *Life*. He pictures how the "Spirit of Grace" leads a disciple from stage to stage, as if moving deeper and deeper into water, with healing coming to each part of the body touched. And at the end, wading gives way to the total immersion of swimming:

> But yet goe another thousand Cubits, and then you shall swimme; there is such a measure of grace in which a man may swimme as fish in the water, with all readiness, and dexterity, gliding an-end, as if we had water enough to swimme in; such a Christian doth not creep or walk, but he runs the ways of Gods Commandments;[29] what ever he

27. Spelling, punctuation, and capitalization in the following citations are as found in the text cited.

28. In *The Application of Redemption by the Effectual Work of the Word, and the Spirit of Christ, for the Bringing Home of Lost Sinners to God.* The text of this and the following citations come from *The Puritans: A Sourcebook of Their Writings*, two volumes bound as one, ed. Perry Miller and Thomas H. Johnson (Mineola, NY: Dover, 2001). This citation is found on p. 306.

29. Consciously or not, this expression echoes the prologue to the *Rule of Saint Benedict*.

is to doe or to suffer he is ready for all, so every way drenched in grace, as let God turn him any way, he is never drawn dry.[30]

Joseph Cotton's inventiveness finds expression as well in his consideration of the use of possessions in "Purchasing Christ":

> Thus much I say, that many times without laying out of money, he cannot be had, without parting with money we cannot get him, the case so stands that sometimes, the holding fast a mans mony lets go the Lord Jesus Christ, you have a famous example in the young man, *Matt. 19.21 to 24.* Where our saviour shewes how hard a thing it is for a rich man to enter into the Kingdom of Heaven, because it is hard for a rich man to part with all that he hath, when God calls for it at his hands, so that without mony sometimes Christ cannot be had; and yet for mony he cannot be had, it was on the point of mony that the Lord Jesus parted with the *Pharisees, Luke 16. 11. 12. If you be unfaithful with the mammon of iniquity, who will trust you with true treasure*; if you do not use outward things well, who will give you saving grace in Jesus Christ? So that sometimes for want of spending money in a right way, many a man looses the Lord Jesus; so that though Christ cannot be had for money, yet sometimes without expence of mony he cannot be had.[31]

Finally, Samuel Willard expresses the classic Christian conviction that present suffering is in view of future bliss:

> Learn hence a reason why the present sufferings of God's Children can neither argue against, nor yet prejudice their felicity: for the time is not yet come wherein they are to appear like themselves . . . when the appointed time for the manifestation of the Sons of God shall come, he can fetch them out in hast, change them in the twinkling of an eye, and cloath them upon with all that excellency and splendid Glory, whereby, they who were but the other day lying among the

---

30. From *The New Covenant, or a Treatise, Unfolding the Order and Manner of the Giving and Receiving of the Covenant of Grace to the Elect*, in *Puritans*, 318.

31. From a collection of sermons called *The Way of Life* (1641), in *Puritans*, 327–35.

pots, shall with their dazling lustre outshine the Sun in the Firma-
ment. It is the Almighty's good pleasure, that their life, for the present, shall be hid with Christ in God: But yet he hath his time, and will
take his opportunity to reveal and make it known.[32]

Anglican Piety

The Reformation in England was marked by the religious/political tension between proponents of more conservative Catholic positions, represented, for example, by Archbishop William Laud of Canterbury (1573–
1645), and advocates of more radical Reformed positions, like the Puritans,
whose great champion would be Oliver Cromwell (1599–1658). The tensions exploded in the Civil War between King and Parliament (1642–1651),
and the fissures are still discernible in the differences in worship between
High Church and Low Church versions of the Episcopal Church.

Jeremy Taylor (1613–1667)—a younger contemporary of John Milton
(1608–1674) and like Milton a master of the English language—was caught
up in these struggles. A protégé of Archbishop Laud, he was briefly imprisoned three times (in 1645, 1655, 1657) for his convictions, before ending as
a bishop in Ireland. His *Rule and Exercises of Holy Living* (1650) and *Rule
and Exercises of Holy Dying* (1651) reveal strong lines of continuity with the
classic tradition. In *Holy Living*, for example, he considers all the vices that
impede and all the virtues that impel Christian discipleship. He states in
his first paragraph, "Therefore as every man is wholly God's own portion
by the title of creation, so all our labours and care, all our powers and
faculties, must be wholly employed in the service of God, even all the days
of our life; that this life being ended, we may live with Him for ever."[33]

Particularly noteworthy as an element of continuity is the attention
he devotes (in section 3) to "the practice of the presence of God," an aspect of piety so emphasized in Catholic teachers like Teresa of Ávila and
Brother Lawrence. He states, "That God is present in all places, that He
sees every action, hears all discourses, and understands every thought, is

---

32. In a sermon entitled "Saints Not Known by Externals," in *The Child's Portion*
(1684); found in *Puritans*, 369–71.

33. Text in Jeremy Taylor, *Selected Writings*, ed. Thomas K. Carroll, Classics of Western Spirituality (New York: Paulist, 1990), 439.

no strange thing to a Christian ear, who hath been taught this doctrine, not only by right reason, but also by God Himself in Holy Scripture" (Taylor, 445). He then discusses in some detail how God is present (1) by His essence, (2) by His power, (3) in special manifestations, (4) by grace and benediction in holy places and assemblies of His people, (5) in the hearts of His people by His Holy Spirit, and (6) in the consciences of all persons by way of testimony and judgment. The consideration of this last mode of presence is particularly pertinent to the disciple:

> Certainly if men would always actually consider and really esteem this truth, that God is the great eye of the world, always watching over our actions, and an ever-open ear to hear all our words, and an unwearied arm ever lifted up to crush a sinner into ruin, it would be the readiest way in the world to make sin to cease from among the children of men, and for men to approach to the blessed estate of the saints in heaven, who cannot sin, for they always walk in the presence and behold the face of God. (Taylor, 448)

Taylor opens his discussion of fasting in section 5 by noting that "Christianity hath to do with it as it may be made an instrument of the spirit, by subduing the lusts of the flesh, or removing any hindrances of religion. And it hath been practiced by all ages of the church, and advised in order to three ministries; to prayer; to mortification of bodily lusts; and to repentance" (Taylor, 458). He concludes with another explicit invocation of the classic tradition: "By the doctors of the church it is called the nourishment of prayer, the restraint of lust, the wings of the soul, the diet of angels, the instruments of humility and self-denial, the purification of the spirit" (Taylor, 460).

In his *Holy Dying*, Taylor reveals his vast learning in ancient Greco-Roman literature when he expatiates on the brevity and misery of mortal existence, as well as his mastery of English prose; but a distinctive note is the sort of social awareness that his older contemporary, John Donne (1572–1631), expressed in the sermon in which he declared, "no man is an island," and, "ask not for whom the bell tolls; it tolls for thee." Taylor says,

> If we could from one of the battlements of heaven espy how many men and women at this time lie fainting and dying from lack of

bread, how many young men are hewn down by the sword of war, how many poor orphans are now weeping over the grace of their father by whose life they were enabled to eat: if we could but hear how many mariners and passengers are at this present in a storm, and shriek out because their keel dashes against a rock, or bulges under them, how many people there are who weep with want, and are mad with oppression, or are desperate by too quick a sense of a constant infelicity; in all reason we should be glad to be out of the noise and participation of so many evils. This is a place of sorrows and tears, of great evils and a constant calamity; let us remove from hence, at least in affection and preparation of mind. (Taylor, 493–94)

Like Jeremy Taylor, William Law (1686–1761) is honored in the liturgical calendar of the Anglican and Episcopal churches, and like him, his life was outwardly defined by the vagaries of religious/political conflict in England. Law lost his university position and then his curacy because of his refusal to swear loyalty to the Hanoverian king, and he spent his life teaching privately and writing, while serving as spiritual director and chaplain in a quasi-monastic domestic setting with two women. The title of the work for which he is most admired states the book's character clearly, *A Serious Call to a Devout and Holy Life Adapted to the State and Condition of all Christians* (1728); his concern is forming genuine disciples, as he says at the beginning: "He therefore is the devout man who lives no longer to his own will, or the way and spirit of the world, but to the sole will of God, who considers God in everything, who serves God in everything, who makes all the parts of his common life parts of piety by doing everything in the name of God and under such rules as are conformable to his glory."[34] What Law means by "devout" is the same as meant by Francis de Sales: it is equivalent to "discipleship." And what he means by "common life" is "ordinary/everyday life."

In a word, being a disciple involves not just worship but the entire disposition of one's life:

34. William Law, *A Serious Call to a Devout and Holy Life; The Spirit of Love*, ed. Paul G. Stanwood, Classics of Western Spirituality (New York: Paulist, 1978), 47.

Our blessed Savior and His Apostles are wholly taken up in doctrines that relate to common life. They call us to renounce the world and differ in every temper and way of life from the spirit and way of the world. To renounce all its goods, to fear none of its evils, to reject its joys, and have no value for its happiness. To be as newborn babes that are born into a new state of things, to live as pilgrims in spiritual watching, in holy fear, and heavenly aspiring after another life. To take up our daily cross, to deny ourselves, to profess the blessedness of mourning, to seek the blessedness of poverty of spirit. To forsake the vanity and pride of riches, to take no thought for the morrow, to live in the profoundest state of humility, to rejoice in worldly sufferings. To reject the lust of the flesh, the pride of life; to bear injuries, to forgive and bless our enemies, and to love mankind as God loveth them. To give up our whole hearts and affections to God and to strive to enter through the strait gate into a life of eternal glory. (Law, ch. 1, 51)

It would be difficult to find a better short summation of the classical vision of discipleship. And Law insists that it is a vision that applies to all believers, indeed, "this is the business of all persons in this world" (Law, ch. 3, 77).

One of the charming aspects of *A Serious Call* is the way in which Law enlivens his teaching through vivid examples, both male and female. In chapters 7 and 8, he examines the contrast between a life of frivolous and thoughtless self-indulgence found in a woman named Flavia, and a life given to almsgiving (works of charity) by her sister Miranda, who responds to every need with compassion and generosity:

If a poor old traveler tells her that he has neither strength, nor food, nor money left, she never bids him go to the place from whence he came, or tells him she cannot relieve him because he may be a cheat, or she does not know him; but she relieves him for that reason because he is a stranger and unknown to her. For it is the most noble part of charity to be kind and tender to those whom we never saw before and perhaps may never see again in this life. "I was a stranger, and ye took me in," saith our blessed Savior; but who can perform this duty that will not relieve persons that are unknown to him? (Law, ch. 8, 118)

One last citation from this admirable teacher reveals once more his immersion in Scripture and the classic mode of reading Scripture as directed to the life (and death) of the believer. Stating that "the Christian's great conquest over the world is all contained in the mystery of Christ upon the cross," he continues,

> Every man therefore is only so far a Christian as he partakes of the Spirit of Christ. It was this that made St. Paul so passionately express himself, "God forbid that I should glory, save in the cross of our Lord Jesus Christ." But why does he glory? Is it because Christ had suffered in his stead, and had excused him from suffering? No, by no means. But it was because his Christian profession had called him to the honor of suffering with Christ, and of dying to the world under reproach and contempt as He had done upon the cross. For he immediately adds, "by whom the world is crucified unto me, and I unto the world" (Gal 6:14). This you see was the reason for his glorying in the cross of Christ because it had called him to a like state of death and crucifixion to the world. (Law, ch. 17, 241)

JONATHAN EDWARDS AND JOHN WESLEY

I close this survey of Protestant teachers with two men who were born the same year (1703), who were both in North America at the time of the First Great Awakening in the 1730s and 1740s,[35] and who both were aware, in a manner earlier writers were not, of the intellectual ferment called the Enlightenment (which I will discuss in the next chapter), and who forged their strong affirmation of traditional piety at a time—as we shall see—when in England some of the best minds were dismissing it.[36] Edwards and Wesley are both robust representatives of a classic vision of discipleship that would shortly begin to suffer erosion.

35. In 1738, the evangelist George Whitefield and John Wesley were working together in the Georgia colony; Edwards met with the evangelist in Massachusetts in 1739–1740, and as Benjamin Franklin notes in his autobiography, he met and was impressed by Whitefield in 1739.

36. The dates of significant British Enlightenment figures: John Locke (1632–1704); Herbert of Cherbury (1583–1648); John Toland (1670–1722); Anthony Collins (1676–1729); Thomas Chubb (1679–1747).

Jonathan Edwards (1703–1758) was intellectually gifted and was strongly engaged in the study of science and philosophy. He read John Locke while a student at Yale, and he was fascinated by the new physics advanced by Isaac Newton. As a boy, he had carried out his own impressive scientific study of spiders. He was, therefore, positively inclined to rational thought. Indeed, his early death (a year after being made president of Princeton University) came about because of a failed smallpox inoculation; his conviction concerning the value of such inoculations was scientifically advanced. Unlike his contemporaries in England, however, who saw classic Christian faith as incompatible with the Enlightenment and resolved that conflict by becoming Deists, Edwards employed his intellectual gifts (and strong aesthetic sense) to develop the deep correspondences between scriptural revelation and the created order.

He was a Puritan to the core and delighted in the severity of a strict Calvinism. His preaching in Northampton in the 1730s, indeed, was a major impetus to the religious revival that swept the Northern states. It was entirely characteristic of Edwards, however, to acknowledge some of the excesses (emotional and behavioral) that the revival had stimulated, and not only analyze them but advance a proper appreciation for the role of affections in the life of the disciple.[37] He argues, for example, that in contrast to inauthentic religious affections, those that derive from faith "are attended with a change in nature," which he sketches by means of a string of New Testament images:

> The scriptural representations of conversion do strongly imply and signify a change in nature; such as being born again; becoming new creatures; rising from the dead; being renewed in the spirit of the mind; dying to sin, and living to righteousness; putting off the old man and putting on the new man; a being ingrafted into a new stock; a having a divine seed implanted in the heart; a being partakers of the divine nature, etc. (3.7)[38]

37. The Yale edition of Edwards's works runs to twenty-six large volumes. He was a preacher who spent up to thirteen hours a day on his sermons and lectures. I do not pretend to have an adequate knowledge of this body of work but base my observations on two of the works that have enjoyed wide readership.

38. *Religious Affections*, ed. John E. Smith, Works of Jonathan Edwards (New Haven:

The "progress of the work of grace," furthermore, is a continued conversion and renovation of nature—a transformation into the character of Jesus Christ: "Truly gracious affections differ from those affections that are false and delusive, in that they tend to, and are attended with the lamblike, dovelike spirit and temper of Jesus Christ; or in other words, they naturally beget and promote such a spirit of love, meekness, quietness, forgiveness and mercy, as appeared in Christ" (3.8).[39] Above all, Edwards insists, religious affections must move from the level of feeling to the arena of action: "Gracious and holy affections have their exercise and fruit in Christian practice," which means (1) living according to Christian norms; (2) making such practice "a business in which he is chiefly engaged in"; and (3) persisting in such practice to the end of life (3.12).[40]

Edwards is popularly associated with the sermon "Sinners in the Hands of an Angry God," which he preached to his congregation in 1741 and which helped catalyze the First Great Awakening. But the image of a fire-breathing ranter is deeply unfortunate, for he was overall a profound and positive interpreter of Scripture for the building up of those wishing to follow Jesus as disciples. A perfect example is the series of sermons "On Charity and Its Fruits," preached to his congregation in Northampton in 1738 and published in 1749. This careful and creative exposition of 1 Corinthians 13 is meant to show "that as a principle of love is the main principle in the heart of a real Christian, so the labour of love is the main business of the Christian life" (1).[41] Here again we find Edwards's conviction that the work of the Holy Spirit in the lives of believers has as its goal transformation into the character of Christ: "The moral image and likeness of Christ does much more consist in having *the same mind in us which was in Christ*; in being of the same Spirit that he was of; in being meek and lowly of heart; in having a spirit of Christian love, and

---

39. *Religious Affections*, 344–45.

40. *Religious Affections*, 383. Edwards develops this critical point at great length, making effective use of the Letter of James's insistence that faith without works is dead (Jas 2:14–26).

41. *Charity and Its Fruits: Christian Love as Manifested in the Heart and Life*, ed. Tryon Edwards (Edinburgh: Banner of Truth Trust, 2000), 25.

walking as Christ walked. This makes a man more like Christ than if he could work ever so many miracles" (2 [*Charity and Its Fruits*, 37]).

When speaking of the terms by which Christians are to be assessed in the last judgment, Edwards strikes the traditional note:

> And when Christ shall come to judgment, and all people shall be gathered before him, then to those who were kind and benevolent, in the true spirit of Christian love, to the suffering and the poor, He shall say (Matt xxv. 34–36, 40), "Come ye blessed of my Father, inherit the kingdom prepared for you from the foundation of the world: for I was hungered, and ye gave me meat; I was thirsty and ye gave me drink; I was a stranger and ye took me in; naked, and ye clothed me; I was sick and ye visited me: I was in prison and ye came unto me. . . . Verily I say unto you, Inasmuch as ye have done it unto one of the least of these my brethren, *ye have done it unto me.*" (5 [*Charity and Its Fruits*, 110])

As a good Calvinist, Edwards also saw charity as encompassing civic responsibility. In parsing Paul's declaration that love seeks not its own (1 Cor 13:5), he declares, "Christian love is opposed to a selfish spirit . . . in this also, that it *disposes a person to be public-spirited* . . . concerned for the community to which he belongs, and particularly of the city or village in which he resides, and for the true welfare of the society of which he is a member" (8 [*Charity and Its Fruits*, 169]). But he speaks for the entire prior tradition when he follows Paul's statement in 1 Corinthians 13:7 that love suffers all things:

> To give ourselves wholly to Christ implies the sacrificing of our own temporal interest wholly to him. But he that wholly sacrifices his temporal interest to Christ, is ready to suffer all things in his worldly interests for him. If God be truly loved, he is loved as God; and to love him as God, is to love him as the supreme good. But he that loves God as the supreme good, is ready to make all other good give place to that; or, which is the same thing, he is willing to suffer all for the sake of this good. (12 [*Charity and Its Fruits*, 256–57])

Like Edwards, John Wesley (1703–1791) was university educated, in his case at Oxford. Like him, he was aware of the Enlightenment. Unlike the

Puritan Edwards, however, Wesley was an heir to Anglican piety and was deeply committed to Arminianism. In the British context, moreover, he was acutely aware of the way the Enlightenment challenged traditional belief and practices. Although he firmly defended the traditional "evidences" for Christianity,[42] therefore, he was eager to advance the "internal evidence" given by the personal experience of God. In *A Plain Account of Genuine Christianity* (1753), for example, he acknowledged that the tradition was under intellectual threat, so much that "in a century or two, the people of England will be fairly divided into real deists and real Christians" (3.6).[43]

So much is Wesley associated with the personal experience of God that the Methodist movement deriving from the work of John and Charles Wesley is notable to outsiders for the Wesleyan Quadrilateral, in which "experience" is added to the Anglican hermeneutical framework of Scripture, tradition, and reason. Theology—and it goes without saying, discipleship—must always be grounded in Scripture, but tradition and reason provide the intellectual means of rightly understanding Scripture, while the experience of God in human lives enlivens the meaning of Scripture. The role of religious experience was important to Wesley personally, since, as he tells us in his *Journal*, before his encounter with Moravians and his Aldergate experience in 1738, he considered his own faith as aridly intellectual,[44] even though as early as 1726, he and his brother (together with George Whitefield) had formed the Holy Club, which anticipated the training in discipleship that so marked the Methodist movement.

Despite, or perhaps because of, his emphasis on the vivifying power of the Holy Spirit in the lives of individuals, Wesley's teachings on dis-

---

42. In 1749, for example, Wesley wrote a lengthy *Letter to Dr. Middleton* in response to Conyers Middleton's *Introductory Discourse and Free Inquiry* of 1747–1748, in which letter he debated the Deist's denial of the miraculous. In that letter, he drew the distinction between the disputable external evidence for the truth of Christianity, and "the strongest evidence" of experience: "Historical evidence can never replace the experiences of our own hearts."

43. Text found in John Wesley and Charles Wesley, *Selected Prayers, Hymns, Sermon Notes, Letters, Sermons, and Treatises*, ed. F. Whaling, Classics of Western Spirituality (New York: Paulist, 1981), 130.

44. The pertinent text can be found in *The Nature of Spiritual Growth: Wesley's Messages on the Holy Spirit*, ed. Clare G. Weakley (Minneapolis: Bethany House, 1977), 17–29.

cipleship are thoroughly within the classic vision I have been tracing. As I noted in my introduction, he pays tribute to *The Imitation of Christ* and publishes an edition of it,[45] and he is generously open to the great spiritual teachers of both the Catholic and Protestant traditions.[46] John and Charles had learned from their reading in monastic literature the importance of disciplined practice and discernment within small groups that met regularly for prayer, study, and mutual edification. In *The Nature, Design, and General Rules of the United Societies* of 1743, Wesley defines the United Society as "a company of men having the form and seeking the power of godliness, united in order to pray together, to receive the word of exhortation, and to watch over one another in love, that they may help each other work out their salvation." The "general rules" are those of classic discipleship: (1) "to do no harm," by avoiding those dispositions and behaviors identified by Scripture as contrary to God's will; (2) "by doing good," that is, carrying out the care for the little ones spelled out by Matthew 25, and "*denying themselves and taking up their cross daily*" (emphasis original)"; and (3) attending upon all the ordinances of God," such as worship, the supper of the Lord, family and private prayer, searching the Scriptures, and fasting, or abstinence.[47]

Consistent with his embrace of the classic tradition wherever he found it, Wesley is consistent in his many sermonic iterations on the demands of true discipleship. To take only one example, his sermon on Jesus's parable of the unjust steward (Luke 16:1–12) develops the theme of God's judgment based on the human stewardship of the gifts God has given each person; every individual must answer for the use of what properly belongs to God: "Our souls, our bodies, our goods, our immortal spirits, and whatever talents we have, are entrusted to us on this condition." Wesley moves relentlessly through every sort of gift at human disposal, showing how they should be directed to God: "there is no use of our time, no action or conversation, which is merely indifferent. All

45. See the introduction, p. 3 and n. 9.

46. In *A Plain Account of Genuine Christianity* 3.11, Wesley lists a number of patristic writers and says in 3.12, "I exceedingly reverence them, and esteem them highly in love. I reverence them because they were Christians, such Christians as are above described. And I reverence their writings, because they describe true, genuine Christianity, and direct us to the strongest evidence of the Christian doctrine."

47. For the text, see Wesley, *Selected Prayers*, 108–10.

is either good or bad, because all our time, as everything we have, is not our own. All of these talents are the property of another. They are the property of God our creator." His conclusion to the sermon shows the plainness of Wesley's language, his acknowledgment of the dedication required to be a true Christian, and his confidence that the Holy Spirit enables believers to do what God asks of them:

> If anyone is to call himself a good steward of the manifold gifts of God, let him see that all of his thoughts, words, and works are agreeable to the post which God has assigned. It is no small thing to lay out for God all we have received from Him. It requires the full infilling of the Holy Spirit and all the gifts and power from His gifts and Spirit. It requires all wisdom, all resolution, all patience, and all constancy. Good stewardship requires a dedication far beyond that which one can have by nature. However, it does not require more than one may have by grace through the Holy Spirit. God's grace is sufficient for us. All things are possible to those who believe. By a living faith through the Holy Spirit, we put on the Lord Jesus Christ. We put on the whole armor of God and are able to glorify Him in all our words and works . . . by grace, we have received a faith which makes this dedication possible.[48]

Conclusion

My goal in this chapter has been to show that what I have called the classical vision of discipleship continued during and after the Reformation of the sixteenth century, not only among Catholic writers but among reformers of every kind. Certainly, the sixteenth, seventeenth, and eighteenth centuries were not notably ecumenical. In addition to the constant polemic between Catholics and Reformers, there was at least as much cross fire between various versions of Protestantism, dealing not only with matters of church organization and ministry but also with such fundamental issues as election and free will, with the divide between strict Calvinists and Arminians on such matters as wide and

48. From "The Good Steward," in *Forty-Four Sermons*; found in *Nature of Spiritual Growth*, 137–48.

deep as between papists and puritans. What is startling, in light of all this division and rancor, is the deep agreement concerning the nature of true discipleship. God's call to the individual was a call to complete devotion that combined love of God and love of neighbor, that in view of the brevity of life and the certainty of judgment, made every disposition and decision of great value, that required the refusal of all vice and the cultivation of every virtue as the work that expressed faith, that demanded self-denial and the willingness to follow Jesus in the carrying of one's own cross, and that did all this in the expectation of a blessed resurrection and an eternal share in heavenly bliss.

Equally surprising, perhaps, is that we nowhere find in this literature the discussion of the church as a social body whose purpose was the amelioration of society at large. The Christian is to be a good citizen, to be sure, but the role of the church was to enable and foster a life of holiness among its members. Similarly, we nowhere find any suggestion that discipleship consists in working toward and effecting political change. But precisely these shifts will manifest themselves full-blown at the beginning of the twentieth century, in a vision of Christian discipleship as the transformation of society—a vision that based itself on the systematic rejection of the classical view, and among many contemporary Christians is taken to be the only authentic vision.

In order to understand this dramatic change, it is necessary to pay the closest attention to the ideological, technological, and societal changes that challenged traditional Christianity, beginning already in the lifetimes of Edwards and Wesley, as well as to the internal changes among Christians consequent upon such challenges.

4

Discipleship under Threat

How did the classic view of discipleship whose goal was the transformation of the self in imitation of Christ—becoming a saint—get eclipsed, rejected, and replaced by a quite different version of discipleship whose goal was the transformation of society?

Many factors were involved, but four were of particular importance in preparing the way to that transition: The first is the birth of modernity, by which I mean the ideology of enlightenment married to technology in the seventeenth and eighteenth centuries. The second is the weakened and fragmented state of Christianity during that same period. The third is the theory and fact of social change during the eighteenth and nineteenth centuries. The fourth is the massive ideological attack on Christianity in the nineteenth century from the side of science and philosophy. These four factors together effected the erosion and then the loss of the scriptural imagination on which the classic vision of discipleship was so firmly based. After a brief sketch of these threatening historical factors in the present chapter, I will turn in the next chapter to the ways in which the alternative vision of discipleship emerged.

The Birth of Modernity

That there should be an irreconcilable clash between the employment of scientific methods and Christian faith was by no means obvious to adventurous thinkers of earlier centuries. The thirteenth-century Franciscan friar Roger Bacon (1219–1292) at Oxford advocated the use of empirical methods in studying the natural world and in his *Opus Maius* of 1267 sketched an entire program for experimental science, including the application of mathematics in physics and astronomy. The polymathic Polish canon Nicolas Copernicus (1473–1543) added expertise in canon law and economics to his revolutionary theory of a heliocentric universe. The Italian Galileo Galilei (1546–1642) had serious struggles with papal authority for espousing the same theory but remained a devout believer his entire life.[1] Similarly, the precocious Blaise Pascal (1623–1662), who made fundamental contributions to math (for example, probability theory) and to physics (for example, principle of falsification), became an intense apologist for the Christian faith (see the *Pensées*). The German Protestant polymath Johannes Kepler (1571–1630) likewise saw his astronomical discoveries to be a confirmation rather than a denial of God's revelation: "The laws [of nature] are within the grasp of the human mind; God wanted us to recognize them by creating us after his own image so that we could share in his thoughts."[2]

However much their ideas would serve to dislodge scriptural revelation, other sixteenth- and seventeenth-century thinkers remained personally (if sometimes idiosyncratically) attached to Christian faith. Such was the case with Francis Bacon (1561–1626), whose *Novum Organum* (1620) advocated seeking truth on the basis of empirical evidence rather than ancient authorities.[3] Such was the case also with René Descartes (1596–1650), who did not consider that starting with the thinking subject rather than the revealing God, a shift in focus that began the modern turn to epistemology as the first and most important philosophical subject, should dislodge revelation. Such was the case with Isaac Newton (1642–1726), who set the ground rules for subsequent physics up to the time of Einstein. Such was the case with Gottfried Wilhelm von Leibnitz

---

1. See Dava Sobel, *Galileo's Daughter: A Historical Account of Science, Faith, and Love* (New York: Walker, 1999).

2. From a letter of 1599, edited by Carola Baumgardt and Jamie Callan, *Johannes Kepler: Life and Letters* (New York: Philosophical Library, 1953), 50. Note that the "image of God" is a thoroughly scriptural trope. For the way in which the same tendency toward harmony continued among Catholic thinkers, see the important study of Ulrich L. Lehner, *The Catholic Enlightenment: The Forgotten History of a Global Movement* (New York: Oxford University Press, 2016).

3. The same can be said of Thomas Hobbes (1589–1679), whose *Leviathan* would prove to be so influential to later political theory. Like the mathematicians and physicists listed in my text, however, it is noteworthy that his theory of social contract is based on an analysis of human subjects in the raw rather than on, say, Rom 1:18–32.

(1646–1716), who regarded his mathematical and philosophical speculations as compatible with and even a celebration of Christian faith.

Such was the case, finally, with John Locke (1632–1704), whose *Essay Concerning Human Understanding* (1690) advanced further the premise that the human subject was the appropriate starting point for philosophy but who remained personally committed to the authority of Scripture.[4] The distinguishing feature of enlightenment in all these figures is that, despite their personal religious allegiance, and despite their desire to have their thought harmonize with scriptural revelation, their point of departure was the observation of the world around them (and within them) rather than the world imagined by Scripture. Locke's work *On the Reasonableness of Christianity as Delivered by the Scriptures* (1695), for example, held Scripture to the measure of human reason, rather than have reason measured by Scripture. His defense of the Bible turned out to be subtly subversive of its authority.

Baruch Spinoza (1632–1677), in contrast, leveled an overt and explicit attack on the Bible—in his case, the Jewish Scriptures (he was himself an apostate Jew). In his *Tractatus Theologico-Politicus* of 1670, he set out to show, by careful critical analysis, that the Torah was not revealed to Moses but had multiple sources, and that it was, in effect, no more than the political justification for the ancient Jewish state. Since (in his view) truth is a matter of the correspondence of an idea to some fact, the lack of such evidentiary material in the Bible means that it should not be read for truth but at most for meaning. Moreover, the pantheistic understanding of nature that Spinoza developed especially in the *Ethics* (1677) left no room for a personal God or special revelation. Basing himself on Cartesian mathematical principles but ranging much more widely than Descartes, Spinoza demanded that everything be judged on the basis of reason alone, and on that basis, the special claims made for Judaism or Christianity must be rejected.[5]

4. Like Isaac Newton, however, Locke was probably Socinian in his view of Christ, an heir to the Arianism that denied the divinity of Christ. Unitarianism, indeed, is the default theological posture of Deism.

5. Following on the work of Spinoza, but with the goal of validating the Catholic tradition rather than the *sola scriptura* principle of Protestantism, the French priest Richard Simon (1638–1712) produced a massive set of books that subjected the entire Bible to critical historical analysis; the most famous and controverted were his *Histoire*

The same rejection of scriptural revelation and relegation of Christianity to being merely one religion among others is a feature of those British, French, and German thinkers who have come to be called Deists, thinkers who affirm the existence of a God, even a Creator God, but a God who remains uninvolved with the world and in particular with human affairs.[6] The soldier and diplomat Herbert of Cherbury (1583–1648), an older contemporary of Spinoza, is generally reckoned as the earliest among them. In his treatise *On Truth* (1624), he argues for the adequacy of human reason in matters religious,[7] and in *On the Religion of the Nations* (1663) carries out a comparison between Christianity and other religions.[8] It is worth noting in these efforts that (1) human reason alone is the criterion of truth; (2) revelation is consequently not the criterion of truth; (3) specifically, biblical revelation is not the source of truth; (4) the topic is not now faith, or even Christianity, but religion. The effect of rational analysis is a distancing from the centuries-old tradition: increasingly, the educated and enlightened will regard all religion, including Christianity, as among the superstitions and errors that must be rejected if one wants to join the new world of rational analysis and control.[9]

In England, Herbert of Cherbury is followed by figures such as Matthew Tindal (1657–1733), whose *Christianity as Old as Creation* (1730) salvaged Christianity by reducing it to the laws of nature embedded from creation; translated into German, this book had a great effect on continental rationalists.[10] A similar line was argued by John Toland (1670–1722) in his *Christianity Not Mysterious* (1696). In this group, Thomas Chubb (1679–1747) is particularly significant for his effort to demystify the Gospels: in *The True Gospel of Jesus Christ Asserted* (1738) and in his

---

critique du Vieux Testament in 3 books (1678) and *Histoire critique du texte du Nouveau Testament* (1689). These were followed by another three studies in 1690, 1693, and 1695.

6. That such a position repristinates ancient Epicureanism is clear and has often been noted, for example, in the case of David Hume.

7. The translation of the full Latin title is *On the Truth, as It Is Distinguished from Revelation, the Probable, the Possible, and the False*, which provides a sense of its tendency.

8. Once more, the full title is candid: *On the Religion of the Nations and the Causes of Their Errors.*

9. See J. Samuel Preus, *Explaining Religion: Criticism and Theory from Bodin to Freud* (New Haven: Yale University Press, 1987).

10. Conyers Middleton (1683–1750), whom we have seen as a correspondent with John Wesley, involved himself in the subsequent debate.

Discourse on Miracles (1741), he distinguished the elements in the gospels that could meet (his) standard of historical accuracy from those that could not (specifically, miracles).[11] The truth of the Gospels, and indeed of Scripture as a whole, is now not to be found in the meaning of their narratives but in their referential accuracy.[12]

By 1748, therefore, when the Enlightenment icon David Hume (1711–1776) wrote his *Inquiry Concerning Human Understanding*, containing in book 2 his detached and ironic disquisition on the impossibility of miracles—including the miracle of divine revelation itself—he was not a bold innovator in the matter of reason and religion but rather a casual tradent of the British intellectual's acceptable worldview. And not only British. In Germany, Gotthold Ephraim Lessing (1729–1781) claimed that "an ugly ditch" separated the facts of history from eternal truths, a ditch that (at least his) human reason could not leap, and he undertook the posthumous publication of the Deist writer H. S. Reimarus's attack (in the name of history) on the supernatural origins of Christianity.[13]

Likewise, French-speaking *philosophes* like the Genevan Jean-Jacques Rousseau (1712–1778), whose *Social Contract* (1762) had such an influence on American political theory, Denis Diderot (1713–1784), who edited the thirty-five-volume monument to enlightenment learning, *l'Encyclopédie*, and the playwright and polemicist Voltaire (1694–1778), who wrote *On Tolerance* (1763) and *On Miracles* (1765),[14] were part of a swelling chorus of those whose grudging Deism was combined with a detestation of traditional Christianity. Voltaire's expostulation against the Catholicism of the *ancien régime*, "Destroy the infamous thing!," says it all.[15] Far more measured was the German philosopher Immanuel Kant (1724–1804),

11. See Charlotte Allen, *The Human Christ: The Quest for the Historical Jesus* (New York: Free Press, 1998), 92–119.

12. This history has been traced by Hans W. Frei, *The Eclipse of Biblical Narrative: A Study of Eighteenth and Nineteenth Century Hermeneutics* (New Haven: Yale University Press, 1974).

13. Albert Schweitzer was not alone in erroneously regarding Reimarus as the starting point for historical inquiry into Jesus. See his *Von Reimarus zu Wrede: Eine Geschichte der Leben-Jesu-Forschung* (Tübingen: Mohr Siebeck, 1906).

14. Note that almost a century earlier, in response to the civil (religious) war in England, John Locke wrote *Letters concerning Tolerance* (1689–1692).

15. In French, *Ecrasez l'Infame*; if the British Deists' attitude toward Christianity was indifference, that of the French Deists was rage. See, for example, E. Claire Cage,

who brought the Enlightenment preoccupation with epistemology to full expression, and the title of whose *Religion within the Bounds of Bare Reason* (1793) effectively reduced religion to a form of ethics thereby perfectly summarizing two centuries of European intellectuals distancing themselves from traditional Christianity.

In North America, where the political stance of the founding fathers owed so much to the reading of Hobbes, Locke, Rousseau, and Hume, it is no surprise to find the dominant religious posture among them to be also a version of Deism. Benjamin Franklin (1706–1790) and Thomas Jefferson (1743–1826) were totally committed to the proposition that the use of human reason guided by empirical facts was the best guarantor of human progress; their invocation of the divine tended to be a somewhat formal afterthought dictated by social expediency. We are not shocked to find Jefferson, late in life, toiling over the New Testament, scissoring out anything miraculous or supernatural, in order to advance *The Life and Morals of Jesus of Nazareth* (1820), based entirely on historical (Enlightenment) grounds.

In sum, by the middle of the eighteenth century—the period when John Wesley was writing—the best and brightest in the English-speaking world and, indeed, in the civilized world of Protestant Europe had dismissed the significance of the Bible as a source of truth, had enthroned reason as the sole path to human flourishing, and had reduced Christianity to a form of superstition that only the benighted (the unenlightened) could take seriously.

Many believers in Europe and America who wanted to cling to the Bible—above all Protestants for whom *sola scriptura* was fundamental—found themselves facing the unhappy options of ignoring the dominant intellectual movement of the age that attacked the Bible (thus confirming the epithet of being benighted) or of seeking to defend the Bible by using the same criteria put forward by their cultured despisers.[16] For a believer aware in any way of the Enlightenment critique, the plausibility

Unnatural Frenchmen: The Politics of Priestly Celibacy and Marriage (1720–1815) (Charlottesville: University of Virginia Press, 2015).

16. In his magisterial *Theology in America: Christian Thought from the Age of the Puritans to the Civil War* (New Haven: Yale University Press, 2003), E. Brooks Holifield convincingly demonstrates how much Protestant theology in the United States was infected with "Baconian Evidentialism."

of imitating Jesus through suffering and death in the hope of sharing in his resurrection life necessarily came into question.

THE WEAKENED STATE OF CHRISTIANITY

The Enlightenment's challenge to traditional belief was the more daunting because Christianity had made itself so vulnerable to a conceptual and moral critique. Four aspects of this weakness can be noted.

The first was the scandal of the European religious wars of the sixteenth to eighteenth century. Going to war was not, at that period, itself considered abnormal or immoral (see the pre-Reformation Hundred Years' War between France and England [1337–1453]), not even war carried out in the name of Christ (see the entire history of the crusades against Islam [between 1096 and 1291]). What made the post-Reformation wars shocking (apart from their savage and sanguinary character) was that Christians were killing other Christians in the name of Christ.[17] In light of the sad spectacle presented by the German Peasants' War (1524–1525), the Eighty Years' War in the Low Countries (1568–1648), the Swiss Civil War of 1712, the French Wars of Religion, pitting Catholics against Huguenots (1562–1598), the English Civil War in which Puritans battled Royalists (1642–1651), and the Thirty Years' War between Catholic France and Protestant Germany (1618–1648), it was natural that thoughtful people should be both morally repulsed and encouraged to think of religion in a fashion that eschewed dogmatic particularity and that should practice tolerance for others.[18] Thus, jurists like Jean Bodin (1530–1596) and Hugo Grotius (1583–1645) sought a path toward peace with good order by subjecting the topic of religion itself to close scrutiny.[19] Their willingness to deal with the fact of religious diversity provided a substantial juridical base for the sort of enlightenment notions advanced by John Locke (government by the consent of the governed) and Hobbes (social contract). The Deist version of Christianity was fueled by the dogmatically inspired wars of religion.

---

17. To be sure, this was a feature of the Fourth Crusade (1202–1204) as well, but in that case the carnage occurred in a far locale rather than at the doorstep.

18. See the works on tolerance by Locke and Voltaire mentioned above.

19. For Bodin, see *Six Books of the Commonwealth* (1576), and for Grotius, *De Jure Belli ac Pacis* (1625).

The second was the spectacle of colonial competition, in which Protestant countries (like England and the Netherlands) vied with Catholic countries (like Portugal and Spain) in establishing their versions of Christianity in the new world(s) that fifteenth- and sixteenth-century exploration had discovered. The violence in this case was not directed at other Christians—at least not overtly—but at the indigenous peoples who were destined to be displaced by the European conquistadors (in South and Central America) and colonialists (in North America). The close connection between Christianity and European colonialism seriously distorted discipleship to the degree that planting the cross as a sign of national expansion eclipsed bearing the cross as a symbol of suffering for the sake of others. In this case as well, critics of traditional Christianity could ask whether the gospel really supported the suppression or destruction of the cultures and religions of others. In the North American colonies, moreover, the religious disputes of England were imported: the Puritans (Congregationalists) so aggressively imposed their version of Reformed Christianity that separate colonies were established to protect the practice of dissenters, like the Baptists (Rhode Island), Quakers (Pennsylvania), and even Roman Catholics (Maryland).

The third weakening was, in fact, the way the divided Christianity of Europe was imported to America, especially in the Protestant colonies of North America. The Pilgrim Congregationalists of 1620 were Puritans whose seventeenth-century dominance in New England was real; they founded Harvard University in 1636 and Yale in 1707.[20] But they did not represent the Reformed tradition alone: the Dutch and German Reformed Church appeared in 1628 and the Presbyterians in 1706. Lutherans located themselves in present-day Delaware in 1619. Anglicans arrived with Sir Francis Drake in 1587 but after the American Revolution (1783) became the Protestant Episcopal Church. Roger Williams (1603–1683) enabled Baptists to find a refuge from Puritan harassment in Rhode Island. In the eighteenth century, the Methodist and Restoration movements spread, as well as other versions of Christian revival. Not only did such denominations represent distinct ways of expressing and representing Christianity, but they in turn also continued to divide and subdivide at a bewildering pace, so that eighteenth- and nineteenth-

---

20. The facts in the following paragraphs are drawn from Roger E. Olson et al., *Handbook of Denominations in the United States*, 14th ed. (Nashville: Abingdon, 2018).

century North America was dotted with different and intensely rivalrous versions of the one faith.

Such divisions did not occur amicably. Congregations split because of intense disagreements on some point or other that, in the eyes of the disputants, made life together impossible. Such fracturing was inevitable, since the principle of "Scripture alone" existed in an intolerable tension with the principles of the priesthood of all believers and the individual's right to interpret Scripture. Efforts at social control exercised by individual congregations and pastors followed naturally from that tension. Heresy trials, harassment, condemnation, excommunication, banishment, and even violence accompanied these denominational divisions. In all such disputes, after all, the issue of who is saved and who is not was paramount. To be the wrong kind of Christian was almost as bad as being no Christian at all.

The question of who is a true Christian was made even more complicated by the appearance of sects that in one way or another connected themselves with the Christian tradition, but with idiosyncratic deletions, alterations, or additions; the principle of individual revelation and authority found itself even further extended. The Religious Society of Friends (Quakers) began in England with the visions of George Fox (1624–1691) and by 1656 was in North America; William Penn (1644–1718) found them a haven in Pennsylvania. The Friends continued what might be called the gnostic strain in Christianity: the inner light guiding each individual was far more important than any external forms such as creed or canon or clergy, with Jesus being the supreme case of such an enlightened soul. The United Society of Believers in Christ's Second Appearing (the Shakers) also began in England and by 1774 had located themselves in Watervliet, New York. A celibate community that believed in an androgynous God and based itself on the spirit letters of Mother Ann Lee, the Shakers sought to anticipate in their communal life the utopian kingdom of the future. In the nineteenth century, the Church of the Latter-Day Saints (Mormons) began with the visions in the 1820s of Joseph Smith, whose Book of Mormon supplemented—and thereby corrected—the Old and New Testaments. Each of these sects also experienced hostility, harassment, and sometimes violence at the hands of denominationally divided Christians.

In light of the rancor and (often) sheer ignorance accompanying such denominational and sectarian disputes, it is not in the least surprising that the influence of the Enlightenment should find expression among the free-thinking Congregationalists of New England. Unitarianism—with its denial of the Trinity and the divinity of Christ—is effectively another name for Deism. It began its life in Boston with the sermons of Henry Ware (1746–1845) and William Ellery Channing (1780–1842), and in 1825, The American Unitarian Association was formed. The Unitarians founded the Harvard Divinity School in 1816 to further its nonsectarian principles.

The fourth aspect of Christianity's weakness—especially in North America—was a consequence of its segmentation into multiple denominations and sects, namely, a lack of structural and intellectual support for traditional beliefs and practices. On the surface, nothing could seem as lively as Christianity in eighteenth-century North America. There were churches and chapels everywhere, and everywhere there were men and women deeply committed to those churches and chapels. As congregations splintered into ever-smaller fragments, however, each with its charismatic leader, attention naturally focused on establishing and maintaining fragile new communities and defending their distinctiveness within a competitive market, more than on the nurturing of mature discipleship.

And as each new version of Christianity appeared, armed with the reasons for its distinctive stance over against every other version (ecumenism was not the order of the day), a coherent connection with older and broader traditions became less possible—and by many even undesirable. Such "making it up as we go along" only became more acute as denominations spread—continuing to divide and subdivide—from the relatively stable environs of the original colonies into the wilder territories of Ohio and Illinois.[21]

For such congregations, Scripture alone was the guide to Christian life, but Scripture was authoritatively proclaimed in sermons by a pastor,

21. For the expansion into the Ohio Territory, see David McCullough, *The Pioneers: The Heroic Story of the Settlers Who Brought the American Ideal West* (New York: Simon & Schuster, 2019). The itinerant and contentious career of the Congregationalist preacher Lyman Beecher (1775–1863) is illuminating. After thirty-five years of ministry in New York, Connecticut, and Boston (1798–1832), he became head of the new Lane Seminary in Cincinnati and spent twenty years in controversy, fighting intemperance, slavery, Unitarianism, and Catholicism (1832–1852), before retreating once more to the east (New York).

who may or may not have received any formal theological training, and whose preaching authority was, in any case, always subject to scrutiny and challenge from congregants who also claimed the authority to read and to instruct. And, in varying degrees, the authority of Scripture itself was under threat, not only from the cultured despisers who represented the Enlightenment but from those calling themselves Christians who found aspects of the Enlightenment liberating. Scripture itself, moreover, lacked reinforcement from such traditional instruments of Christian identity as the creed, the sacraments, and the liturgical year.

Important Reformation creeds lacked the virtue of parsimony displayed by the Apostles' and Nicene Creeds and tended toward an extravagant excess of definition.[22] When they ventured definitions of disputed theological and ecclesiastical points (and issues of civic government!), they functioned more to divide than to unite, and some free-church movements eschewed the use of creeds altogether. As for the sacraments, both baptism and the Lord's Supper sometimes served less as means of spiritual transformation than as foci of disputation and dissent. The great seasonal cycle of the liturgy was likewise but a shadow: whether and how to observe the birth of Jesus, Lent, and even Easter were matters of debate more than consensus. Traditions of the communal study of the Bible and prayer appeared (as with the Methodists), but instruction on discipleship—with a heavy emphasis on keeping the commandments—mainly came through home lessons, sermons, and Sunday school; individual Christians claimed their authority to read and interpret the Bible for themselves, and the practice of bibliomancy (divination through random scriptural verses) was not unknown.

In sum, the process of division and disputation among North American Protestant Christians weakened the capacity of scattered churches to form disciples according to the mind of Christ. The atmosphere of contention among Christians of different stripes, indeed, covered over a pervasive sense of anxiety regarding two central points. First, if the Bible is the sole source of truth, and we read the Bible in a manner directly opposed to the way our neighboring congregation reads it, how

22. See, for example, the Augsburg Confession (1530), the Dordrecht Confession (1632), the Thirty-Nine Articles (1571), the Westminster Confession (1646), the Savoy Declaration (1658), the Second London Baptist Confession (1689), and many more.

can we be secure in our claim to be living truly according to Scripture, or that Scripture is perspicuous? Second, if the point of being a believer is salvation, and our neighbors claim an exclusive hold on the means to salvation in a manner distinct from our own claim to such an exclusive hold, how can we possibly be sure of being saved? The effect of competing exclusive claims is to relativize what ought to be certain.[23] The pluralistic and competitive state of Christianity made its claims to absolute truth less and less plausible.

Political and Social Change

The Enlightenment had as its goal not only a changed way of thinking—shifting once for all from the superstitious realms of metaphysics and religion to reasoning on the basis of empirical evidence—but equally to use such empirically based reasoning to change the structures of the world. The changes that were accomplished in the eighteenth and nineteenth century were in fact momentous, making the world an entirely different place than that inhabited by Luther and Calvin and challenging traditional belief by showing how, in contrast to prayer and fasting, politics and technology could actually change things for the better in the present world. No need, the Enlightenment declared, to wait for heaven to liberate humans from a vale of tears: politics and technology can vastly improve the human condition here and now. It is the combination of Enlightenment thinking with political and technological change that constitutes modernity.

Thus, each in its fashion, the American and French revolutions (1776 and 1789) were expressions of Enlightenment aspiration. The American version looked to Locke, Hume, and British constitutional precedents to bring about a democratic republic in which those who governed did so at the consent of the governed and were bound by the constitution of 1789 to protect the "inalienable rights" of those by whom they were chosen to govern (for a time). Among those rights of the people was the free practice of religion, without any version of religion enjoying establishment privilege. Although in the eyes of the English the American declaration of independence was a form of internal sedition, in the eyes

---

23. See Peter L. Berger, *The Sacred Canopy: Elements of a Sociological Theory of Religion* (New York: Doubleday, 1967).

of the colonists it was genuinely the birth of a new nation, one that was, in the words of Lincoln's Gettysburg Address, "conceived in Liberty and dedicated to the proposition that all men are created equal." The tenor of the American initiative is nowhere better expressed than in *The Federalist Papers* composed by John Jay, James Madison, and Alexander Hamilton; they are entirely instruments of persuasion rather than coercion.

In sharp contrast, the French Revolution was a rage-fueled and violent paroxysm against the *ancien régime* of monarch, nobility, and church in the name of the "liberty, fraternity, and equality" learned from Voltaire, Rousseau, and the other *philosophes*, and led by the goddess Reason through years of savage internecine conflict that ended finally in the ascension of Napoleon (first consul, 1799; emperor, 1804) and the restoration of Catholicism as the official religion of France.[24] Nevertheless, France after the revolution was demonstrably not the same as France before the revolution, and, as in North America, Enlightenment aspiration demonstrated the power of humans to change the world rather than simply contemplate it. In the process, the people became the subjects of political action and not merely the subjects of monarchical whim.[25] And religion became a right exercised by individuals according to their lights rather than a universal truth imposed by authority.

What was called natural philosophy turned the empirical principles of Bacon, Descartes, and Spinoza to the empirical facts of the material world—now viewed as the only real world worth considering—to improve them. Benjamin Franklin was regarded by the British and French as a great philosopher and invited to the circles of their great thinkers, not because he created a system of thought but because he changed the world around him for the better. His study of the Gulf Stream contributed to better and speedier travel on the Atlantic; his experimentations with electricity leading to the invention of the lightning rod saved countless homes from destruction; his Franklin Stove improved the circulation of hot air in houses; his invention of bifocals saved the sight of the elderly.[26]

24. See the *Concordat of 1801*. For this whole history, see Simon Schama, *Citizens: A Chronicle of the French Revolution* (New York: Vintage Books, 1989).

25. In this respect, the opening words of the Constitution of the United States, "We, the People," mark the most decisive change in world politics.

26. See Walter Isaacson, *Benjamin Franklin: An American Life* (New York: Simon & Schuster, 2004).

In virtually all fields apart from medicine, the eighteenth and nineteenth centuries were without parallel in the range of their inventions.[27] From the seed drill (1701) to the spinning jenny (1764), steam engine (1769), hot-air balloon (1784), steamboat (1786), gas lighting (1792), cotton gin (1794), and lathe (1797), the eighteenth century spun out invention after invention, each of which led to still further inventions that led, it seemed, to a mastery of the material world rivaling even that ascribed to the biblical deity.[28] The pace of world-altering invention only increased,[29] leading to the industrial revolution (1760–1840), which employed new processes of chemical and metal processing, steam and waterpower, machine tools, and a mechanized factory system, to enable the manufacture of material goods at a previously unimagined efficiency, while at the same time requiring ever more extensive mining of mineral resources, and fostering patterns of exploitation (for example, child labor) and social dislocation (for example, the growth of urban slums).[30]

It took some time for the negative aspects of modernity to be recognized,[31] and until they were, its claim to make the world better through politics and technology appeared convincing—far more persuasive (at the evidentiary level) than the promises stated in the Bible. And it is fair to say that in the realms of science, technology, politics, and above all

27. William Harvey published his epochal findings on circulation in 1628, but apart from the development of the smallpox vaccine in 1796, the invention of the stethoscope in 1819, of anesthesia in 1846, antiseptics in 1847, pasteurization in 1856, and of the first contact lenses in 1887, medical research and practice lagged behind inventions directed to the external world until the twentieth century.

28. For such pretension, see William F. Lynch, *Christ and Prometheus: A New Vision of the Secular* (Notre Dame: University of Notre Dame Press, 1970).

29. In the first half of the nineteenth century, inventions include the battery (1800) and steam locomotive (1814), photograph (1814), reaper (1831), telegraph and morse code (1837–1838), bicycle (1839), and gyroscope (1852).

30. The novelist Charles Dickens (1812–1870) was a child laborer in a bootblack factory, and in works such as *Oliver Twist* (1839), *Bleak House* (1853), and *Hard Times* (1854), he exposed the dark underside of that era.

31. For the epistemological and moral overreach of modernity, see Luke Timothy Johnson, *Miracles: God's Presence and Power in Creation* (Louisville: Westminster John Knox, 2018), and Christian Smith, *Atheist Overreach: What Atheism Can't Deliver* (New York: Oxford University Press, 2018).

commerce, the premises of modernity continue to dominate: the control and manipulation of material reality through dispassionate reason has been, up to the very near present, the distinguishing mark of the first world. Those premises do not include consideration of a divine will, and religion is relegated to a private (and increasingly idiosyncratic) preference. The ideology of the Enlightenment eclipsed, among the intellectual elite, the world imagined by Scripture. The politics of the Enlightenment marginalized religion. The technology enabled by Enlightenment principles demonstrated the superiority of science to religion.

NINETEENTH-CENTURY IDEOLOGICAL CHALLENGES

European intellectuals, however, were far from done in their savaging of traditional Christianity, religion, and finally the premises of the Enlightenment itself. In this section, I consider a series of hammer blows delivered on believers by Christianity's cultured despisers, ranging from the scientific historical-critical study of the Bible to the dismantling of religion's illusion by psychoanalysis. The effect of these nineteenth-century European challenges was not felt all at once or universally, even in Europe. But through the medium of universities (and their divinity schools!), these ideas filtered into the minds of American ministers and further eroded—for many, indeed, destroyed—any traditional grounds for discipleship. Taken together, the ideologies of nineteenth-century European intellectuals provide the necessary backdrop to the formation of the second vision of Christian discipleship.

Historical-Critical Analysis of the Bible

The first of these hammer blows was the invention of the so-called historical-critical study of the Bible. Believers had always asked historical questions of the Bible and had, especially in figures like Origen, understood the Bible's limits as a historical source.[32] The Enlightenment, however, made history a weapon for demystifying all of Scripture and reducing it to an inadequate and untrue set of human compositions. The

---

32. See Origen, *On First Principles* 4.1.8, 15–18; *Against Celsus* 1.63; Augustine, *The Literal Meaning of Genesis*.

approach had its roots in Spinoza's challenge to the traditional authorship of the Old Testament, and in the efforts of British Deists like John
Toland and Thomas Chubb to find a nonmiraculous Jesus, but in 1835
was raised from amateur to scientific status and directed specifically at
the New Testament, in the German University of Tübingen.

In that year, David Friedrich Strauss (1808–1874) produced his monumental *Life of Jesus Critically Examined*, in which every gospel passage
was subjected to rigorous examination for its historicity (by this point,
historical referentiality was taken to be the only meaningful mark of
truth). By bracketing anything miraculous as outside historical pur-
view—while implying that anything miraculous was also untrue—
Strauss concluded that the Jesus of the Gospels was woven whole cloth
out of the mythological notions of the first believers.[33] The subsequent
"quest of the historical Jesus" was the supreme Enlightenment project
directed against traditional Christianity and, although declared dead by
Albert Schweitzer, resurrected itself, to the confusion of many believers,
in the late twentieth century.[34]

In the same year of 1835, Ferdinand Christian Baur (1792–1860), the
real founder of the Tübingen school, published his challenge to the
authenticity of Paul's Pastoral Letters,[35] and in 1845, he extended his
inquiry to Paul and the Acts of the Apostles,[36] and then the entire
early history of Christianity,[37] which he read reductively as a form of
ideological and institutional conflict. Baur's disciple, Albert Schwegler
(1819–1857), elaborated these theories into a comprehensive interpre-

33. *Das Leben Jesu, kritisch bearbeitet*; the 1846 translation into English by George
Eliot made a particularly strong impact.

34. Albert Schweitzer, *The Quest of the Historical Jesus: A Critical Study of Its Progress
from Reimarus to Wrede* (New York: Macmillan, 1968); see Luke Timothy Johnson, "The
Humanity of Jesus: What's at Stake in the Quest for the Historical Jesus," in *Contested
Issues in Christian Origins and the New Testament: Collected Essays*, Supplements to
Novum Testamentum 146 (Leiden: Brill, 2013), 3–28.

35. *Die sogennanten Pastoralbriefe*; the same year, F. H. Kern challenged the authenticity of the Letter of James, in *Der Character und Ursprung des Briefes Jacobi* (Tübingen:
Fues, 1835).

36. Ferdinand Christian Baur, *Paulus, der Apostel Jesu Christi* (Leipzig: Fues,
1866–1867).

37. *The Church History of the First Three Centuries*, 3rd ed., trans. Allan Menzies
(Edinburgh: Williams & Norgate, 1878).

tation of Christianity's birth and growth.[38] Although the specific conclusions of the Tübingen school eventually gave way to later and better
scholarship, its overall approach continued to dominate New Testament
scholarship until very recently, and at the beginning of the twentieth
century (labeled as the higher criticism), it entered the curricula of the
North American divinity schools at Harvard, Yale, and Union, stimulated
opposition from the Princeton School of Theology, and settled in for
the never-ending modernist-fundamentalist conflict in twentieth- and
twenty-first-century American Christianity.[39] For the purposes of this
study, the historical-critical approach to the entire Bible will be a fundamental element in the new vision of discipleship that also emerges
fully at the start of the twentieth century.

German Philosophy

The second ideological challenge came from nineteenth-century German
philosophy, which was an indirect but powerful contributor to the shaping of the second vision of discipleship. The topic is notoriously complex
and arcane, resisting any simplified treatment.[40] But a few notes can be
offered on the German Idealism that built on the work of Immanuel Kant
(1724–1804), especially in the *Critique of Pure Reason* (1781).

First, no sooner was reason enthroned over revelation than reason
itself was brought into question. Distinguishing between "things in
themselves" (*noumena*) and "things as they appear" (*phenomena*), Kant
considered the human mind capable of knowing only the appearances,
signaling a retreat from the hard empiricism of the British philosophers
even as the natural world was then being altered through technology.

Second, rather than embrace a complete skepticism, idealists like
Johann Gottlieb Fichte (1762–1814) moved easily from a purported law
of human reason—that it moved dialectically from thesis to antithesis

---

38. Albert Schwegler, *Das nachapostolischer Zeitalter in den Hauptmomentum seiner
Entwicklung* (Tübingen: Fues, 1846); for a critical study of the Tübingen school, see
Horton Harris, *The Tübingen School: A Historical and Theological Investigation of the
School of F. C. Baur* (Grand Rapids: Baker Books, 1990).

39. For the modernist-fundamentalist conflict, see George M. Marsden, *Fundamentalism and American Culture*, 2nd ed. (New York: Oxford University Press, 2006).

40. For a fuller discussion of these figures, see Frederick Copleston, *18th and 19th Century German Philosophy*, vol. 7 of *A History of Philosophy* (New York: Doubleday, 1963).

to synthesis—to speculation concerning the world of ideas that evolved according to the same pattern.

Third, such a systematizing (metaphysical) passion found full expression in Georg Wilhelm Hegel (1770–1831), whose appropriation of Fichte's dialectic was worked out in the inevitable progress of the world-spirit (*Weltgeist*) through human history, which now became the manifestation of an immanent (even divine?) idea; see his *Lectures on the Philosophy of History* (1837; published posthumously).

Fourth, building on the same Kantian basis, Arthur Schopenhauer (1788–1860) in *The World as Will and Representation* (1818–1819) moved in a less optimistic direction: world history is the immanent working out (within the *noumena*) of a blind will that humans are powerless to resist. In different ways, Hegel and Schopenhauer powerfully influenced later thinkers.

It is important to pause here to consider just how these speculative exercises represented a threat to a scripturally based Christianity: (1) They all proceed on the basis of human reason alone; revelation is not a factor in their thought; (2) if there is an element of the divine in their systems, it is far removed from the Creator and Savior spoken of in Scripture; (3) rather than a personal God who creates and cares for creation and humanity, the divine is an impersonal force within the system; (4) human destiny is not a consequence of free choices but is determined by a process over which humans have no control—a process that moves inexorably on its own tracks. In sum, the best and brightest of continental philosophers in the first half of the nineteenth century simply found Christianity irrelevant.

In three other German philosophers, however, Christianity is not simply bypassed; it is explicitly rejected as a form of false consciousness. Ludwig Feuerbach (1804–1872) turned Hegelianism in a materialist direction, paying attention in particular to religious belief as nothing more than the psychological projection of human desire (see *The Essence of Christianity* [1841]). Religious belief is true insofar as it is rooted in human psychology, but it is false (and worse, a falsification) insofar as it pretends to pertain to any reality beyond human consciousness. To treat a psychological projection as something more than a human phenomenon is a form of self-alienation. Christianity (and for that matter any other religion) is of interest only as it tells us something about human need and longing. Theology *is* anthropology and nothing more.

Karl Marx (1818–1883) rejected German idealism of the Hegelian sort and applauded Feuerbach for definitively identifying all religion as a form of self-alienation.[41] But he considered Feuerbach to have fallen short, since the point of philosophy was, in his view, to be freeing humans from their economic self-alienation: "The philosophers have only interpreted the world, in various ways; the point is to change it" (*Theses on Feuerbach* 11 [1845]). Considering the challenges to property such as that of Pierre-Joseph Proudhon to be utopian and insufficiently scientific, Marx (and his collaborator Friedrich Engels [1820–1895]) analyzed the disruptions to society created by the industrial revolution and developed a "dialectical materialism" that applied the thesis-antithesis-synthesis of Fichte and Hegel to the analysis of social and economic realities, arguing that a historical necessity drove humans inexorably toward a "classless society" in which the enlightenment ideals of fraternity, liberty, and equality could be achieved through a communistic society. To accomplish this end, however, a revolutionary fervor and commitment is required of those seeking liberation from the shackles of capitalism: "Workers of all countries, Unite!" (*Communist Manifesto* [1848]). Marxism's compelling analysis and almost prophetic call had a powerful impact on the eventual shaping of the new vision of discipleship (as the transformation of society), as Christians tried to filter out Marx's atheism and materialism while retaining the critique of capitalism and the conviction that some form of socialism represented the only humane future for mankind, forgetting, perhaps, that disenchantment from religion was an essential premise for Marx himself.

The final German philosopher of the nineteenth century who showed animus toward Christianity was the brilliant epigrammatist, Friedrich Nietzsche (1844–1900). When he declared in *The Gay Science* (1882) that "God is dead," he meant that the Enlightenment had made traditional belief in the biblical God, who had buttressed all European civilization, no longer possible for people like himself:

---

41. "He is in fact the true conqueror of the old philosophy" (*The Economic and Philosophic Manuscripts of 1844*). "The foundation of irreligious criticism is: *man makes religion*, religion does not make man" (*A Contribution to the Critique of Hegel's Philosophy of Right* [1843]).

God is dead. God remains dead. And we have killed him. How shall we comfort ourselves, the murderers of all murderers? . . . must we ourselves not become gods simply to appear worthy of it? (section 125)[42]

Nietzsche found religious faith to be antithetical to intelligence, which requires humans "to reason in a way diametrically opposed to the traditional one: whenever we find strength of faith too prominent, we are led to infer a lack of demonstrability, even something improbable, in the matter to be believed" (*Genealogy of Morals* 24). And for him, the Christian faith is particularly reprehensible: "In the Christian world of ideas there is nothing that has the least contact with reality—and it is in the instinctive hatred of reality that we have recognized as the only motivating force at the root of Christianity" (*The Antichrist* 39). Nietzsche's wrath was directed especially toward Paul for the way in which—in contrast to the nobility that Nietzsche associated with antiquity and advocated for the present—Paul advocated a "slave mentality."[43] Nietzsche perfectly represents the humanistic atheism that rejects Christianity precisely for the way in which it inculcated a form of discipleship that degraded humans.[44]

Evolutionary Theory

In contrast to the solitary German humanist Nietzsche who raged against Christianity, Charles Darwin (1809–1882) was a British natural scientist of the first order whose investigations were carried out in conversation with others (for example, Alfred Russel Wallace) and who only gradually came to a personal position of agnosticism with regard to God. Part of the impact of his studies, in fact, can be ascribed to their disinterested and objective character. Nevertheless, the publication of *On the Origin*

42. See also *Thus Spoke Zarathustra*, prologue 2.

43. See the excerpts from Nietzsche on Paul in Wayne A. Meeks and John T. Fitzgerald, *The Writings of Saint Paul*, 2nd ed., Norton Critical Edition (New York: Norton, 2007), 408–14.

44. The great exception to these philosophical trends was the Danish thinker Søren Kierkegaard, whose literary brilliance and existential analysis of life in defense of Christianity came to light (and influence) only in the twentieth century.

of Species (1859) after decades of hands-on research met with wide and wild controversy, making him represent for many the best and worst in the scientific approach unleashed by the Enlightenment. Not through abstract debate but through empirical research, Darwin's propositions challenged the biblical worldview more fundamentally than all German polemics combined: the age of the earth, the process of natural selection, and the survival of the fittest all provided an interpretation of the world that countered biblical chronology, the divine guidance of history, and the special character of humans as created in the image of God.

The controversy only intensified with the publication of *The Descent of Man, and Selection's Relation to Sex* in 1871. If Darwin was correct, if humans descended from the apes over a period of millions of years through a blind biological process, then indeed the biblical story could no longer be read (even by believers) in the same naive fashion as it had been. For many believers, the choice was stark: you could believe in evolution, or you could believe the Bible.[45]

Since Darwin was not an isolated figure, but one whose ideas (and experiments) were taken up by many other scientists, the threat posed by evolutionary theory loomed even larger, especially when concepts like survival of the fittest came to be applied to contemporary society in forms of social Darwinism, such as the eugenics movement associated with the scientist Francis Galton (1822–1911).[46] Controversy concerning the mechanisms of change continued even among those who accepted evolution's broad outlines; Lamarckism, for example—the proposition that acquired characteristics can be inherited—enjoyed a long minority life. Despite all the controversy, however, evolutionary theory became the reigning scientific and social paradigm in succeeding decades, making the premises of development and progress the mark of enlightened public discourse.[47]

45. For a sense of the original (and continuing) controversy, see Alister McGrath, *The Big Questions: Why We Can't Stop Talking about Science, Faith, and God* (London: Saint Martin's, 2015). It is striking that some Christian defensive responses, such as creation science or creationism, fell into the trap of trying to read Genesis as though it was ever intended to be read in such literalistic fashion. Once more, the Enlightenment dictated the terms of debate even over Scripture.

46. See *Heredity and Genius* (1869) and *Inquiries into Human Faculty and Its Development* (1914).

47. Acceptance of a paradigm does not mean agreement on its applications. Some

Sociological Theory

France contributed to this already thick stew of ideology with the theories of socialism advanced by Henri de Saint-Simon (1760–1825) and Joseph Pierre Proudhon (1809–1865)—the theories thought by Marx to be utopian rather than scientific—but above all the invention of the discipline called sociology. Auguste Comte (1798–1857) considered humans to evolve through three stages: the theological, the metaphysical, and the positive, by which he meant not only the study of society but also its change—for the better—through the application of empirical methods he termed "positivism." He distinguished between natural science and social science (sociology), which he termed, in a clear troping of medieval theology, "the queen of the sciences." It was the task of positivism to construct a positive form of society on the basis of truly rational principles—a purely secular humanism. Comte considered, however, that an appeal to reason alone was insufficient for the creation of a coherent society and so invented a "religion of humanity," complete with calendar and rituals, as a utopian glue for the social order. It was not a great success.

Émile Durkheim (1858–1917), however, was the true originator of proper sociology as the scientific study of social forms and institutions, using such tools as statistics, surveys, and analysis of historical phenomena. Like other thinkers in this survey, he looked at human behavior strictly on its own terms without any reference to God. In 1895, he published *The Rules of Sociological Method*, and in 1897, he published a groundbreaking study of *Suicide*, comparing statistics in Catholic and Protestant populations. Sociology as practiced by Durkheim not only observed social phenomena but sought the causes of them and what function they might serve within a group. Thus, his final work on *The Elementary Forms of the Religious Life* (1912) brought to the subject of religion all the dispassionate analysis he brought to suicide; he argues that all religions share a common concept of the sacred, or the holy, but in the end, all religion represents the "collective consciousness" of

---

aspects of evolutionary theory, such as the legitimacy of evolutionary psychology, have been the subject of vigorous and sometimes angry debate among members of the guild (see the debate between Stephen Jay Gould and Richard Dawkins).

the group itself. Religion and a society are not merely interconnected; religion is the expression of the social cohesion of the group. The effect of the study is to reduce all religion—as in other ways we have seen with Feuerbach and Marx—to the epiphenomenal. For Feuerbach, the real subject was human psychology; for Marx, the real subject was human economics; for Durkheim, the real subject was human society.

Depth Psychology

Sigmund Freud (1856–1939) must be included among the nineteenth-century ideological challengers to religion, even though his *Interpretation of Dreams*, the book that revealed his discovery of the unconscious, did not appear until 1899, and his overt reductionistic treatments of religion were published only in the early twentieth century.[48] Like Auguste Comte's positivism, Freud's psychoanalysis became in its early years something much like a religious cult, complete with initiations, defined rituals, group reinforcement, and excommunications (see Jung and Adler), all directed by the hieratic father figure of Freud himself.[49] Freud's work was paradoxical in that it applied the most rigorous rationality of the Enlightenment to the criticism of Enlightenment rationality itself. Humans are driven by dark forces within them over which they have little (sometimes no) control. Even the minute dissection of the conflicts between libido and superego, for example, yields only slowly if at all to the insights that liberate the ego from unconscious drives. Not only is there no God in control of things; there is no real human control either. Religion is at best an illusion that comforts humans in their captive condition, that enables them to bear the discontents of civilized life. At best a very poor anthropologist, Freud sought in human prehistory (*Totem and Taboo*) and in the psychoanalytic reading of the Bible (*Moses and Monotheism*) the etiology of a structure of meaning through which humans alienate themselves.

In the twenty-first century, after the dominance of talking therapies has been displaced by the chemical treatment of chemical imbalance,

---

48. *Totem and Taboo* (1913), *The Future of an Illusion* (1927), *Civilization and Its Discontents* (1930), and *Moses and Monotheism* (1939).

49. See Peter Gay, *Freud: A Life for Our Time* (London: Dent & Sons, 1988), for the intense dynamics among first-generation analysts.

and now that psychoanalytic theory subsists only as a form of literary fashion in universities, it is difficult to remember just how much Freudian premises and jargon formed the default discourse of the chattering classes through virtually the entire twentieth century.

Conclusion

The effect of the four factors I have described in this chapter is clear. In the eighteenth and nineteenth centuries, modernity swept everything before it in Europe and North America. The politics and technology based in Enlightenment reason changed the way humans saw themselves and the world around them. Increasingly, the educated elite either dismissed the Bible (and the Christianity based on it) or reduced it to a rhetorical support for a vague humanism. Taking the Bible seriously as an account of the world or as the basis for life was, in that view, the refuge of the unevolved and undereducated. The split between the educated elite and the many (so despised by Nietzsche) grew deeper with the passage of time. Christian faith, in the eyes of the enlightened, was the very embodiment of ignorance and resistance to progress.

In the view of the enlightened, it was not the law of a loving God as expressed by Scripture that counted but the inexorable laws of nature, or the dialectical laws of economics, or the inevitable laws of societies, or the laws of unconscious impulses; these were the forces that needed to be taken into account. To a remarkable degree, the ideologies espoused in the nineteenth century combined a form of rigid determinism together with a commitment to progress, which was to be accomplished through changes in the material world.

And as the world was demystified by removing God—although God's place was frequently taken by lesser forms of divinity—so was any understanding of humans as created in the image of God. Indeed, instead of the infinite value of the individual soul, there was the pragmatic value of societal and economic classes. Rather than the liberation of each person from the slavery that is sin, the gift of salvation through Jesus Christ, and a future life with God, the point of human endeavor is the liberation of all humanity from the diverse enslavements of society and a march toward a classless and neurosis-free future. Bearing one's cross in imitation of Jesus and in service to others is, in this view, a form of masochism, delusion, and self-alienation; it is especially to be despised because it resists the call to universal progress through the manipulation of material goods.

Such a massive attack on the traditional vision of discipleship was the natural concomitant of the rejection of the world imagined by the Bible. If heaven and earth are fantasies, if Jesus is a fiction, if God is only a projection, then the entire premise of discipleship is void. Those acting as though they were as real as the steam engine or telegraph were fools or charlatans.

The effects of modernity were the more corrosive because, as I have suggested, Christianity itself from the seventeenth century forward was a fragmented and fragile target. Especially in North America, the continuing segmentation of Protestant denominations—very often precisely on the basis of the correct interpretation of the Bible—led in two main directions. In one direction, Bible-based belief tended to ignore modernity or to accommodate to modernity's technological (and economic) benefits while bracketing its challenge to the Bible. In the other direction, Christians who accommodated actively to modernity tended to fit the Bible and belief within modernity's framework.

All of this is the backdrop to the development of the second vision of discipleship. The stages of that development now need to be described.

5

Shaping a New Vision

By the end of the nineteenth century, the material benefits brought by modernity were clear. Science and technology made astonishing and obvious progress, changing in fundamental ways how people lived. Such was certainly the case in Europe but was even more sensationally evident in North America, where the transition from coastline colonies to a continent-straddling nation happened with breathtaking speed.

Steamships, railroads, and (very shortly) automobiles and airplanes made the transportation of goods and of people more rapid and efficient than ever dreamed possible. Communication between distant places was accomplished by means of the telegraph (1837) and telephone (1876). The production of petroleum (1859) abetted the development of the internal combustion engine. Developments in metallurgy made the erection of great bridges and buildings possible.[1] The invention of the electric light and its use (from 1882) in private homes profoundly affected patterns of domestic life and commerce. All these inventions, indeed, had as a goal and a consequence the rapid expansion of commerce.

The ever-growing demand to produce material goods shifted the center of commerce from agrarian and craft manufacture to urban factories, and the demand in such factories for raw materials in coal and ore and petroleum spurred the expansive extraction of minerals from the earth. The pace of discovery and invention, in turn, enabled entrepreneurial

1. For the engineering and manufacturing involved in great spans like the Brooklyn Bridge (1883), see David McCullough, *The Great Bridge: The Epic Story of the Building of the Brooklyn Bridge* (New York: Simon & Schuster, 1983). The Home Insurance Company building in Chicago is considered the first genuine American skyscraper (1885).

capitalists to exploit resources and technologies to create huge fortunes: Carnegie in steel, Rockefeller in oil, Vanderbilt in transportation, Astor in furs, and—revealingly—J. P. Morgan in finance. The extravagant wealth of the few, once the privilege of royalty and nobility, now displayed itself in the "conspicuous consumption" of land, mansions, jewels, and servants by aggressive entrepreneurs.[2] Some of this wealth found its way into philanthropy (as in the case of Carnegie), but most of it did not. Still, for the ordinary American in the nineteenth century, material existence was on the surface much better—safer, more comfortable, more pleasurable, more filled with possibility—because of the successes of modernity.[3]

But there was also a dark side of modernity. Wars were no longer fought in the name of religion, to be sure (everyone, after all, was enlightened), but they by no means ceased, and armaments technology made them even more lethal. The nineteenth century featured almost constant dynastic war in Europe.[4] Colonial powers fought countless "little" wars as they sought to secure their imperial ambitions around the globe.[5] And in North America, a great civil war tested the ability of a nation founded on Enlightenment convictions to survive. The American Civil War provided a foretaste of the horrors of total war that would mark twentieth-century conflicts, when not only the defeat of armies but the destruction of entire populations and cultures became the goal.

Modernity also brought with it massive social dislocation. The enlightened European nations made the age-old phenomenon of slavery

2. The term was coined by sociologist Thorstein Veblen in *The Theory of the Leisure Class: An Economic Study in the Evolution of Institutions* (1899).

3. As I noted in the previous chapter, medical science trailed all these spectacular manipulations of the external world. Many children did not survive to adulthood, and even at the end of the century, average life expectancy was under fifty years. Bloodletting was still widely practiced. Diseases such as pneumonia and tuberculosis remained without remedy, and infectious diseases such as smallpox, yellow fever, scarlet fever, cholera, and even influenza could wipe out entire populations. Germ theory only advanced under Pasteur and Koch from the middle of the nineteenth century and found some practical application with Lister at the end of the century.

4. A short list: the Napoleonic Wars (1803–1815), the Crimean War (1853–1856), the Franco-Austrian War (1859), the Austro-Prussian War (1866), the Franco-Prussian War (1870), the Russo-Turkish War (1877–1878), and the Wars of Italian Unification (1848–1859).

5. See especially Byron Farwell, *Queen Victoria's Little Wars* (New York: Norton, 1985).

a lucrative commercial enterprise, bringing some ten million Africans to the Caribbean islands and North America to supply the labor for an expanding market for tobacco and cotton. The tendency of modernity to objectify and commodify found perfect expression in the slave trade of the middle Atlantic.

Some thirty million people also migrated to the United States over the course of the nineteenth century, with the pace of immigration increasing after 1830. The Irish potato famine between 1845 and 1849 killed a million people, and millions of Irish people fled to America in search of a better life. Irish Catholicism was not a welcome arrival in the predominantly Protestant nation. But the melting pot became even more a mixed stew with the influx of millions of eastern Europeans (mostly Jews) and Italians (mostly Catholic) in the second half of the century.[6] Clashes between populations drawn from such disparate (and often hostile) European populations continued in the promised land of America, with a segment of the United States adopting a know-nothing attitude that was hostile to all newcomers.[7]

The huge influx of immigrants in the second half of the century also swelled the population of cities, above all New York, where the growth of slums rivaled those of midcentury London. But immigration was not the only cause of city slums with teeming tenements. The nineteenth century also saw increasing numbers of rural Americans seeking and finding work in urban factories. Even as the myth of the frontier was being formed in the late nineteenth century, the flight from the countryside to the cities had begun.

While the capitalist entrepreneurs made great fortunes and lived in luxury, moreover, the overall economy in the United States was chaotic, alternating between boom and bust, with the booms advancing the wealth of the rich and the busts exacerbating the misery of the poor.[8] Work on the (building and running of) railroads, in coal, copper, and

6. One source for the (s)melting pot metaphor is an 1845 entry in the journal of Ralph Waldo Emerson.

7. The sometimes violent clashes between ethnic groups are brilliantly evoked in Annie Proulx's novel, *Accordion Crimes* (New York: Scribner, 1996). The know-nothings of 1844–1855 were officially the Native American Party.

8. A short list of economic panics and recessions in the nineteenth century: 1802–1804; 1807–1810; 1815–1821; 1836–1838; 1857; 1873–1879; 1882–1885.

silver mines, and in factories was hard, dangerous, and unregulated. Cities were choked by the toxic fumes spewed by those "dark Satanic mills."[9] Child labor in mines and factories was common, with diseases like tuberculosis and black lung a common fate. Owners and managers were in complete control, supported by the power of (often) corrupt government. The struggle to form labor unions was accompanied by violence and murder.[10]

Not surprisingly, the overcrowded urban tenements that housed laborers—usually every member of a family—displayed the inevitable corollaries of systemic destitution and despair: crime, prostitution, and drunkenness helped to make the slums of New York and Chicago the dark underside of the late nineteenth century that Mark Twain called "the Gilded Age."[11] The period was also the heyday of American journalism, and while many newspapers indulged in yellow journalism, there were nevertheless stalwart writers such as Lincoln Steffens, Ida Tarbell, and Ray Stannard Baker, who published in journals like *McClure's Magazine* lengthy and devastating investigative exposés of corporate corruption, earning for themselves the (at first, pejorative) label of "muckrakers."[12]

CHANGING SOCIETY

Partly in reaction to the negative conditions brought about by modernity, and partly as an expression of modernity's own urge to change the world, many in the nineteenth century, both in Europe and in North

9. William Blake, "Jerusalem" (1810)—he was speaking, to be sure, of London. In the previous chapter, I noted the exposure of London's dehumanizing social conditions in the novels of Charles Dickens.

10. The degrading nature of life in the New York slums was brought home to many by the photographic work of the journalist Jacob A. Riis (1849–1914), especially in his book, *How the Other Half Lives: Studies among the Tenements of New York* (New York: Scribner's Sons, 1890). For the violent riots, bombings, and murders in Chicago during this period, see John A. Farrow, *Clarence Darrow: Attorney for the Damned* (New York: Vintage Books, 2012), 144–213.

11. Mark Twain and Charles Dudley Warner, *The Gilded Age: A Tale for Today* (1873).

12. Included in their number slightly later were muckraking novelists like Upton Sinclair (1878–1968) and Theodore Dreiser (1871–1945), as well as the lawyer Clarence Darrow (1857–1938).

America, turned their energies to politics (in the broadest sense) as the means to human improvement. The most radical among them sought to overturn or replace the existing social order, while others aimed at improving the human condition by regulating behavior through the passage of laws. But all these reformers shared the essential conviction of modernity: that society itself is malleable and subject to manipulation by human ingenuity.

Structural Change

The influence of the French Revolution of 1789 continued in Europe after the Napoleonic interlude. Between 1848 and 1850, a series of liberal revolutions against monarchical structures spread from Italy to France and enveloped a dozen other European nations before collapsing and disappointing the romantic expectations of the enlightened elite ranging from George Sand to Karl Marx.[13] The socialistic theories of Pierre-Joseph Proudhon (1809–1865), Henri de Saint-Simon (1760–1825), and Charles Fourier (1772–1837) were so widespread and so popular that Marx and Engels found it necessary to distinguish between the utopian socialism of such writers and the explicitly revolutionary, scientific, socialism advanced by the communists (see Engels, *Socialism, Utopian and Scientific* [1880]). Even in England between 1838 and 1848, the Chartist movement was a form of political protest that sought relief for ordinary citizens within a constitutional framework.[14]

In the nineteenth-century United States, despite fears of a rampant revolutionary socialism among workers, especially in labor unions, and despite the fervent efforts of some like the anarchist Emma Goldman, who were committed to that vision, the main expression of socialism was the spread of utopian communities founded on the principles of utopian socialism. By midcentury, there were at least eighty such communities started in the eastern United States. Some were dedicated to the prin-

13. For Sand and her involvement in the movement, see Elizabeth Harland, *George Sand* (New Haven: Yale University Press, 2004). *The Communist Manifesto* by Marx and Engels was composed at the outbreak of revolution in Germany. Marx's response to the restoration of monarchy is found in *The 18th Brumaire of Louis Napoleon* (1852).

14. See Dorothy Thompson, *The Chartists* (London: Pantheon, 1984).

ciples of Robert Owen (1771–1858), a Welsh philanthropist, such as the one at New Harmony, Indiana. Some embraced transcendentalism, like Brook Farm in Massachusetts. Some extended the sharing of property, in good Platonic fashion, to the sharing of spouses, like the Oneida Community in New York. Many communities, like the Wisconsin Phalanx, were part of the Fourierist movement. By the mid-nineteenth century, the Shakers had established eighteen communities in New England and the Midwest. Whatever the overarching ideological motivations (transcendental, anarchist, Christian), such communes shared a rejection of the competitive capitalist society and sought a more meaningful life in the sharing of possessions, in this, not unlike the adherents of monastic orders. But unlike monastic orders, these communes sought a material kingdom now rather than a spiritual kingdom in the future. They also lacked the brilliant practical guidance of the *Rule of Saint Benedict*, and most soon failed. Very few of them survived to the twentieth century. Like earlier and later idealists, they discovered that socialism tends either toward dissolution or toward oppressive social controls.[15] Despite all these failures, however, and despite the (later) lessons to be drawn from state-controlled socialism, the dream of a life that could combine freedom, equality, and fraternity remained strong. For many, socialism rather than capitalism seemed to represent the best future for humanity.

Changing Laws

Others in the nineteenth century sought to remedy social ills through the politics of persuasion and the passage of laws. Many of these social reformers were committed Christians who increasingly directed their religious fervor to changing the behavior of their neighbors; others were non-Christian or only nominally Christian, who sought to better society as an expression of their humanistic ideals. In these efforts, above all, we

15. See, for example, Luke Timothy Johnson, *Sharing Possessions: What Faith Demands*, 2nd ed. (Grand Rapids: Eerdmans, 2011); Rosabeth Moss Kantor, *Commitment and Community: Communes and Utopias in Sociological Perspective* (Cambridge: Harvard University Press, 1972); Benjamin Zablocki, *The Joyful Community: An Account of the Bruderhof—a Communal Movement Now in Its Third Generation* (New York: Penguin Books, 1971). Socialism shares wealth but is notoriously unable to create wealth; see George Gilder, *Wealth and Poverty* (New York: Regnery, 1981).

increasingly find an emphasis on politics (transforming society) as the defining element of discipleship.

Abolition

Moral revulsion at slavery took hold first in England—which, to be sure, had been one of the main European traders in slaves. James Oglethorpe (1696–1785) disallowed the practice of slavery in the colony of Georgia, which he had founded. William Wilberforce (1759–1833) was an evangelical Christian who led the fight for abolition in England for twenty years, until the Slave Trade Act was passed in 1807. England subsequently passed the Slavery Abolition Act in 1833. In the United States, the campaign for abolition was led by the fiery William Lloyd Garrison (1805–1875), a devout Christian with Quaker and Baptist antecedents, who read the Bible daily and based his rejection of slavery on such reading. For some thirty years, his newspaper, *The Liberator* (1831–1865), agitated for abolition, and he was one of the founders of the American Anti-Slavery Society (1833–1870).[16] Other abolitionists like Harriet Beecher Stowe (author of *Uncle Tom's Cabin* [1852]), Frederick Douglass, Theodore Parker, Wendell Phillips, and Sojourner Truth joined him in the work of the society, which combined political agitation through the press, and political pressure through public meetings. Garrison was very much an either-or person: slavery was an absolute evil, and anyone associated with it was an evil person. Based on his reading of the Bible, he was even willing to abandon the American Constitution since it condoned slavery.

Nothing could seem like such a clear-cut case of an evil system as slavery, nor any cause more righteous than abolition. Yet for Christian participants in the cause, there were ambiguities. Despite Garrison's conviction that the Bible spoke against slavery, its witness is in fact at best mixed, and slaveholders were well able to hold their own in strictly exegetical debates.[17] Some Protestant denominations (such as Methodism in 1844)

16. For Garrison's remarkably intense and focused life, see Henry Mayer, *All on Fire: William Lloyd Garrison and the Abolition of Slavery* (New York: Saint Martin's, 1998).

17. See, for example, Nellie Norton, *Southern Slavery and the Bible: A Scriptural Refutation of the Principal Arguments on Which Abolitionists Rely* (Macon, GA: Burke, Boykin, 1864).

experienced schism over the issue. Abolitionists sometimes slipped from hating the system of slavery to the straightforward hatred of slaveholders and were willing to support violence to establish the abolitionist position in disputed territories like Kansas,[18] and they considered the insurrectionist John Brown to be a martyr. Such hatred, to be sure, was reciprocated, and it took a great civil war and the deaths of some 600,000 American men and boys to secure the emancipation of the slaves. The cause once won, Garrison was able at last to shut down the presses at *The Liberator*.[19]

Despite such ambiguities, abolitionism was the clear model for other efforts by the righteous to reform society by changing the behavior of others. There is little evidence that participants engaged in extensive examination of their own behavior or motivations; being on the right side was sufficient. The political/moral cause enabled both biblical and enlightened Christians to join the cause—as well as other enlightened ones (like the transcendentalists) whose attachment even to an attenuated Christianity was mostly rhetorical.[20] For those not willing to engage in revolution or join utopian communities, abolitionism showed the way to discipleship as the transformation of society through a politics driven by Christian ideals. Other movements of the nineteenth century would follow.

Suffragism/Feminism

Here again, England anticipated: Mary Wollstonecraft's *A Vindication of the Rights of Women* (1792) established on Enlightenment grounds that women were equal to men and ought to have the same rights to education and suffrage.[21] In the United States, the first movement for

18. The minister Henry Ward Beecher (Lyman Beecher's son) financed the sending of rifles—called Beecher's Bibles—to abolitionists in Kansas.

19. The Union victory in the Civil War and the Emancipation Proclamation by no means eliminated the oppression of former slaves in the South or the scourge of racism in the nation as a whole, as the entire history of the next century and a half demonstrated. Changing laws, it turns out, is much easier than changing cultures or human dispositions.

20. The case of Theodore Parker (1810–1860) is illustrative. Beginning as a Unitarian pastor and transcendentalist, he increasingly devoted his idealistic energies and brilliant rhetoric to the cause of abolitionism.

21. She was slightly preceded by John Stuart Mill's *The Subjection of Women* (London: Longmans, Green, Reader & Dyer, 1869).

women's rights was linked to and in some ways emerged from abolition-ism. Elizabeth Cady Stanton and Lucretia Mott, for example, met at the World Anti-Slavery Convention in 1840, and Sojourner Truth was deeply committed to both movements.[22] As in the abolitionist movement, the religious background and motivation of early feminists was mixed, but the influence of Quakerism was clear in the case of Mott, Susan B. Anthony, and the Grimke Sisters.[23]

The logic linking abolition and suffragism is obvious. Women working for the relief from oppression to slaveholders would naturally apply the same principle of emancipation to the half of humanity that remained legally the property of their fathers or husbands, with no vote and little voice. Sadly, the passage in 1870 of the Fifteenth Amendment to the Constitution, giving the vote to all males regardless of race (but not to women), caused a rift between the two movements and within suffragism itself. After decades of further struggle, women finally got the vote in 1920 with the ratification of the Nineteenth Amendment.

It is also logical that early suffragism should be supported by female Quakers, members of the Christian sect that was least hierarchical and emphasized the divine presence in every person. As in the case of abolition, however, biblical support for the proposition that women should be equal to men was scarce. Scripture seemed overwhelmingly to make women subordinate to men, from the opening stories in Genesis to the letters of Saint Paul. The feminist movement therefore experienced tensions between those like Susan B. Anthony, who wanted to focus solely on achieving the vote (leaving the Bible to the side), and those like Elizabeth Cady Stanton, who wanted to challenge the authority of Scripture directly. In 1895 and 1898, the two volumes of *The Woman's Bible* were published under her leadership to considerable controversy. The volumes commented on those portions of the Bible that spoke of women in order to counter their sexism. In response to criticism from some women, Stanton replied, "the only difference between us is, we say

22. Her famous speech, "Ain't I a Woman?," was delivered at the Ohio Women's Rights Convention in 1851.

23. Other important leaders (and signers of the Declaration of Sentiments at the Seneca Falls Convention in 1848) were Quakers, including Mary Ann McClintock, Martha Wright, Jane Clothier Hunt, and Amy Kirby Post.

that these degrading ideas of women emanated from the brain of man, while the church says they came from God."[24]

Temperance Movement

Drunkenness was widely considered to be a major cause of violence (especially domestic violence) and crime in the blighted slums of the nineteenth century. But the urge to eliminate the abuse of alcohol preceded awareness of places like Hell's Kitchen. As early as 1813, the Massachusetts Society for the Suppression of Intemperance was founded, and by 1818 had forty groups averaging about a hundred members each. The temperance movement was ardently supported by Mormons, Adventists, and Millerites. In 1826, the Congregationalist pastor Lyman Beecher delivered an influential series of sermons on temperance, and in the same year, the American Temperance Society was established in Boston. By 1838, it could claim to have over a million members. The Presbyterian revivalist Charles Grandison Finney in 1831 demanded the signing of a temperance pledge as a condition of salvation. The Methodist Church was a strong advocate of temperance. By the 1860s, temperance had become a mass movement that sought not simply a change of moral dispositions and habits but the passing of legislation that would enforce abstinence.

It is not in the least surprising that women should have been especially active in the temperance movement, because women were so often the victims of alcohol-fueled violence.[25] The suffragists Susan B. Anthony and Elizabeth Cady Stanton were advocates for temperance, and in 1874, the Women's Christian Temperance Union was founded. Under the presidency of the feminist Frances Willard, the Women's Christian Temperance Union became by 1898 the largest women's organization in the world. Among its most famous members was the activist

24. *The Selected Papers of Elizabeth Cady Stanton and Susan B. Anthony*, ed. Ann D. Gordon, vol. 6 (New Brunswick: Rutgers, 2013), 114. Stanton's lively mind and feisty spirit pervade her autobiography, *Eighty Years and More: Reminiscences (1815–1897)* (New York: European, 1898).

25. See Holly Berkley Fletcher, *Gender and the American Temperance Movement of the Nineteenth Century*, Studies in American Popular History and Culture (London: Routledge, 2007).

Carrie Nation (Caroline Amelia Nation [1846–1911]), a Methodist who, in response to a direct call from God, began to harass taverns in various ways, ultimately attacking them with a hatchet and leading rallies and marches against intemperance.

The movement achieved success with the passing of the Eighteenth Amendment to the Constitution in 1919, prohibiting the making, sale, or transportation of alcohol in the United States. This legal victory, however, proved pyrrhic, since prohibition initiated a decade-long spree of bootlegging, inebriation, and organized crime. The ratification of the Twenty-First Amendment in 1933, which cancelled national prohibition, was a welcome relief and a reminder that trying to change moral attitudes and behavior through draconian laws is not an unambiguous good, or one without shadow.[26]

Workers' Rights

Already in his 1776 classic, *The Wealth of Nations*, section 1, the Scottish economist Adam Smith recognized the difficulties attending the division of labor in the industrial age, especially regarding the distribution of wealth among owners and laborers. If laborers compete individually for wages, their wages will fall; if they combine in their demand for wages, their wages will rise. It is to their benefit, therefore, to form combinations—a united front—when negotiating with owners. Similarly, owners who form combinations among themselves can resist workers' demands. Smith's analysis sets the frame for the intense struggles between labor and management through the nineteenth and much of the twentieth centuries. Especially as the disparity between the wealth of owners and workers grew greater, and as the lives of workers grew meaner, the conflicts between them became sharper.

In England, trade unions (a very ancient concept) were formed and strikes against owners were staged from early in the century.[27] In 1834,

26. See, for example, Joseph R. Gusfeld, *Symbolic Crusade: Status Politics and the American Temperance Movement*, 2nd ed. (Urbana: University of Illinois Press, 1986).

27. There were *collegia* made up of similar trades in the Roman Empire, and trade guilds in the medieval period, but they were not formed, as were the unions in the wake of the industrial revolution, to gain a greater share of the profits of owners.

the philanthropist Robert Owen tried to form a National Consolidated Trades Union to bring some order out of chaos. There was a wave of strikes in 1842, and, as noted earlier, Marx and Engels called in 1848 for the workers of the world to unite in revolution. In the United States, violent strikes gave impetus to the formation of effective unions and collective bargaining: the Homestead Strike of 1892 against Carnegie Steel led to the murder of strikers by owners' goons; the strike of bituminous coal miners in 1894 was similarly stymied by the owners' strongarm methods; the Pullman Strike of 1894 against the railroads was suppressed only by the intervention of federal troops. The Knights of Labor union was formed in 1869 and became the American Federation of Labor (AFL) in 1886. A more anarchist/socialist union, the Industrial Workers of the World (popularly called the wobblies) was organized in Chicago in 1905.

Many of these American laborers were men traditionally raised in rural settings (like the miners in Appalachia) but forced by poverty into backbreaking and health-depleting labor in mines and factories. Often, their children likewise were kept in ignorance and ill-health through similar labor, while their wives did piecework in miserable slums. Other laborers were immigrants who came to America because of the impoverishment of their home country. Such were the four million Irish who immigrated between 1820 and 1900, many of them driven out of Ireland by the great famine of 1845–1852.

The Congregationalist pastor Washington Gladden (1836–1918) was one of the first Christian leaders to give explicit attention to the struggles of American laborers, helping to form the American Economic Association in 1885, and working side by side with workers in the effort to secure economic justice. Gladden was a key figure in the social gospel movement—which I discuss below—and the Progressive movement, each of which envisaged a synergy between Christianity and social (political/economic) progress. From the side of Roman Catholicism, Pope Leo XIII (1810–1903) issued the encyclical *Rerum Novarum* in 1893, stating the legitimacy and desirability of labor unions as a middle way between savage capitalism and dehumanizing socialism.

Eugenics

The connection between the theory and practice of eugenics and Aryan race-theory under the Nazis is so well established that many are unaware of how massive the eugenics movement was in late nineteenth- and early twentieth-century Britain and United States. But eugenics represented perhaps the most logical of all applications of modernity's favorite child, the theory of evolution. If humans evolve in the manner of other animals by natural selection, then it makes perfectly good sense that the change-the-world mentality of the enlightened should extend itself to the controlled breeding of the human species. The eugenics movement is social Darwinism at its starkest. The father of the movement was not Darwin, however, but one of his disciples (and his cousin), the polymathic psychologist Francis Galton (1822–1911), who coined the term "eugenics" and spelled out its aims in *Inquiries into Human Nature and Its Development* (1883). The theory was to improve human stock by encouraging "the better sort of people" to have more children, while discouraging others—the poor, the mentally deficient, the criminal—from breeding. Such a program would, if implemented, lead naturally to the sterilization of "unworthy" parents and the aborting of unwanted children. A quick and efficient way toward a perfect society!

It is perhaps startling to realize today just how much classist and racist premises drove both the theory and practice of eugenics. All the "better people" were in favor. In England, the Eugenics Education Society was founded in 1907, and in 1921, the American Eugenics Society was established. Courses on eugenics were taught in universities and research into the subject was funded by wealthy donors like the Rockefellers, Harrimans, Carnegies, Fords, and Kelloggs—the same corporations that fought the rights of workers to form unions! In the United States, the premises of eugenics drove the sterilization of African American and Native American populations.[28] The publication in 1912 of *The Kallikak Family* by Henry Goddard helped make the case for the segregation of the lower classes and lesser races, sterilization, and birth control, as well as restrictions on the immigration of undesirables from eastern and southern Europe (that is, Jews and Italians).

Eugenics was the darling cause of those calling themselves Progressives in the late nineteenth and early twentieth centuries. The Women's Christian Temperance League, for example, supported it, and Margaret Sanger (1879–1966), the founder of the organization that later was named

---

28. See Edwin Black, *War against the Weak: Eugenics and America's Campaign to Create a Master Race*, exp. ed. (New York: Dialog, 2012).

Planned Parenthood, was a firm adherent of negative eugenics.[29] While more biblically based Christians silently refrained from joining the movement, more progressive Christian clergy like the Anglicans James Inge and William Piele endorsed eugenics conferences, as did the Roman Catholic archbishop of New York, Patrick Hayes.[30] Among Christian intellectuals, G. K. Chesterton was an isolated voice of protest.[31]

And it was not just talk. Between 1907 and 1932, explicit eugenics laws were passed by thirty-two states, allowing the forced sterilization of the "insane," "feebleminded," "dependent," and "diseased," and over 100,000 Black, Latina, and Native American women were in fact sterilized during that period.[32]

The turn toward activism taken by Christian disciples in nineteenth-century America can perhaps best be illustrated by the Beecher family. Lyman Beecher (1775–1863), as I have noted, was a Congregationalist preacher from Massachusetts who as president of Lane Seminary in Cincinnati, spent decades in an active ministry against intemperance (and Catholics). His daughter Harriet Beecher Stowe (1811–1896) became famous for her abolitionist novel, *Uncle Tom's Cabin*, and was later an advocate for women's rights. His daughter Catharine (1800–1878) was an educator who wrote and spoke in favor of females in higher education (but not of suffragism). Most notably, Lyman Beecher's son Henry Ward Beecher (1813–1887), also a Congregationalist minister, moved considerably away from his father's Calvinism, becoming famous for his rhetorically impressive sermons stressing the love of God. Before the Civil War, he was an avid abolitionist—sending, as we have seen, rifles to militants in Kansas. After the war, he joined in the suffragist and temperance movements. And he embraced Darwin's theory of evolution, stating

29. See, for example, the chapter "The Fertility of the Feebleminded," in *The Pivot of Civilization* (1922).

30. See Christine Rosen, *Preaching Eugenics: Religious Leaders and the American Eugenics Movement* (New York: Oxford University Press, 2004).

31. G. K. Chesterton, *Eugenics and Other Evils: An Argument against the Scientifically Organized State* (1922).

32. See Linda Villarosa, "The Long Shadow of Eugenics in America," *New York Times*, June 8, 2022, https://www.nytimes.com/2022/06/08/magazine/eugenics-movement-america.html.

its compatibility with Christianity (*Evolution and Religion* [1885]). With Henry Ward Beecher, we see how the constraints of "biblical Christianity" gave way to a "progressive Christianity," which consisted mainly in the love of neighbor expressed in social activism.[33]

Among many nineteenth-century reformers, indeed, Christianity was effectively replaced by such activism, as Elizabeth Cady Stanton—who constantly revels in her own escape from dark religious superstition—clearly celebrates in a tribute to her colleague Susan B. Anthony:

> Today Miss Anthony is an agnostic. As to the nature of the Godhead and the life beyond her horizon she does not profess to know anything. Every energy of her soul is centered upon the needs of this world. To her, work is worship. She ... has done the good given her to do. And thus, in darkest hours, has been sustained by an unfaltering faith in the final perfection of all things. Her belief is not orthodox, but it is religious ... she is a Reformer.[34]

THE SOCIAL GOSPEL

The Progressive movement in American politics is usually considered to have been launched by the great success of Henry George's treatise *Progress and Poverty* in 1879. The economist's book proposed a simple way to solve the problem of the boom-and-bust character of a capitalist economy, namely, a single land-tax that would tend to reduce poverty and enable the progress and prosperity of ordinary people. The book sold millions of copies and encouraged among readers the sense that with sufficient good will and effort, true economic progress could also be a socially just progress. What came to be called the social gospel was in effect an embrace of this progressive vision by many Christian clergy, and their willingness to identify their Christian commitment with progressive social and political programs.

The Congregationalist pastor Washington Gladden (1836–1918), for example, was a leading Progressive, who served on the city council of

33. See especially Debby Applegate, *The Most Famous Man in America: The Biography of Henry Ward Beecher* (New York: Doubleday, 2006).
34. Stanton, *Eighty Years and More*, 161.

Columbus, Ohio, and as the religion editor of the *New York Independent*, leveled criticisms at Boss Tweed. Gladden was a prolific writer, advocating the unionization of labor and opposing racial segregation. His 1877 book, *The Christian Way: Whither It Leads and How to Go On*, is regarded as a foundational text for the social gospel movement. Similarly, Charles Henry Parkhurst (1842–1933) was a Presbyterian pastor in New York city who served as president of the Society for the Prevention of Crime (1891). In 1892, he preached against the corruption that underlay the crime in the slum known as Hell's Kitchen. These were the years during which Jacob Riis was using flash photography to expose the subhuman conditions of the slums radiating out from New York's Five Points, heightening public awareness of the conditions of life for the destitute packed into rat-infested tenements (see note 10, above).

The social gospel is most associated, however, with the name Walter Rauschenbusch (1861–1918), a Baptist minister who spent ten years of his early ministry in New York's Hell's Kitchen (1886–1896) and was profoundly moved by this firsthand experience of the inner city.[35] In 1893, he founded with Leighton Williams the Brotherhood of the Kingdom, a group of pastors, writers, and politicians who met together for the exchange of papers and discussion until 1915, animated by the conviction that the Christian idea of church needed to be corrected by the image of the kingdom of God, and that the church should "assist in its [the kingdom's] practical realization in the world." Among the goals of the group (after keeping Jesus always in their own lives) was to "lay special stress on the social aims of Christianity," with each member endeavoring "to make Christ's teaching concerning wealth operative in the church."[36]

35. For a lively study of the time and place, see Richard O'Connor, *Hell's Kitchen: The Roaring Days of New York's Wild West Side* (Philadelphia: Lippincott, 1958).

36. See Ronald C. White Jr. and C. Howard Hopkins, *The Social Gospel: Religion and Reform in Changing America* (Philadelphia: Temple University Press, 1976), 73. By focusing on Rauschenbusch, I do not mean to ignore the important contributions made by other members of the group, especially those of Samuel Zane Batten (1859–1925), who wrote *The Social Task of Christianity: A Summons to the New Crusade* (1909) and *The Christian State: The State, Democracy, and Christianity* (1909). Nor do I mean to diminish the work of other scholars, such as the Baptist Shailer Mathews (1863–1941), whose works *The Social Teachings of Jesus* (1897) and *The Social Gospel* (1909) were foundational.

When he was a seminarian at Rochester Theological Seminary in New York, Rauschenbusch had already been converted to the historical-critical method of reading Scripture, and when he returned to that school in 1897, he became professor of New Testament until 1902; he then became professor of church history, a position he held until his death in 1918. On the basis of his studies, he published in 1907 the book that truly marks the full articulation of the social gospel, *Christianity and the Social Crisis*.[37]

Writing in a clear and accessible prose that at every point evinces calm rationality, Rauschenbusch not only proposes an entirely new conception of Christian discipleship but does so on the basis of a thoroughgoing critique of the traditional understanding. The church, he proposes, is not an institution whose practices are meant to transform its members according to the image of Christ. It is, rather, a social organization whose vision should be outward, not inward; the church must exercise a prophetic role in the world and work to transform society into the kingdom of God. His study shows that "the essential purpose of Christianity was to transform human society into the kingdom of God by regenerating all human relations and reconstituting them in accordance with the will of God."[38]

Several points can quickly be made concerning Rauschenbusch's rich and complex argument.

First, he completely accepted Enlightenment epistemology. Critical history and science set the boundaries and the criteria of truth. Religion must operate within the framework of reason thus defined. Specifically, Rauschenbusch regarded sociology as the most advanced and important of conceptual tools.

Second, he read Scripture—both Old Testament and New Testament—solely as historical sources. In line with the Enlightenment critique of the Bible, referentiality ruled.

Third, Rauschenbusch thought exclusively in terms of social systems and social dynamics; his language at times sounds positively Durkheim-

37. In 1917, he delivered the Taylor Lectures at Yale Divinity School, which were published during the same year as *A Theology for the Social Gospel*.

38. I use the hundredth-anniversary edition edited by Paul Rauschenbusch with the title *Christianity and the Social Crisis in the 21st Century* (New York: HarperOne, 2007), which includes essays by contemporary scholars. The quotation is on p. xxi of the introduction.

ian.[39] Thus, sin is defined in terms of evil social structures and systems, and the church is defined as an organization that must combat such evil social structures and systems.

Fourth, Rauschenbusch located the heart of the Old Testament in the prophets, who are understood to be social critics, while the heart of the New Testament is the synoptic portrayal of Jesus as the prophet whose vision of the kingdom of God challenged the social order of his day (*Social Crisis*, 1–80). Paul's letters are read not as normative for Christian discipleship but exclusively as witnesses to early Christian social practice.

Fifth, Rauschenbusch's lengthy review of church history argues that while the primitive church managed to maintain something of Jesus's vision concerning the kingdom of God, the entire subsequent history of Christianity consisted in compromising and suppressing that vision. Certain external factors made the proclamation of a new social order problematic: Christians were in the beginning powerless and persecuted; they expected an imminent parousia, and they viewed the empire as demonic (*Social Crisis*, 123–31). But other distorting elements were internal and persistent. Rauschenbusch specifically blames otherworldliness, asceticism, monasticism, sacramentalism, dogmatism, churchliness, and subservience to the state. The church lost any sense of democracy, internally, and had no scientific comprehension of society (133–62). He is kindly and gentle in his scathing dismissal of traditional piety but is dismissive, nonetheless. In effect, he regards all the hortatory literature and pious practice of Christianity's existence up to the twentieth century as a disastrous mistake.

Sixth, Rauschenbusch calls for the church to align itself with modernity to work for the right kind of social changes (such as temperance, an end to racial segregation, and the unionization of workers) (*Social Crisis*, 280–330). The gospel and social progress—concerning which, he is sunnily optimistic—go hand in hand; perhaps better, social progress is the authentic expression of the gospel. Hence, ministers should preach the social gospel from the pulpit (Rauschenbusch calls it "social evangelization") and should engage the politics of social change in their actions (288–300).[40]

39. "The conception of God held by a social group is a social product." See Walter Rauschenbusch, *A Theology for the Social Gospel* (New York: Macmillan, 1918), 167.

40. In effect, Rauschenbusch is calling for what later liberation theologians would call conscientization.

If Christianity would now add its moral force to the social and economic forces making for a nobler organization of society, it could render such help to the cause of justice and the people as would make this a proud page in the history of the church for our sons to read. (*Social Crisis*, 270)

Seventh, he is convinced that the economic and organizational expressions of socialism represent the best future hope for the realization of the kingdom of God on earth. He is critical of the Catholic Church because, although it supported unions, it opposed socialism (*Social Crisis*, 259). He thinks that many Protestant clergy are already more or less socialistic in their thought (260) and that Protestantism in America is deeply sympathetic to socialism (261). He states,

Theology must become Christocentric; political economy must become anthropocentric. Man is christianized when he puts God before self; political economy will be christianized when it puts man before wealth. Socialistic political economy does that. It is materialistic in its theory of human life and history,[41] but it is humane in its aims, and to that extent is closer to Christianity than the orthodox science has been. (*Social Crisis*, 301–2)

He argues that trade unions, however important, are but a step in the direction of a socialistic social order (*Social Crisis*, 328). He desires, in fact, a society that will be organized communistically:

The question is now, how quickly Christian thought will realize that individualism is coming to be an inadequate and antiquated form of social organization which must give place to a higher form of communistic organization, and how thoroughly it will comprehend that this new communism will afford a far nobler social basis for the spiritual temple of Christianity. . . . It would seem, therefore, that one of the greatest services which Christianity could render to humanity in the throes of the present transition would be to aid those social forces which are making for the increase of communism. (*Social Crisis*, 320–21)

41. The allusion here to Marxism cannot be missed, in contrast to the "orthodox science" of capitalism deriving from Adam Smith.

Fairness demands the recognition that Rauschenbusch wrote *Social Crisis* at a time of considerable general confidence in social progress before the shock of World War I and before the horrors of totalitarian communistic societies, initiated by the Russian Revolution of 1917, could be known. Even the lectures that formed the basis of *A Theology of the Social Gospel* were delivered at Yale months before the October Revolution and the imposition of Leninist ideology on the people of Russia.[42]

A Theology for the Social Gospel, in turn, is an unembarrassedly pragmatic attempt to theologically buttress the positions advanced in *Social Crisis*: He begins, "We have a social gospel. We need a systematic theology large enough to match it and vital enough to back it." As in his earlier book, Rauschenbusch identifies evil with evil social systems (*Theology*, 69–94), and the role of the church is to fight those evil systems as "the social factor of salvation" (118–30). As for individual salvation, it is attained through one's participation in this social process. Although Rauschenbusch affirms prayer, he thinks of mysticism as a form of immature individualism (104–5); activism is the most mature expression of discipleship (95–109): "Salvation is the voluntary socializing of the soul."[43] As might be expected, his understanding of Jesus is Socinian. It is the personality of Jesus that is significant (151); he experienced God in a new way: "all his mind was set on God and one with him" (155). Jesus was truly free and was thus able to be "the initiator of the kingdom." Classic elements of the creed, such as the incarnation or the death and resurrection of Jesus, play no role in this theology.

Only after all this does he turn to "the conception of God" (*Theology*, 167–87). I have already noted that he considers every notion of God to be a social product (167), and he proposes that Christianity's conception should accord with its social mission:

> Its God must join the social movement. The real God has been in it long ago. The development of a Christian social order would be the highest proof of God's saving power. The failure of the social movement would impugn his existence. (*Theology*, 178)

---

42. He does, however, call the earlier Russian Revolution in the spring and summer of 1917 "on behalf of democracy and peace" the work of God (*Theology*, 165).
43. *Theology*, 99.

God, indeed, is the power that works through human working: "Through the conception of evolution and through the social movement we have come to see human life in its totality, and our consciousness of God is the spiritual counterpart of our social consciousness" (*Theology*, 179). Not surprisingly, this God is against capitalism: "If we can trust the Bible, God is against capitalism, its methods, spirit, and results" (184).[44] His position on eschatology is consistent with his conviction that God is another way of thinking about social progress. After dismissing traditional eschatology as "stupid,"[45] Rauschenbusch proposes an eschatology that is simply the end point of social transformation:

> Our chief interest in any millennium is the desire for a social order in which the worth and freedom of every least human being will be honored and protected; in which the brotherhood of man will be expressed in the common possession of the economic resources of society; and in which the spiritual good of humanity will be set high above the private profit interests of all materialistic groups. (*Theology*, 224)

The boldness and clarity of Rauschenbusch's articulation of the social gospel are striking, but it is important to note that he mainly brought to full and explicit expression elements that had been stirring among socially engaged Christians through much of the nineteenth century. Such a progressive vision of a steady march toward the kingdom of God on earth was, however, occluded by the events of the twentieth century. The rise of totalitarian fascism and communism, the devastating effect of two world wars and a nuclear-armed cold war, and the revolts and revolutions among colonial populations were a shock to the sort of optimism evinced by Rauschenbusch and his colleagues. In response to such seismic catastrophes, academic theologians followed the lead of Karl Barth, whose *Letter to the Romans* (1918) initiated what came to

---

44. This broad sort of reference to Scripture is typical of the book, which nowhere seriously engages actual texts.

45. His dismissal reveals a contempt for believers who do not share his own view: "eschatology is usually loved in inverse proportion to the square of the mental diameter of those who do the loving" (209).

be called dialectical theology and eventually neoorthodoxy. Not human progress but God's sovereignty defined the kingdom of God, while God says "*Nein*" (no) to any presumption of human progress.[46]

Yet the influence of Rauschenbusch is detectable in the work of the young Reinhold Niebuhr in the 1920s and 1930s, in the activism of a John Frederick Steinbruck (1930–2015), a Martin Luther King (1929–1968), a Bishop Desmond Tutu (1931–2021), and even the contemporary evangelical pastor Jim Wallis (b. 1948), the founder of the *Sojourners* journal and community, although Wallis's explicit and constant use of Scripture as the basis for his social radicalism represents a real departure from earlier progressivism.[47] Mainly, however, Rauschenbusch's vision of discipleship as working to transform the world seeped into the minds of all the ministers in America trained in seminaries where the historical-critical method of reading the Bible and some version of the social gospel pervaded the curriculum.

The real heir of Rauschenbusch's vision of discipleship and the role of the church, though, appeared in the late 1960s with the development of liberation theology. Rauschenbusch saw the kingdom in terms of liberation:

> Those who have derived their spiritual freedom and social spirit from Jesus are most likely to have the combination of freedom with love and gentleness. This ought to be the distinctive mark of Christ within the social movement. Is it true that Jesus has been experienced as a Liberator more frequently apart from theology than within it? If so, why?[48]

Liberation theology picked up and carried the torch of the social gospel.

LIBERATION THEOLOGY

Liberation theology emerged in the late 1960s from the Christian-Marxist dialogues in Germany. The ideas of Marxist philosophers like Ernst Bloch

---

46. See David F. Ford, *The Modern Theologians*, 3rd ed. (Oxford: Blackwell, 2005); Douglas John Hall, *Remembered Voices: Reclaiming the Legacy of "Neo-Orthodoxy"* (Louisville: Westminster John Knox, 1998).

47. See, for example, *Agenda for Biblical People* (New York: Harper & Row, 1976) and *Faith Works: How to Live Your Beliefs and Ignite Positive Social Change* (New York: Random House, 2005).

48. *Theology*, 163.

(1885–1977), Emil Fuchs (1874–1971), and Walter Benjamin (1892–1940) were engaged by Christian theologians who sought once more to connect eschatological hope to actual historical processes, specifically through politics.[49] European pioneers include Johannes Baptist Metz (1928–2003), a student of Karl Rahner, who spoke explicitly of a "political theology" in which theory was grounded in and expressed through praxis;[50] Jürgen Moltmann (b. 1926), whose "theology of hope" was expressly in conversation with Ernst Bloch;[51] and Dorothee Sölle (1929–2003), who made every form of oppression a target for her impassioned protest.[52]

The term "liberation theology" came to be associated particularly with the Catholic (and eventually also Protestant) theologians of Latin America, who combined the political theology they learned in Europe to a sense of mission to the wretched poverty of the *campesinos* in Central and South America, and who formed base communities as a form of resistance to corrupt capitalistic regimes. Gustavo Gutiérrez (b. 1928), for example, a Peruvian priest who was influenced by Metz, among others, in his groundbreaking book *A Theology of Liberation* articulated God's "preferential option for the poor."[53] Juan Luis Segundo (1925–1996) was a Jesuit who also studied in Europe before beginning work on social and religious issues in Uruguay.[54] A Spanish Jesuit, Jon Sobrino (b. 1938) did his doctoral work in Germany before working in El Salvador.[55] The Brazilian Leonardo Boff (b. 1938) likewise did doctoral work in Germany before leaving the Franciscan order and becoming a leading figure in Latin liberation theology.[56]

49. Dorothee Sölle: "Every theological statement must be a political statement as well" (*Against the Wind: Memoir of a Radical Christian* [1999]).

50. As in Johannes B. Metz, *Theology of the World*, trans. W. Glen-Doepel (New York: Seabury, 1969).

51. Jürgen Moltmann, *Theology of Hope: On the Ground and the Implications of a Christian Eschatology* (London: SCM, 1967).

52. Dorothee Sölle, *Beyond Mere Obedience: Reflections on a Christian Ethic for the Future* (Minneapolis: Augsburg, 1970); *Political Theology* (Philadelphia: Fortress, 1974).

53. Gustavo Gutiérrez, *A Theology of Liberation: History, Politics, and Salvation* (Maryknoll, NY: Orbis Books, 1973).

54. See his *Liberation of Theology* (Maryknoll, NY: Orbis Books, 1976).

55. See his *Jesus the Liberator: A Historical-Theological Reading of Jesus of Nazareth* (Maryknoll, NY: Orbis Books, 1994).

56. See his *Church: Charism and Power; Liberation Theology and the Institutional Church* (London: SCM, 1985).

Other ideological influences from outside theology—all with Marxist premises—affected the development of liberation theology by identifying forms of oppression and seeking to empower those oppressed. Frantz Fanon (1925–1968), for example, was a French psychiatrist from Martinique who studied the psychopathology of colonialization and argued in defense of violence in efforts to decolonize.[57] Paulo Freire (1921–1997) was a Brazilian educator who advocated "critical pedagogy" and employed the concept of conscientization—being made aware of one's condition of oppression—as the necessary precondition to social change.[58] Edward Said (1935–2003) was a Palestinian advocate for postcolonialism—rejecting the cultural hegemony of Western colonial powers and asserting the validity (perhaps superiority) of non-European perspectives.[59] These and other voices helped make the intellectual context of the late twentieth century one in which Marxism, which had failed so visibly as a way of organizing actual societies, thrived among academics as a utopian (even eschatological) vision for the future.

In twentieth- and twenty-first-century North American universities and schools of theology, liberation theology subdivided according to categories of the oppressed, whose victimhood is perhaps less overt than in the nineteenth century but is protested with equal vigor. Thus, feminist theologians continue the tradition of the suffragists, but now with an eye not to achieving the vote but to equalizing language;[60] Black theologians continue the tradition of abolitionists and civil rights activists, but now with an eye to the subtle manifestations of systemic racism;[61]

57. Frantz Fanon, *The Wretched of the Earth*, trans. C. Farrington (New York: Grove Wiedenfeld, 1963).

58. Paulo Freire, *Pedagogy of the Oppressed*, trans. Myra Bergman Ramos (New York: Herder & Herder, 1970).

59. Edward W. Said, *Orientalism* (New York: Pantheon, 1978).

60. See, for example, Mary Daly, *Beyond God the Father: Toward a Philosophy of Women's Liberation* (Boston: Beacon, 1973); Letty M. Russell, *Human Liberation from a Feminist Perspective: A Theology* (Philadelphia: Westminster, 1974); Rosemary Radford Ruether, *Sexism and God-Talk: Toward a Feminist Theology* (Boston: Beacon, 1983); Elisabeth Schüssler Fiorenza, *In Memory of Her: A Feminist Theological Reconstruction of Christian Origins* (New York: Crossroad, 1983).

61. See, for example, James Cone, *Black Theology and Black Power* (Maryknoll, NY: Orbis Books, 1969); Cone, *A Black Theology of Liberation* (Maryknoll, NY: Orbis Books, 1970); Dwight N. Hopkins, *Introducing Black Theology of Liberation* (Maryknoll, NY: Orbis Books, 1999).

and Black female theologians—womanists who have been excluded by both feminists and Black male thinkers—object to being the lowest rung on an affluent society's ladder.[62]

Despite these variations, liberation theology has a number of shared characteristics. It deals primarily with categories or classes of people rather than with individuals and focuses on issues of power (who has it and who has not). Its perspective and premises are fundamentally Marxist, with attention paid particularly to conditions of alienation/oppression, with a horizontal (this-world) rather than vertical (next-world) eschatology, with a passionate commitment to socialism rather than capitalism. It advocates conscientization or consciousness-raising among groups that are not aware of their oppressed/alienated condition. It emphasizes the need for praxis, that is, forms of practical political activism by those empowered with new awareness, in the form of base communities, protests, or even revolution. It interprets Scripture on the basis of such praxis, suppressing texts that are not liberating; using broad general images (the exodus experience, Jesus the liberator); and making silent voices speak, that is, giving power to those who are suppressed within the text by racist or sexist authors. Finally, it is much clearer on liberation from than it is on liberation for: the vision of a liberated future is much hazier than the protest against the nonliberated present.

All liberation theology, indeed, stands squarely on the shoulders of the social gospel. Liberation theology pays little or no attention to the first vision of Christian discipleship, not even bothering to engage in Rauschenbusch's dismantling of it. Liberation theology shares with the social gospel a fundamental acceptance of the epistemological and axiological premises of modernity; thus, the uncritical use of the historical-critical method, with the historical Jesus rather than the resurrected Lord serving as norm. And like the social gospel, it despises capitalism and embraces socialism as the authentic expression of the good news, with this difference, that liberation theology is much more emphatically Marxist and is less optimistic about progress as an incremental process within a democracy.

Finally, liberation theology shares with the social gospel the paradox of being the product of elitists speaking in behalf of the downtrodden.

---

62. See, for example, bell hooks, *Ain't I a Woman? Black Women and Feminism* (Boston: South End, 1981); Delores Williams, *Sisters in the Wilderness: The Challenge of Womanist God-Talk* (Maryknoll, NY: Orbis Books, 1993).

Neither was genuinely a movement from under. In the case of the social gospel, it was primarily Protestant ministers, who observed but scarcely participated in the lives of the urban poor. In the case of liberation theology, it was some clergy (as in Latin America) but primarily academics whose main experience of oppression was the tenure system of universities. Consequently, the social gospel and liberation theology succeeded primarily in raising the consciousness of ministers trained within the context of university seminaries and (partially) those to whom they ministered. The great majority of Christians were either unaffected or repelled by the understanding of discipleship as social activism. Those who clung to the more traditional vision, however, were increasingly alienated from their progressive clergy and were at the same time alienated from the deep resources concerning discipleship that they were no longer taught.

6

A Critical Analysis of the Two Visions

In the first five chapters of this book, I have engaged in a straightforward history of ideas, seeking to trace out the stages of a monumental shift in Christian consciousness that occurred in the nineteenth and twentieth centuries. I began with an extensive exposition of the first vision of discipleship, the imitation of Christ as the transformation of the human person, a transformation that demanded asceticism, prayer, and self-denial, which follows in the path of the crucified and raised Messiah, Jesus. By reviewing centuries of hortatory literature in chapters 2–3, I then showed how that ancient vision remained steady, despite societal upheavals, up to, through, and after the Reformation, and found significant expression even in the first part of the nineteenth century.

In chapter 4, I examined the structural and ideological forces that from the time of the Enlightenment threatened the first vision of discipleship by eroding the biblical way of imagining the world. And in the last chapter, I showed how many Christians embraced modernity, with its impulse to change the world, so that a second vision of discipleship emerged during the nineteenth century, which consisted in the transformation of society, now in imitation of the Jesus who overthrew the tables in the temple. This second vision, I noted, was more than a response to changing social conditions. It was based on an explicit rejection of the premises and practices of the traditional vision.

It is this element of rejection that now invites closer attention. If the second model of discipleship were advanced simply as an adaptation of the first model to changing circumstances, then we could ask how successfully the adaptation responded to contemporary concerns as well as how faithfully it was able to maintain what was valid and true in the earlier conception. But a point-by-point rejection of the traditional vision, such as we found argued in Rauschenbusch and as assumed by liberation theologians? Any claim to a contemporary truth that rests on a judgment of the past as false demands interrogation. True in what respect and by what norms? False in what respect and by what norms?

In this part of the book, then, my perspective shifts from that of the historian to that of the Christian theologian, who has a stake in the game. By comparing the two visions, I undertake a critical analysis of them. I point out the differences between them and evaluate their strengths and weaknesses. I inquire specifically into their respective understanding and use of Scripture, their theological convictions, and their characteristic practices. Given their premises, are the respective visions internally consistent and coherent? If they are, then a choice between the sets of premises is demanded. I think it is important to bear in mind, as I examine the two visions, that the overriding concern for every Christian ought not to be which vision seems most attractive or popular or relevant but which vision best corresponds to the truth of the good news that we confess.

THE USE OF SCRIPTURE

The traditional understanding of discipleship based itself on Scripture as the inspired word of God, a word that was in turn enacted and reinforced by the sacramental life of the church. Human authorship was acknowledged but was not considered definitive; the human authors were led to write by the Holy Spirit and in some fashion, God spoke through these compositions. The word of Scripture was therefore authoritative, the necessary starting point and essential framework for all thought and practice within the Christian community. Although other sources of wisdom might be read by Christians, they could never displace the canonical writings. The constant citation, allusion, and echoing of scriptural texts that we find in writers from Origen to Jonathan Edwards is more than rhetorical flourish; it is the imaginative world within which such Christian teachers lived.[1]

---

1. See Luke Timothy Johnson, "Rejoining a Long Conversation," in *The Future of Catholic Biblical Scholarship: A Constructive Conversation* (Grand Rapids: Eerdmans, 2002), 35–63.

The writings of the New Testament, mainly the Four Gospels, the Letters of Paul, and Hebrews, provided the most important texts guiding life within this world. Although the Old Testament was universally recognized as the fundamental shaper of believers' shared imagination (above all in the Psalms), it took a secondary place as the norm of Christian discipleship. It was valued mainly for foretelling the Messiah, for its narratives full of moral import, and for its wisdom concerning life before the living God. But the Old Testament was always read from the perspective of the New Testament. It was the writings of the new covenant above all that believers regarded as immediately applicable to every circumstance because they spoke of, and to, the conditions of believers in every age. Believers in every era, after all, worshiped the exalted Christ, lived by the power of the Holy Spirit, and celebrated the presence and power of God in miracle and sacrament alike. No matter the passage of time, no matter the circumstances of life, these remained constant: the power of the resurrection was as new in every generation as it was on the first Easter.

The Gospels' portrayal of Jesus's character, then, expressed above all in his ministry of healing and care for others, revealed the path that they also were to follow. They, too, were called to self-denial and suffering as they looked to the redemption of their bodies. In sum, disciples of Jesus sought, through the power of the Holy Spirit, to be transformed in their own character according to the image of Christ.

Traditional modes of reading Scripture were correspondingly complex, involving the discovery of truths about the historical past, about the moral present, and about the eschatological future. Christians through many centuries read at what might be called a mythical-mystical-moral mode of cognitive receptivity. Old Testament stories about the past, for example, are true not because they always corresponded to empirical fact (Origen says that Scripture sometimes says impossible things) but because the God-shaped *narrative* yields truth about God's creation and humans within it. Human intelligence always struggles to catch up to the inexhaustible riches of the wisdom disclosed by the sacred page.[2] The essential truth of Scripture, disciples thought, did not need adjusting because of changed social circumstances. Imitating Jesus in his suffering,

2. See Johnson, "Origen and the Transformation of the Mind," and "Augustine and the Demands of Charity," in *The Future of Catholic Biblical Scholarship*, 64–118.

death, and resurrection was an absolute unaffected by the contingencies of time and place.

The second model of discipleship also makes use of Scripture but with significant differences. Rather than read Scripture from within a shared imagination, it approaches the Bible from the outside, specifically from the perspective of modernity.[3] Thus, from the start, all aspects of the miraculous, which means a great portion of Scripture, are eliminated, including such basics of the Christian creed as the incarnation and the resurrection of Christ.[4] Thus, if the creation account in Genesis does not correspond to scientific conclusions—which it certainly does not—then it has nothing to say at all. It is consigned to the rubbish bin.

In line with the epistemological premises of modernity, furthermore, the historical-critical manner of reading alone is thought to have validity. In the traditional vision, the historical (i.e., literal) sense of Scripture was considered far less significant than the moral and mystical senses, for the historical sense simply described the actions and circumstances of people in the past whereas the moral and mystical meanings addressed present-day readers in all circumstances. For the second model, in contrast, the historical reigns supreme. Indeed, moral imperatives are sought from historical precedents. But it must be said that, even if complete historical accuracy could ever be achieved, historical reconstruction itself is an inadequate guide to present action.

The newer model also assigns greater prominence to a different set of biblical texts. The Old Testament takes on a significance at least equal to the New. Not all the Old Testament, to be sure; not the legal and sapiential text but only those history-like narratives that are taken to serve as moral paradigms. Thus, for liberation theology in particular, the story of the exodus stands as a model for challenging evil social systems and the liberation of the oppressed. Conveniently, the example does not include the next part of the narrative, namely, the conquest of the land of Canaan by the Israelites, with its attendant ethnic displacement and

3. See Henning Graf Reventlow, *The Authority of the Bible and the Rise of the Modern World* (Philadelphia: Fortress, 1984).

4. See the lengthy analysis of and response to the epistemological premises of modernity in Luke Timothy Johnson, *Miracles: God's Presence and Power in Creation*, Resources for the Use of Scripture in the Church (Louisville: Westminster John Knox, 2018), 21–78.

violence. The prophets of Israel, in turn, are not read as pointers to the Messiah Jesus but as voices of protest against economic injustice. Jesus, in turn, is no longer the suffering Son of Man who gives his life for others but also as a first-century prophet who rails against the crime of empire and the corruption of the temple administration. The most important word of Jesus is his promise of good news to the poor and liberty to the oppressed. The most meaningful act of Jesus is his taking a whip to the money changers in the temple.

The central importance of Paul and Hebrews—as well as that of the other epistolary and visionary compositions of the New Testament—is dismissed or diminished, while the more history-like Synoptic Gospels replace the traditional place of honor held by John. The dismissal of Paul and Hebrews, in particular, has everything to do with the premise that they distort the historical Jesus in a mythical direction. Their portrayal of a suffering and exalted Messiah is regarded as a retrojection on the historical Jesus by the early church and therefore as historically false. The image of the suffering Son of Man in the Gospels is part of this retrojected image and can therefore safely be ignored in favor of the social justice warrior.

Above all, the new model's approach to Scripture is governed by praxis. As the creed provided a hermeneutical frame for traditional readings,[5] so does the perspective given by specific social commitments direct the employment of scriptural texts. The feminist theologian Rosemary Radford Ruether is perhaps the most candid on this commitment, when she declares that only those texts that lead to the liberation of women are to be regarded as authoritative.[6]

It need not be stressed, I think, that such relegation of formerly decisive and formative texts represents an essential rupture with the entire mythical/moral/mystical connection to the risen Christ—and the sacramental life of the church. The bracketing of all discourse except the historical, moreover, eliminates most of what the New Testament

5. Luke Timothy Johnson, *The Creed: What Christians Believe and Why It Matters* (New York: Doubleday, 2002), 40–64.

6. Rosemary Radford Ruether, "The Feminist Critique in Religious Studies," *Soundings* 64 (1981): 388–402, and *Sexism and God-Talk: Toward a Feminist Theology* (Boston: Beacon, 1983).

explicitly addresses, namely, the moral dispositions of humans; from the Sermon on the Mount to the First Letter of Peter, the main *topic* is the transformation of character.

In sum, each vision of discipleship claims to be biblically based. Each privileges certain texts over others. Each is guided in its reading by the convictions and commitments of those who read. Each elevates one level of textual meaning over other levels.

The critical questions to be posed concerning the use of Scripture must, I think, include whether the privileging of certain texts demands the actual suppression or cancellation of others; whether the convictions and commitments of readers correspond adequately to the full import of the New Testament in particular (which for Christians must always remain more normative than the Old); and, finally, whether the mode of reading selected enables an active and dialectical engagement with all the texts of Scripture. On all these points, it seems clear that the newer understanding falls short.

THEOLOGICAL CONVICTIONS

The convictions animating the two visions of discipleship are logically interconnected, so that the cosmology, anthropology, theology, Christology, and eschatology of each version makes better sense within its overall conception than within the other's. The visions are alike in this respect, that they place discipleship within a soteriology. Every soteriology (system of salvation) involves a cosmology (a conception of the world), an anthropology (an understanding of humanity), and an eschatology (an understanding of the telos or end point) and addresses the questions of why saving is necessary, who saves, and what is to be saved.

In broad terms, the traditional conception of discipleship sits within a biblical construal of reality, even if the precise apprehension of that reality is conditioned by changing experience and thought within the body of believers. In sharp contrast, the second model—as Rauschenbusch makes clear in his *Theology for the Social Gospel* (1917)—completely embraces modernity's construal of reality as determinative of all thought and experience, with the Bible fitting in as best it can. All the advances accomplished by human ingenuity from the eighteenth to twentieth century establish the epistemological baseline for theology. What humans regard as useful to the present generation determines what is salvageable from unpromising ancient texts, in contrast to the conviction that Scripture, taken as a whole, prescribes what is good—not always useful or pleasant, but good—for humans in every age and circumstance.

The World

The distance between the premises of the two visions is immediately evident in this most basic question. For the traditional understanding of discipleship, the world and all that is in it are God's creation. The *how* of creation was never, for earlier believers, a matter of interest; the habit of reading Genesis as a scientific account was an unfortunate defensive reflex in response to the challenge of modernity. Not the *how* of creation but the *that* was what mattered; God is the source and goal of all that exists. As Psalm 24:1 declares, "The earth is the LORD's and all that is in it, the world and all who live in it." The statement is taken by the classic vision as religious truth. Creation bears the mark of God's supreme intelligence and therefore can be read as a source of revelation. Humans are created in the likeness of God and therefore occupy a special place within creation as stewards (to care for the earth) and priests (to give God praise in the name of all beings). The traditional understanding consequently provided boundaries to claims of ownership (over land, over other humans) and to modes of exploitation (of land, of persons).

The world as created by God is derived, dependent, contingent. It need not exist, and therefore its very existence is a gift from the Creator. The prayer of offering at the Catholic Eucharist expresses the conviction effectively: "Blessed are you, Lord God of all creation, for through your goodness we have received the bread we offer you, fruit of the earth and the work of human hands. It will become for us the bread of life." The world, and above all humans as representing the world, stands always under the judgment of God and is answerable to its Creator.[7]

The view of the world in the second version of discipleship is entirely shaped by the premises of modernity. The poetry of Genesis and the Psalms and of Paul are regarded as the Enlightenment viewed all poetry,

7. See Luke Timothy Johnson, "Creation," *Perspectives on Science and Christian Faith* 59 (2007): 3–9.

pleasant but not serious, merely mythic and not true according to the canons of scientific inquiry. Astrophysics provides knowledge concerning the age of the universe. Geology tells us the age of the earth. Archaeology offers the evidence for the earliest humans. Above all, evolutionary biology and evolutionary psychology explain the origin and development of the human species. On one side, all such knowledge reveals the laws of nature; but on the other side, those laws keep changing as new discoveries are made. Standing within the world as defined by science, then, one has the options of a radical determinism or a random indeterminacy (uncertainty), depending on what level of the material world one analyzes.[8]

The most important accommodation to modernity made by this vision of Christianity is to accept its thoroughgoing materialism. The world is not a gift disclosing spirit; it is an intricately interconnected set of physical systems, whose ultimate origin—and whose innate order—do not demand an appeal to spirit or soul, or, more recently, even mind, which has largely been displaced by brain chemistry. Human behavior only appears to be free; human creativity is an illusion. Despite such a pessimistic-seeming determinism offered by the physical and social sciences they espouse, the social gospel and liberation theology insouciantly define authentic Christianity in terms of a progress toward the material improvement of the human condition.

God

That God is the source of all that is and the goal of all that exists is fundamental for the classic vision of discipleship. God not only *is*; God is the underived power who brings every creature into being at every moment. God is the living God of Scripture, the Creator, Revealer, Savior, and Sanctifier, who in his work among humans has revealed a complex inner life as Father, Son, and Spirit, a complex inner life into which, by grace, humans have been incorporated. The traditional understanding of God is based on Scripture but is enriched by the experience and thought of believers through the ages, because the living God is not absent from creation but is intimately if implicitly present in all that exists. The prayer

8. See Sara Maitland, *A Big-Enough God: A Feminist's Search for a Joyful Theology* (New York: Holt, 1995).

and practice of disciples is shaped by Scripture, to be sure, but also by the sacramental and ascetical rhythms of the community, the creed, and the hard thinking of theologians from Origen to Calvin. God *is* the topic, because God is what is most real.

The second version of discipleship tends to speak of God, when it does speak, more in terms of an afterthought than as the first thought. God is not the all-powerful presence whose will is sovereign but is the less-than-all-powerful telos of human social progress. Rather than the one beyond all becoming who is nevertheless the source of all becoming, God is Godself in the process of becoming as the omega point of human aspiration. Indeed, both the social gospel and liberation theology embrace a form of process theology, in which "God" is a way of speaking about human social progress. Relieving God of the burden of omnipotence is thought to relieve God also from any responsibility for the evil in the world. Such a limited God, to be sure, cannot really be addressed in prayer—does it make sense to pray to our best future selves?—or thanked for signs and wonders in creation. Even the simple plea of the Lord's prayer, "Your will be done on earth as it is in heaven," turns out to be empty if there is no "you" or "will" or "heaven."

It is sometimes claimed by adherents of the second model of discipleship that the transcendent, omnipotent God of classical theology is more abstract and remote than the version of God as the one coming into being with our own best efforts to reshape the world. The truth is the opposite. The God of traditional devotion was not remote but intimate to humans, even terrifyingly close to human hearts, while the God of the second vision is completely abstract and distant, if indeed God is only us on the way to bringing about "God's" kingdom. Traditional piety, moreover, was not nourished by the lucubrations of Thomas Aquinas or Duns Scotus but by the reading and praying of Scripture, which everywhere speaks of and to God as living and present, accessible through prayer, constantly active and self-revealing through signs and wonders, powerful enough to transform sinners into saints. Within this vision, it was possible to practice the presence of God as something more than a fantasy and to consider human life as under the loving judgment of God. Neither of these makes sense within the framework of a God-in-process.

We see, then, the sharpest of contrasts. In the newer model of discipleship, humanity needs liberation, and humans themselves must accomplish that liberation. In the older version, humans have been fundamentally set free by the living God, and individuals await the further liberation of their souls and bodies.

Christ

The contrast carries over into Christology. A caricature of the traditional understanding of Christ is that the creedal definition of him in ontological terms—"God from God, true God from true God, begotten not made"—diminished an appreciation of his humanity. But in modernity, the opposite has happened: the assertion of the mere humanity of Jesus has had as a corollary the complete abandonment of his divine nature. The incarnation, like the resurrection, is a myth that scientific thought must abandon.[9] The social gospel and liberation theology base themselves squarely on that supreme Enlightenment project, the quest for the historical Jesus, stripped of everything supernatural and superstitious, and depicted in scientifically reliable terms. Such a Jesus, it is claimed, is more human, more accessible, more meaningful. Robert Funk infamously boasted that his Jesus Seminar freed Jesus from the "tyranny" of the creed and "filled the gap" left by the creed.[10]

Is that cartoon version accurate? Not in the least. Devotional literature through the ages reveals a sense of Christ's living presence among believers that is real and instant. The risen Jesus is experienced in prayer (and visions), in the Eucharist, and in the miracle of human transformation. The belief that Jesus is the Son of God by no means implied that he was less than fully human (except, perhaps, in some versions of monophysitism), but it did mean that the human Jesus revealed the face of God. The contemplation of Jesus, above all in his passion and death, was the means of allowing the transforming power of Christ's suffering fully into human consciousness. Teresa of Ávila (1515–1582), who practically defines classic Christian mysticism, complete with ecstatic experiences, speaks in chapter 22 of her *Life* (1565) of turning away from advice that she leave behind meditation on Jesus in order to contemplate God alone:

9. See John Hick, ed., *The Myth of God Incarnate* (Philadelphia: Westminster, 1977).
10. Robert W. Funk, Roy W. Hoover, and the Jesus Seminar, *The Five Gospels: The Search for the Authentic Words of Jesus* (New York: Macmillan, 1993), 7–8.

It is through this Lord of ours that all blessings come. He will show us the way; we must look at His life—that is our best pattern. What more do we need than to have at our side so good a friend, who will not leave us in trials and tribulations, as earthly friends do? Blessed is he who loves Him in truth and has Him always at his side. Let us consider the glorious Saint Paul, from whose lips the name of Jesus never seems to have been absent, because he was firmly enshrined in his heart. Since realizing this, I have looked carefully at the lives of a number of saints who were great contemplatives and I find that they follow exactly the same road. Saint Francis, with his stigmata, illustrates this, as does Saint Anthony of Padua with the Divine Infant. Saint Bernard, too, delighted in Christ's humanity, and so did Saint Catherine of Siena and many others of whom Your Reverence will know better than I.[11]

The so-called historical Jesus offered by modernity, in turn, is clearly not more human than the Jesus of traditional piety.[12] It is constructed by means of a selection of the words and deeds of the Jesus depicted in the Gospels, rather than on the character of Jesus revealed through his obedient faith. The result is not a living and complex person but a form of sociological construct. But the claim to have located *the* historical Jesus is itself bogus, as a review of the many different Jesuses offered by a supposedly scientific method makes plain.[13] Eliminating from the Gospels the incarnation and resurrection, the miracles wrought by Jesus, and even the narrative structure of the Gospels themselves, reveals not the real Jesus but the sad projection of the scholar's fond desires.

And given that the Jesus constructed by scholars is not to be found in the Gospels as such, or is divine in any fashion greater than us, it remains a very real question why the political or moral example offered by a

11. *Autobiography of St. Teresa of Avila*, trans. and ed. E. Allison Peers (Mineola, NY: Dover, 2010), 139. Note that Teresa characteristically appeals not only to Scripture (Paul) but also to the saints before her.

12. See Luke Timothy Johnson, "The Humanity of Jesus: What's at Stake in the Quest for the Historical Jesus," in *Contested Issues in Christian Origins and the New Testament: Collected Essays*, Supplements to Novum Testamentum 146 (Leiden: Brill, 2013), 3–28.

13. Luke Timothy Johnson, *The Real Jesus: The Misguided Quest for the Historical Jesus and the Truth of the Traditional Gospels* (San Francisco: HarperSanFrancisco, 1996), 1–56.

historical reconstruction should be more significant to contemporaries than that of a Socrates or Hillel. The appeal to Jesus in the newer version of discipleship, sadly, amounts to not much more than rhetoric.

Salvation

For the traditional model of discipleship, salvation is both present and future and in both dimensions is thoroughly *extra nos*, brought about by God through the grace of Jesus Christ. Salvation in the present is being liberated from the power of sin and being empowered to live according to the will of God in imitation of Jesus. Being saved in this sense means also turning away from the snares of the devil in the secular world and joining other disciples in the body of Christ, the church. Together, such disciples seek to learn Jesus through their shared participation in the Holy Spirit, in a process of personal and communal transformation that is called sanctification. Salvation in the future means to be freed from the bondage of death through resurrection and a share in God's eternal life. This is all accomplished through the presence and power of God and, although demanding the cooperation of human effort, does not derive from any work done by believers themselves.

Perhaps because it is so central to the first model, the second vision of discipleship minimizes personal salvation, whereas the salvation/liberation of entire populations under oppressive systems is emphasized. Such liberation is both present and future, in that it is in process. This model is much clearer on the nature of "freedom from" the evils of capitalism, racism, and sexism than it is on the shape of "freedom for." Not only are the precise lineaments of the utopian condition left unclear—what is the character of a liberated woman or a classless society?—but the notion that sin is also personal and not only social is left almost completely unexamined. Indeed, salvation is not through the grace of God—the process God is much too supine for that—but entirely through human effort. The social gospel and liberation theology are, to use a traditional term, totally Pelagian.

Anthropology and Eschatology

The anthropology and eschatology of each model is especially revealing, because in them the divergent cosmological perspectives become clear.

The traditional conception of reality, for example, privileges the spiritual over the material, the eternal over the temporal. The brevity and inevitable suffering of human life is considered worth enduring in view of eternal joy. The newer model adopts, sometimes without noticing, the thoroughgoing materialism of modernity; the fact of the body is unquestioned, but the existence of the spirit is elusive and perhaps even illusory. And since all material reality is bound by physical laws, hope for eternal life must likewise be an example of neurotic wish-fulfillment.

In the classic model, each human person is created in the image of God and is called individually to be transformed into the image of Christ. But discipleship is not solitary: each person is part of the body of Christ with other believers and, through the communion of saints, is intimately joined to the believers of all ages. The social gospel and liberation theology think mainly in terms of human society as a whole and of distinct groups within society, distinguished by wealth, gender, and class, often in oppositional binaries.

In the traditional view, then, the mortal existence of humans is fleeting when compared to eternity; suffering is endemic to human life, and suffering can—when embraced in faith—be transforming of the self and even salvific for others. For the second version, human life is brief, true, but it can be extended indefinitely and made more comfortable through technological progress. Suffering is needless and meaningless, is indeed evil. Eliminating human suffering—material suffering to be sure—is a chief goal of discipleship.

Consistent with its cosmology, the traditional vision of discipleship has an eschatology in which God's ultimate victory over evil in the empirical order is affirmed but, apart from millennialist outbreaks, not emphasized. For most of Christian history, eschatology has tended to be vertical, personal, and immediate: the classic four last things that disciples expect to face are death, judgment, heaven, or hell. Although the bodily resurrection is affirmed, many traditional Christians think in terms of the salvation of their souls and expect a share in the spiritual existence that is God's. Corresponding to these convictions is an emphasis on living righteously in the presence, and under the gaze, of the living God who is the discerner of human hearts. Not only virtuous actions matter, although they certainly do, but even more the dispositions of the human heart count in such judgment. Intention and motivation are not secondary to moral reckoning but primary.

The eschatology of the social gospel model rejects the prior tradition on all these points. It expresses little or no interest in the destiny of the individual person. Its focus is on the future well-being of humanity as a whole within the mortal arena. But this future is not conceived in terms of the return of Jesus, or the great assize. It is rather imagined as the emergence of social conditions that are optimal for human thriving and happiness. Thus, we see the importance of liberation and the centrality of the exodus story. The human pilgrimage is emphatically not toward the heaven envisaged by the Letter to the Hebrews; that is fantasy. The pilgrimage, rather, is toward a world in which disparities in wealth, oppression, and the discrimination and degradation resulting from such disparities are eliminated. It is very much a movement toward an earthly city, made by human hands. The human future thus imagined is unambiguously utopian. The book of Revelation's vision of God wiping away all tears, "with no more death or mourning or crying or pain" (Rev 21:4), would, in this reckoning, be accomplished through human effort in the historical (horizontal) future.

Sin

Each vision of discipleship involves a battle against sin. In the traditional model, which thinks more in terms of individuals than in terms of social structures and systems, sin is viewed primarily in terms of a personal rebellion against God's will, a cognitive and volitional rejection of God's claim on humans. Such rebellion manifests itself in the corruption of a person's relationship to God, creation, and other humans (Rom 1:18–32). It thus has a broadly social dimension, but that social infection is secondary—that is, it derives from personal sin—rather than primary. In the classic model, humans are seduced into such rebellion and corruption by the father of lies, the devil. The struggle for personal transformation in faith therefore demands a constant resistance to the demonic impulses that distort thinking and misdirect moral dispositions. Conversion is a lifelong process that can never be taken for granted. The spiritual change of even one person demands an asceticism of attentiveness at every moment, as well as the assistance of spiritual mentors, for the danger of self-deception is both real and subtle.

The social gospel (and liberation theology) views sin in quite a different manner. It thinks in terms of social groups and systems rather than in terms of individuals. Groups are categorized according to wealth, class, race, and gender. The elements of what is today called intersectionality can be located already in Rauschenbusch's social gospel: on one side of the equity imbalance stands the impoverished, Black, female factory workers, and on the other side stands the rich, male, White, factory owners. The emphasis is not on the vice or virtue of individuals but on whether one belongs to an oppressed or an oppressing category. Sin is found in evil social systems (capitalism, sexism, racism, speciesism), and demonology is attached to such systems. They are the "powers and principalities" of which Paul speaks (see Eph 6:12), the suprapersonal energies active in all the systems that hold humans captive and oppose their full development.

Such evil systems, in this view, can be conquered only through identification and resistance. In the previous chapter, I noted how the social gospel emerged from Christians' participation in such nineteenth-century movements of social reform as abolitionism, suffragism, and temperance. In each case, it was believed that a massive change of behavior mandated by law would effect a victory over evil. The supreme example of an evil social system, however, has been capitalism, regarded as the engine of greed, corruption, and oppression, the ideological cover for imperialism and colonialism. From William Blake's "dark satanic mills" at the birth of the industrial revolution (1806) to the *Lumpenproletariat* invoked by Frantz Fanon (1961), protest against the stratification of society, blamed precisely on capitalism, has energized Christian reformers.

True justice and peace, the argument goes, can only be a concomitant of equity; the imbalance among people is by its very nature sinful. And if equity is the goal, then socialism must be the best of all social arrangements and the best basis for genuine equality. Rauschenbusch and all the liberation theologians in his wake take it as axiomatic that socialism (or, even better, communism) is not only the appropriate telos of Christian progressivism but even the embodiment of the kingdom of God. In his 1917 Taylor lectures, as I have shown, Rauschenbusch waxed rhapsodic about the social revolutions in Europe and Russia that had socialism as their goal. The sad and sanguinary experiments in state socialism that dominated the twentieth century have done little to quell progressive zeal for this utopian dream.

On the question of sin, it appears that each version's strength has a corresponding weakness. The traditional model is impressive in its diagnosis and prescriptions for personal sin, but it has paid little attention to social systems as such. This is not to say that the traditional view lacked a concern for others, or practical expressions of such concern. On the other side, the social gospel (liberation theology) stands as a powerful voice of protest against oppressive social realities. But it is, based on the literature I have read, correspondingly weak concerning the impact of personal sinfulness. Beyond calling for a recognition of one's collusion in oppressive systems, it has little to say about how individuals can combat sin in their own lives and allow God to transform them according to the image of Christ.

Considered purely from a theoretical perspective, as here, I conclude that the second model of discipleship, while internally fairly consistent, is incoherent as a specifically Christian theology, deficient in its construal of Scripture, in its conception of the world, in its theology, Christology, soteriology, and eschatology. The traditional model has its weaknesses, to be sure, but if one had to choose a vision of discipleship that is authentically *Christian* in character, one would choose the first vision over the second.

PRACTICES

Each vision demands of disciples certain practices that are consonant with that vision. The classic form of discipleship asks of believers more than formal presence and participation in the church's worship and other common activities. It demands of individuals a personal commitment to the ascetical practices of prayer, fasting, and almsgiving, all of which are regarded as expressions of faith toward God and love toward neighbor. Preeminent among these, however, is certainly prayer, which makes perfect sense, given the theological premises I have described.

Since God is the all-powerful presence permeating all of creation and is more intimate to humans than they are to themselves, then prayer of every sort is the privileged medium of access to that presence and power: praise, petition, confession, and doxology, all the public and private expostulations of faith, are channels through which God's word and will can be articulated, activated, and embodied by believers. The reason why the Psalms have always held a special place in the piety of believers is that they give voice to all these forms of prayer. Of all the modes of prayer, however, the classic model has held up contemplation as the most excellent, for such silent attendance on God's presence opens believers most fully to the transforming power of the Holy Spirit.

If prayer can be taken as shorthand for the traditional model, then politics can be taken as the summary of the social gospel and its heirs. The active engagement of disciples with social structures and systems is at the heart of discipleship: siding with the oppressed, organizing communities of resistance, agitating for legal change, mandating the change of public behavior, and supporting (righteous) revolutionary fervor—all these are not secondary but primary to authentic Christian identity. Working for progress, for the improvement of society in structural terms, is the entire point of discipleship.

Prayer and fasting are not in this model explicitly rejected, but neither do they play any significant role, and when they are practiced, it is often with a public and political goal: a fast for the release of prisoners, a day of prayer for national healing, and the like. Contemplation as the highest expression of prayer disappears completely. Fasting, when it is practiced, does not serve as a means of revealing the complex and destructive drives that lie below people's superficial control and is characteristically undertaken as a tool of public shaming and coercion: we will not eat until prisoner X is released, until dogs are not euthanized, until global warming is halted.

As for almsgiving, it is too awkwardly connected to structural inequality and patronage. This vision focuses instead on the reform of entire economic systems: out with the greed of Wall Street, in with the equal sharing of goods. The example of almsgiving is especially revealing. The giving of alms—which in the tradition means not only the largesse of individuals but also forms of community assistance—is meant to be a direct expression of care and concern between individual persons and groups. But it does not eliminate the social and economic differences between those who have and those who have not. The political character of the social gospel, however, is interested not in such deeds of mercy among individuals but in the elimination of a capitalist system that, it argues, creates such disparities in wealth and status and makes almsgiving into a paltry palliative.

Much more can be said on the topic of characteristic practices, but for the moment, this quick sketch does the job. In sum, the two visions of Christian discipleship can be distinguished in this fashion: in the first, the love of God is primary and leads to the love of neighbor; in the second, the love of neighbor is paramount and expresses love for God.

QUALIFICATIONS

As my brief synopsis suggests, each of the models of discipleship, when taken in isolation, can be caricatured. The traditional model can be parodied as a narcissistic self-preoccupation that is oblivious to the needs of others, much less the plight of the world: "It is my time of prayer; I can't be bothered with your plea for help." Contemplatives in particular can be dismissed—as they often have been—as social parasites who contribute nothing good to the world. Likewise, the social gospel model can be accused of making the church seem little more than an ethical society, or worse, one political interest group among others: "Our worship this Sunday will be distributing pamphlets for PETA in the mall." Such activists have no more reason to be taken seriously than any other political interest group simply because they call themselves Christian.

Actual representatives of the respective visions, to be sure, tend to confound such caricatures. On one side, Rauschenbusch himself was a person of deep piety, whose faith was expressed in his prayerful poetry. Warriors for social justice like Martin Luther King and Desmond Tutu were similarly steeped in the traditions of communal worship and prayer and were far from espousing positions that could in any sense be considered heterodox. Likewise, the priests who first shaped Latin liberation theology were men of prayer and pastors.

On the other side, history shows that a life centered in prayer can issue in an astonishing range of good works directed at other humans. The traditional mode of discipleship, after all, generated the founding and sustaining of countless hospitals and hospices and leprosaria and refuges for the devastated and displaced, of orphanages and homes for the elderly, of schools and universities, and of soup kitchens and shelters for the homeless. It might be asked, indeed, if the more recent Christian agitation for social change through persuasion and legislation in the political realm has brought the kingdom of God any evidently closer than had the social contributions of the earlier model.

Ideally, we would think that the love of God and the love of neighbor should be deeply connected within the prayer and action of Christian disciples. The life of prayer and the life of social engagement ought not to be antithetical but complementary. The careful reading of Matthew's Gospel should encourage Christians to be as convicted by Jesus's teaching on prayer in the Sermon on the Mount (Matt 6) as they are by Jesus's demand of material assistance "for the least of these my little ones" in the parable of the final judgment (Matt 26). Christian discipleship, we think, is distorted when such mutuality is abandoned. It is lost when proponents of liberation theology not only make politics central but regard contemplation as counterrevolutionary. It is likewise lost when advocates for prayer and worship dismiss political engagement as nonevangelical.

The reason I have taken such pains to examine the theological convictions grounding each vision of discipleship is that I consider the more ancient and (in my view) more profound vision of discipleship to have been eclipsed among many contemporary first-world Christians. It is not that social activist believers do not pray or even fast. It is that they seem increasingly unaware of the need for personal transformation if social engagement is not to be frustrating if not fatuous. They appear increasingly ignorant of the sort of rigorous asceticism required of humans to truly transform consciousness and character if they are not, in the words of Eliot's Becket, to commit "the greatest treason, to do the right thing for the wrong reason."[14]

Before considering how a more adequate vision of discipleship can be envisaged, one further question must be answered: Is my disjunction between the transformation of the person and the transformation of society the whole story, or has discipleship fallen into an even more incoherent state, so that those who think of themselves as traditional may not be so in the least, may be, in fact, as alienated from the great tradition of discipleship that extended from the first to the nineteenth century as those who explicitly reject and replace it? To approach this question, a cursory review of some more contemporary hortatory literature is necessary, and I turn to that in the next chapter.

14. T. S. Eliot, *Murder in the Cathedral* (New York: Harcourt Brace, 1935), 44.

Discipleship in Churches

The social gospel/liberation model of Christian discipleship, I have shown, represents a dramatic break with the entire prior tradition in its engagement with Scripture, in its theological premises, and even in its characteristic practices. Fully accepting the epistemological and axiological outlook of modernity, this model considers the disciple's challenge to be the change of society (incrementally or suddenly) through progressive politics or sudden revolution. The church's call, in turn, is to combat capitalism and its imperialistic, colonializing, and oppressive expressions and to work toward a socialistic future. Politics more than prayer is the instrument through which the (ever-evolving) God of process will achieve humanity's best hope for a paradise on earth.

Although this vision explicitly bases itself on the experience of the oppressed (as perceived and interpreted by intellectuals), it has been from the beginning, and remains, an elitist phenomenon, located primarily in universities and in liberal schools of theology attached to universities. Its not insignificant influence within mainstream Protestantism and post–Vatican Council Roman Catholicism has been extended through the ministry of pastors whose theological training took place in schools where the historical-critical approach to the Bible has been mandatory and where, increasingly, the Marxist habit of thinking in terms of class, gender, and race rather than in terms of individual souls has become dominant. Within the last decades, such seminaries speak and teach in the name of social justice far more than they do of the salvation of souls.

The headline-capturing tensions and divisions within mainline Protestant and Catholic churches within the same period have much to do with the acceptance or rejection of the vision of discipleship advanced by liberally educated teachers and ministers, who are sometimes stunned to find congregants less willing than their seminary colleagues to identify the gospel with social activism.[1]

But what alternative do churches that reject the social-justice version offer? To what extent do the vast number of Christians who think of themselves as traditional, or conservative, or evangelical truly represent that classic tradition in a coherent and convincing fashion? To what extent do Christians who reject modernity (perhaps in the name of some form of fundamentalism) carry forward the vision of discipleship of a Jonathan Edwards or John Wesley? Is the sharpness of their rejection matched by the power of their affirmation? Would a Teresa of Ávila or a Martin Luther be able to converse with such contemporary believers within a shared framework of conviction and practice?

An answer to these questions must be sought, I think, in the same sort of hortatory literature that I have examined in earlier chapters. This means that I exclude from consideration all the polemics and infighting within which basic principles and points of difference are debated. I do not, for example, analyze the modernist-fundamentalist conflict within American Protestantism,[2] although that war continues in both explicit and implicit ways.[3] I am not here concerned with the theoretical issues—having analyzed them in the previous chapter—or with battle-lines and combatants but rather with the positive vision of Christian discipleship being advanced by those who consider themselves traditional Christians. How connected to the classic tradition are they?

Because the reading of Scripture plays such a pivotal role, however, a preliminary clarification may be helpful. All the writers I examine in

1. A personal example: traveling to an economically depressed Allentown, Pennsylvania, to deliver a lecture, I was met by a former student from Yale Divinity School, who told me, "I could be a better pastor, but my people won't let me." Turns out that he had taken every liberation theology class available at Yale Divinity School and then found that castigating American policy in Central America did not resonate with the out-of-work former miners in his congregation.

2. See, for example, James Barr, *Fundamentalism* (Philadelphia: Westminster, 1974); D. G. Hart, *Defending the Faith: J. Gresham Machen and the Crisis of Conservative Protestantism in Modern America* (Phillipsburg, NJ: P&R, 2003).

3. As in Francis A. Schaeffer, *A Christian Manifesto* (Westchester, IL: Crossway, 1981); see also the championing of biblical inerrancy in "The Chicago Statement on Biblical Inerrancy" by the Reformed pastor and theologian R. C. Sproul.

this chapter consider Scripture to be the word of God and authoritative for Christian life. They treat Scripture as a precious revelation that is inspired by God. In this sense, they can be said to continue the traditional vision of discipleship.

By no means, however, are all of them fundamentalists, believers who affirm the verbal inspiration and inerrancy of the Bible, not only in matters pertaining to faith and morals but in all matters whatsoever, including history—a position, by the way, that is supported neither by Scripture itself nor by the tradition.[4] Christians espousing such a theory of verbal inspiration and inerrancy seek to oppose the historical reductionism of modernity, but they overcompensate and find themselves fighting on modernity's own terms, by reducing truth to the merely referential. They correctly reject the quest for the historical Jesus as a rejection of the gospel's witness, for example, but they are willing to construct a life of Jesus that itself draws indiscriminately and uncritically from the Gospels.[5] At an extreme, their position demands a defense of the creation story in Genesis as a form of science, and the search for a sea beast large enough to have swallowed Jonah.[6]

The authors I consider in this chapter either do not explicitly adhere to the theory of verbal inspiration and inerrancy, or such a theory has little or no effect on their teaching concerning discipleship. Scripture's teaching on how to live life before God, after all, is the most direct and accessible to readers in every age, is the least subject to historical criticism, and is a wisdom that can be considered as true, not because it corresponds to a set of facts in the empirical realm but because it proposes a mode of human life that can be embodied in the empirical realm.

4. See B. B. Warfield, *The Inspiration and Authority of the Bible* (New York: Oxford University Press, 1927) and *The Divine Origin of the Bible* (Philadelphia: Presbyterian Board of Publication, 1882).

5. At a sophisticated level, see *The History of the Christ: The Foundation for New Testament Theology* by the great New Testament scholar Adolf Schlatter, the first volume of his *Theology of the New Testament*, trans. Andreas J. Köstenberger (Grand Rapids: Baker Books, 1997); at a more popular level, see R. C. Sproul, *Following Christ* (Wheaton, IL: Tyndale House, 1991).

6. See Edward B. Davis, "A Whale of a Tale: Fundamentalist Fish Stories," *Perspectives on Science and Christian Faith* 43 (1991): 224-37.

A Daunting Complexity

At least three kinds of complexity make any assessment of disciple-ship—specifically the teaching of discipleship—in the twentieth and early twenty-first century daunting: the first is the rapidity and extent of political and social change, driven by the engines of modernity; the second is the divided, disputed, and discredited witness of American Christianity; the third is proliferation of media through which diverse versions of discipleship are promulgated.

Modernity's World

Over the twentieth and early twenty-first centuries, modernity contin-ued its triumphant shaping of a secular world. Technological progress was breathtaking in its pace and scope. Einstein's *annus mirabilis* in 1905 revolutionized physics and led to a century in which not only travel by land, sea, and air was speedy and safe,[7] but also, with the assistance of rocket technology, space travel moved from the realm of the imagination to an empirical fact. Microchip technology, in turn, revolutionized all communication, with the internet establishing (with the help of satel-lites in space) the World Wide Web of interconnectivity,[8] sucking into its maw all earlier electronic advances (radio, radar, cinema, television), and, through smartphones in the hands of adults and adolescents, cre-ated a self-reinforcing frame of plausibility supporting what Mircea Eli-ade called a hominized world,[9] one invented and sustained by human effort with no need or desire to turn to God.

The biological sciences finally caught up. The Green Revolution in ag-riculture, for example, enabled the production of food for an exploding

7. In *Modern Times: The World from the Twenties to the Eighties* (London: Weidenfeld & Nicolson, 1983), Paul Johnson brilliantly sketches the way in which the demonstration of Einstein's theory of relativity shaped the first world in the twentieth century.

8. The Canadian philosopher Marshall McLuhan perceived the systemic implica-tions of modern media in *Understanding Media: The Extensions of Man* (New York: Mc-Graw Hill, 1964), coining the expressions, "the medium is the message," and "global vil-lage," predicting the development of the World Wide Web decades before its invention.

9. Mircea Eliade, *The Sacred and the Profane: The Nature of Religion* (New York: Harcourt, Brace, 1959), 204.

global population. Above all, medical science offered through nutrition and medication the possibility of healthier living and greater longevity. Surgeons could replace limbs and organs and even cosmetically reshape faces and bodies. Above all, the discovery of DNA and the birth of molecular genetics gave rise to the Human Genome Project, introducing new possibilities not only for understanding organisms but also for even further transforming interventions in organisms.

At least in the first world, modernity's focus on the material and the manipulable appeared to yield a healthier, longer, richer, and altogether happier life. Those formed through the omnipresent media reinforcement of such a materialistic mantra found it plausible that religion, when not a harmless eccentricity, was a bothersome remnant of a less advanced, superstitious age.

There is, to be sure, another side to secularism's triumph. Christianity might be numerically the world's largest religion, but it was forces opposed to Christianity that dominated social and political change; nationalism (imperialism, colonialism), racism, Marxism, and other ideologies spawned by the nineteenth century drove the cataclysmic adventures of crazed leaders; fascism was the twentieth century's particular invention. The fearsome lethality of modern warfare did not deter dictators and tyrants from its passionate exercise; during this time, armed conflict was the norm rather than the exception. The two world wars of the twentieth century killed millions of young men, devastated lands, destroyed cultures, displaced populations, and ruined the lives of those soldiers and civilians they did not kill.

But we can add to those attention-grabbing conflicts the decades-long wars in Korea, Vietnam, Laos, Cambodia, Central America, the Middle East, Africa, Sri Lanka, and China—wars fought in the name of liberation, national security, racial purity, or access to mineral wealth. The technology of war—a primary manifestation of secular science—invented modes of killing never before imagined, including the nuclear weapons that froze great powers into a decades-long cold war of armed competition, with a lucrative arms industry encouraging the stockpiling of such armaments under the Cold War's slogan of "mutually assured destruction."

To be sure, the twentieth century also spawned international organizations whose goal was to secure peace and counter such political and social factionalism, among them the League of Nations, the United Nations, the World Council of Churches, the European Union, and the form of international capitalism known as globalization.[10] The main accomplishment of such efforts, alas, was the creation of bureaucracies that combined inefficiency with a tone deafness to the concerns of ordinary people.[11]

The same ideological impulses that led to war also sponsored the genocidal slaughter of entire populations in Turkey (the Armenians), the Soviet Union (Kulaks and all those standing in the way of Stalin), Europe (the Holocaust), China (Mao's Cultural Revolution), and Rwanda (with Hutu massacring Tutsi). Racial politics excluded and oppressed Jews and Romani in Europe, as well as Black people in the United States (Jim Crow laws of segregation) and in South Africa (apartheid). Ethnic conflicts dominated the recent histories of Myanmar and Sri Lanka. All such exclusionary (and murderous) policies relied on racial and class premises that stemmed not from Christian principles but from the ideologies of modernity.[12] Some Christians were coopted by such ideologies; see the German National Church under Hitler, or the segregated churches of the United States. The voices of Christians who protested such practices were weak and mostly symbolic;[13] the world was being run by modernity, and appeals to the gospel were, in the eyes of the tyrants, powerless and, indeed, pitiful.

10. The World Economic Forum founded in 1971 is the perfect exemplification. For a (not entirely successful) effort to put a positive spin on globalization, see Miroslav Volf, *Flourishing: Why We Need Religion in a Globalized World* (New Haven: Yale University Press, 2017).

11. The early decades of the twenty-first century have seen the emergence of populist politics both in Europe (exemplified by Brexit, the withdrawal of Great Britain from the European Union) and in the United States (exemplified by "America first" Republicans).

12. See the acute analysis by Miroslav Volf, *Exclusion and Embrace: A Theological Exploration of Identity, Otherness, and Reconciliation* (Nashville: Abingdon, 1996).

13. The Civil Rights Movement in the United States led by Martin Luther King and associates from the Black church was the obvious exception, except that, even before King's assassination, that movement began to fragment. For the troubles faced by peacenik protestors like the Catholic priest brothers Daniel and Philip Berrigan, see Jim Forest, *At Play in the Lions' Den: A Biography and Memoir of Daniel Berrigan* (Maryknoll, NY: Orbis Books, 2017).

Despite the impressive advances in agricultural productivity (the Green Revolution), destitution and starvation prevailed in such war-torn lands as Somalia and the Sudan, while the donations of food from international agencies went into the hands of the competing warlords. And despite the astonishing progress in medical sciences like epidemiology, devastating epidemics and pandemics (the Spanish influenza, AIDS, Ebola, Covid-19) continued to resist efforts at control, proving lethal to many millions. In the eyes of many in the prosperous first world, indeed, the planet itself seemed diseased, and apocalyptic visions of the end of humanity due to global warming or climate change stirred quasi-religious responses of panic and protest.[14]

Other social diseases flourished during this period, abetted by the same power brokers who stood behind war and famine: drug trafficking and forms of addiction that preyed on the weakest and festered within the violence of gangs and drug cartels; human trafficking as an element in an ever more pervasive sexualization through pornography and prostitution; addiction to gambling and other forms of high risk behavior; the narcotization of populations through pain-relieving and anxiety-avoiding medicines and therapeutic interventions. Modernity has created a world that is in some respects spectacularly successful and in other respects has made many people weaker and more vulnerable.

My analysis must take such complexity into account as it pertains to the state of Christianity in the United States at the start of the twenty-first century. The most prosperous and privileged of the first-world nations, it is sadly divided between the rich and educated elite and the forgotten laboring poor; between the worldly sophisticates in urban centers (for whom religion is the stuff of sarcasm and humor) and the traditionalists of small towns and farms (for whom church is the only available source of meaning); between those narcotized by entertainment and life-enhancing drugs and those anaesthetized by illegal and lethal drugs; between the young and healthy who have mutated comfortably along with their digital gadgets and the elderly and ailing who feel

14. The quasi-religious nature of the movement is exemplified, as others have noted, by the strange elevation of an obscure Swedish adolescent (Greta Thunberg) into an oracle reverenced by international agencies; the mythological distance from Joan of Arc is not great.

(correctly) that they have been left behind; between those who swim in secular waters like fish in the sea and those who regard themselves as cast off and gasping for life on a deserted beach. It is a world desperately in need of God's word. But where can it hear that word in an intellectually responsible and morally convincing fashion?

Discredited Christian Witness

In my sketch of nineteenth-century Christianity in America, I emphasized its tendency to divide and subdivide, so that the answer to the question, Where is the authentic voice of the gospel to be heard? was drowned by the clamor of opposing claimants to (exclusive) Christian authenticity. Christians did not speak to the world with a single voice; they seldom even conversed among themselves with civility. In the United States, the same individualism that championed free enterprise in commerce led not only to denominational conflicts but also to the invention of totally new versions of Christianity in storefronts and tents and auditoriums across the country.

The same fissiparous frenzy continued through the twentieth and into the twenty-first century but took on a new shape because the flood of immigrants in the nineteenth and twentieth century had brought so many Catholics from Ireland, Italy, and eastern Europe that Roman Catholicism was in the twenty-first century the largest single denomination in the country (approximately seventy million, 21 percent of the population); although Protestantism taken as a whole still comprised 40 percent of the population calling itself Christian (approximately 140 million), no single denomination came close to the size of Catholicism. Given the historical hostility between Catholics and Protestants, the divisions within Christianity became the more obvious.

Some ecumenical efforts were undertaken to partially heal the disedifying spectacle of Christians hating each other. The World Council of Churches founded in 1937 drew participation from major Protestant denominations but did not include Roman Catholics or the countless nonlegacy churches. The Second Vatican Council (1962–1965), in turn, reached out in friendship to the "separated brothers" within Protestant churches, recognizing the legitimacy of their specific modes of discipleship. But it was only after the conspicuous ugliness of the John F. Kennedy presidential campaign—when anti-Catholic polemic reached a peak—that genuine (if superficial) amity was achieved between Catholics and Protestants in the United States. The ecumenical spirit was expressed as well by formal dialogues between Catholic and specific Protestant traditions, above all the Lutheran and Episcopal.

The fragmentation of American Christianity, however, went beyond separation into different sects and rivalry among denominations. It included bitter fights within denominations, leading to many and opposing versions of the (ostensibly) same body of believers, so that multiple adjectives were required to identify just which brand of Presbyterian or Lutheran or Baptist was meant. In the nineteenth century, as I have shown, the issue of race—specifically the abolition of slavery—divided denominations. That issue scarcely disappeared in the twentieth century, leading to the designation of Sunday as the most segregated day in America, with Black and White Christians gathering separately and developing distinct styles of worship.

In the twentieth and twenty-first century, however, the modernist/fundamentalist battle extended itself past the formal issue of the authority of Scripture to embrace conflicts over sexual orientation and gender. On one side, the language of civil rights found expression in the modernist argument that women should be ordained and exercise authority in the church, while on the other side, biblical authority was invoked in the rejection of such innovation. Baptists, Presbyterians, Lutherans, and Episcopalians all suffered schism because of an inability to negotiate gender issues. On the heels of the contentious problem of gender inclusivity came the modernist claim that those practicing same-sex love ought not only to be accepted but ought also to have the right to ordination and episcopal consecration; once more, denominations like the Methodists and Presbyterians found themselves in hostile camps, fighting not only the moral/theological issue but rights over ecclesiastical property (who owns the churches?). More recently still, transsexual rights have been asserted, with the outcome again being predictable.

Whatever the legitimacy of the various claims,[15] it is clear that the spirit of modernity—with its language of rights and its concern for ec-

---

15. My own position on the issues and the process for resolving them can be found in Luke Timothy Johnson, *Scripture and Discernment: Decision Making in the Church* (Nashville: Abingdon, 1996) and *A Catholic Consciousness: Scripture, Theology, and the Church* (New York: Paulist, 2021), 147–94.

clesiastical power—had entered fully into (mainly) mainline Protestant denominations in the United States, affecting not only the shaping of the issues but as well the processes by which churches sought to resolve them (for example, by voting). To outside observers, the struggles seemed distressingly political, with power and the disposal of property providing more than a little amount of motivation on every side. It is equally clear that the attention given to internal conflicts over the rights and privileges of members both deflected attention away from training in discipleship and presented to an already skeptical secular world the spectacle of a deeply conflicted Christianity.

American Roman Catholics, in turn, had been the very model of uniformity and compliance to church authority before the Second Vatican Council but then found themselves also divided—if not to the point of outright schism—over the council's call to *aggiornamento*; in the eyes of some, that call was a capitulation to modernity. Catholics in the United States were whipsawed between, on one side, angry activists who embraced liberation theology and liturgical reforms and, on the other, equally angry resisters to change, some of them to the extent of returning to the celebration of the Mass in Latin. Given the hierarchical structure of Catholicism, the direction in which the sitting bishop of Rome gazed either rejoiced or dismayed pious Catholics who were as fundamentalist regarding the papacy as many Protestants were toward the Bible.

To top off all this ecclesiastical infighting, the late twentieth and early twenty-first century also exposed widespread moral corruption among Christian ministers. That ministers and priests had historically been less than shining moral exemplars is well established and had been the stuff of antireligious polemic for a very long time.[16] But the exposure of financial fraud practiced by well-known Protestant ministers—and the Vatican itself—had a powerful effect against the backdrop of self-righteous posturing. A hostile media examined the lives of evangelists with fervor and was delighted to announce new examples of clerical hypocrisy. But the most devastating form of moral collapse was sexual: the media revelation of decades-long pedophilia carried out by Catholic priests,[17] and worse, the decades-long coverup of those sins by the hi-

---

16. One can start with Boccaccio's *Decameron* or Chaucer's *Canterbury Tales* and work one's way to H. L. Mencken and Sinclair Lewis (*Elmer Gantry*).

17. It is certainly the case that only a small percentage of priests were guilty of such

erarchy, was for many (including many Catholics) the final straw. Many Catholics simply stopped going to Mass or confession. Many Protestants worriedly shopped for a pastor whose life matched his or her words. The witness of American Christianity was severely compromised at a time when it most needed to be authentic.

Diffused Proclamation

A final factor making the examination of discipleship in the twentieth and twenty-first centuries complicated is the diffusion of means by which Christian leaders sought to communicate their message. Every denomination had its own publishing house, pumping out hundreds of books of sermons, meditation, guidance, Bible study, and devotions. Every denomination had its own journals filled with sermons, meditation, guidance, Bible study and devotions. Christian newspapers and broadsheets proliferated, and the freelance founding of churches was matched by a freelance pattern of publication in print. The question becomes pressing: What must be read and what can safely be ignored when assessing teaching on discipleship in present-day Christianity?

But publications in print are only a fraction of the problem, for technological advances in electronic communication were also exploited by Christian teachers. In the 1930s, the radio priest Charles Coughlin was heard by millions every week, and the young Catholic theologian Fulton J. Sheen had a weekly broadcast on NBC from the 1930s to the 1950s that was heard by a large and enthusiastic audience. Protestant evangelists like Oral Roberts followed suit; he began broadcasting in 1947 before shifting to television in 1954, where his emotive healing sessions could be seen even in the most remote Mississippi village.[18] Sheen also moved over to television in 1952 with his enormously popular show, *Life is Worth Living*. These early success stories encouraged countless other

---

abuse and that Protestant ministers—as well as teachers and coaches and others with access to children—were statistically as likely to be pedophiles as priests, but those empirical facts do not affect the scandalous impact of the systemic coverup practiced by the Catholic hierarchy. For my own response to that scandal, see Luke Timothy Johnson, "Jesus and the Little Children: A Gospel Perspective on the Church Scandal," in *The Living Gospel* (New York: Continuum, 2004), 51–58.

18. I vividly recall watching Roberts perform healings in 1955 on a black-and-white TV set in the home of my brother's hardshell Baptist in-laws in Ludlow, Mississippi.

ministers to broadcast their sermons and services on radio and television, as any surfing across radio stations or television channels attests. The reach of successful programs was astounding. Robert H. Schuller's *Hour of Power*, for example, began broadcasting in 1970 and over the next four decades was viewed each week by millions around the world. Billy Graham's weekly radio broadcast, *Hour of Decision*, was similarly heard around the world from 1950 to 2016.

Digital technology enabled a still further step: using the satellites spun into space, evangelists constructed their own networks, enabling them to offer a menu of Christian instruction or entertainment twenty-four hours a day. Pat Robertson founded the Christian Broadcasting Network in 1960; the Trinity Broadcast Network was started by Paul and Jan Crouch in 1973; a Catholic nun, Mother Angelica, began the Eternal Word Television Network in 1981; and the indefatigable Oral Roberts founded Golden Eagle Broadcasting in 1996. Such specifically Christian networks provided a home for the widest variety of preaching, instruction, and conversation. The internet, in turn, has enabled other entrepreneurial evangelists to establish websites and podcasts. What, in all this mélange, is wheat, and what is chaff? Surely some sort of winnowing is required.

Necessary Exclusions

Since my interest is the teaching of discipleship in the church—as distinct from universities and schools of theology—and my question concerns the degree to which the first, traditional, vision of discipleship continues in the church, so that it can be authentically termed "traditional," I must begin with some preemptory exclusions. And since my examination from the first has been primarily literary—analyzing hortatory writings—I will focus on literary evidence that seeks specifically to transmit the ancient vision to new generations and comes closest, in my view, to fully represent that ancient vision.[19] I exclude, therefore, evangelists and teachers whose ministry (in part or whole) focuses on

19. Many televangelists, from Fulton Sheen to Billy Graham, also wrote extensively. Sheen published twenty-two widely read books; Graham published thirty-four books, many of them bestsellers. Excluding them from detailed consideration is for the sake of economy rather than a judgment on their worth.

one element to the implicit suppression of others, to the degree that the full understanding of Christianity (and of discipleship) is occluded.[20]

The most difficult exclusion is of those whose ministry or teaching is largely in service of a political agenda. This list would embrace such unlikely fellows as Fulton Sheen (for whom American democracy was threatened by atheistic communism), Martin Luther King (for whom the gospel demanded a commitment to civil rights), and Jerry Falwell (for whom the moral majority of conservative believers were called to save America).[21] The list would certainly include Pat Robertson, whose televised *700 Club* supported conservative politics, and the Roman Catholic bishops, whose entire message seemed at times to be reduced to the single issue of abortion. The list might also include Jim Wallis and the Sojourner movement, which is evangelical in spirit while being strongly committed to social change through political means. The exclusion is necessary because the gospel cannot (should not) be equated with specific political goals, but it is difficult because the efforts of these teachers at least called for positive social engagement by disciples. Other excluded categories do not.

Much easier to exclude as a heretical narrowing of the gospel is the phenomenon of end-of-world prophecy, the distinctive twentieth-century recrudescence of millenarianism based on the Scofield Bible.[22] The list of writers and televangelists whose entire message consists in discerning the signs of the times before Armageddon must include Garner Ted Armstrong (*The World Tomorrow*), Irvin Baxter, Greg Laurie, Jack Van Impe, John Hagee, and Hal Lindsey, whose 1970 nail-biter *The Late Great Planet Earth* (with Carole C. Carlson) was the best-selling religious book of the 1970s and 1980s, selling some twenty-eight million copies before 1990. Even more financially successful was the series of sixteen novels and four movies making up the *Left Behind* franchise, which purveyed

20. The reader will understand, I hope, that these categories, and the names I include within them, are not comprehensive but suggestive. Some examples, like the ubiquitous and multifaceted Oral Roberts, appear in several lists.

21. See the insightful study by James M. Patterson, *Religion in the Public Square: Sheen, King, Falwell* (Philadelphia: University of Pennsylvania Press, 2019).

22. *The Scofield Reference Bible* (Oxford: Oxford University Press, 1909) was a version of the King James Version annotated by Cyrus Scofield according to the principles of dispensationalism, which sold over two million copies before 1945.

dispensationalism to the masses, especially the young, so successfully that some of the volumes in the series reached sixty-five million in sales worldwide.[23] There is good money to be made in end-time fantasies. But the entire enterprise is a sad and delusional distortion of Christian faith. Its stress on knowing the future is not accompanied by a serious shaping of discipleship in the present.

Easier still to exclude from serious consideration is the grotesque distortion of Christian discipleship called the prosperity gospel. Its classic literary expression is Bruce Wilkinson's *Prayer of Jabez* (2000), which takes an obscure verse from the Old Testament and erects it into a vision of discipleship as a trouble-free path to material wealth.[24] Once more, Oral Roberts was a pioneer in calling for "seed faith" that God could grow, the seeds being basically contributions to Oral Roberts's ministry. The financial success of Roberts (if not of those whose tithes he received) was evident in the establishment of Oral Roberts University in 1963. Other televangelists peddling some version of the prosperity gospel (sometimes accompanied by miracle healings) include Benny Hinn, Joel Osteen, Creflo Dollar, Kenneth Copeland, and Joseph Prince. Drawing their own wealth from the poor and disadvantaged, they most resemble the scribes whom Jesus described as "swallowing the houses of widows" (Luke 20:47), and their message has no gospel character to it.

Less egregious than the prosperity gospel but nevertheless one-sided and falling short of a genuinely traditional grasp of discipleship are all those preachers and teachers (often Pentecostal) whose version of the good news so emphasizes the joys of conversion and the delights of fellowship that, even when lacking a financially fraudulent intent, serve more as a source of solace than of challenge, offering a Jesus who is both savior and problem solver. Music, personal witness, emotional preaching, and the shedding of tears often characterize the worship in which congregants participate voyeuristically through the medium of television. This broad category includes Robert Schuller, Joyce Meyer, Jimmy Swaggart, James and Tammy Bakker, and the great majority of African American evangelists that I have seen. In contrast to the severe

23. Tim LaHaye and Jerry B. Jenkins (Carol Stream, IL: Tyndale House, 1995–2007).
24. *The Prayer of Jabez: Breaking through to the Blessed Life* (Colorado Springs: Multnomah Books, 2000).

evangelism of, say, Billy Graham, which focuses in a straightforward fashion on the state of sin and the need to confess Jesus as one's Savior, such evangelism appears as a form of entertainment, so focused on the benefits of Christian membership that a continuing struggle against sin and for transformation is little in evidence.

Last, I exclude the vast collection of books, guides, workshops, and videos devoted to what is called "discipling" and is devoted mainly to the training of converts to become makers of other disciples.[25] The motivating biblical text is Matthew 28:20, "Go make disciples of all nations," and the underlying aspiration is the conversion of all humans to the gospel. In the literature of this sort I have read, far less attention is given to discipleship in the traditional sense as the transformation of the self in imitation of Christ than to making disciples in the way Jesus did.[26] Church growth and maintenance seems the point, and the target audience are pastors who want to learn the best techniques for accomplishing this. It is a form of how-to literature.

The Classic Tradition

Once the deck has been cleared, what remains? Is the alternative to the social gospel/liberation model of discipleship only this chaotic outpouring of product? Or are there sparks of genuine tradition in this dark and noisome echo chamber (see Phil 2:15)? There are, and they continue their quiet work of forming disciples according to the mind of Christ away from the commercial commotion of megachurch growth and full-service religious catering. In the remainder of this chapter, I indicate

25. A sampling: Billie Hanks Jr. and William A. Shell, eds., *Discipleship: The Best Writing from the Most Experienced Disciple Makers* (Grand Rapids: Zondervan, 1981); Bill Hull, *The Disciple-Making Pastor: The Key to Building Healthy Christians in Today's Church* (Grand Rapids: Baker Books, 1999); Leroy Eims, *The Lost Art of Disciple-Making* (Grand Rapids: Zondervan, 1978); Greg Ogden, *Transforming Discipleship: Making Disciples a Few at a Time* (Downers Grove, IL: InterVarsity Press, 2016); Jim Putman, *Real-Life Discipleship: Building Churches That Make Disciples* (Colorado Springs: NavPress, 2010).

26. A partial exception is the phenomenally successful book—it sold over thirty million copies—by Rick Warren, *The Purpose-Driven Life: What on Earth Am I Here For?* (Grand Rapids: Zondervan, 2002). It is an exception because his contents are basically solidly traditional, although done up in a streamlined, how-to fashion; it is only a partial exception because the end point for the disciple is the making of other disciples.

some of the resources that both Catholic and Protestant believers can turn to for sure guidance.

What are the criteria I use for considering something being genuine tradition? (1) An embrace of the world imagined by Scripture rather than that postulated by modernity, with Scripture taken as the norm of truth, not in every matter but in everything that pertains to faith and morals and therefore the nature of discipleship. (2) The premise that, together with the canon of Scripture, the creed is the framework of Christian identity. (3) The conviction that the goal of every human life is to share eternal life with God and that this present transitory existence is in no way ultimate and must not be treated as such. (4) The realization that sharing in God's life comes about through God's gift, which empowers humans to imitate Christ and become transformed in their character according to the mind of Christ. (5) The firm resolution that such transformation requires the exercise of prayer more than politics, fasting rather than the acquisition of power, and almsgiving that shares all possessions (material and spiritual) with those in need. (6) Finally, the appreciation that the absolute and final criterion of true discipleship is the love of neighbor, expressed not only in disposition but in positive action, not according to the premises of our own utopian visions but according to the true needs of the neighbor here and now. (7) The appreciation that such imitation of Christ's self-emptying obedience and servant love inevitably involves suffering.

Shining Lights: Chesterton and Lewis

Without question, two of the most influential twentieth-century figures representing classical Christianity, men whose writings continue to be read and studied by serious Christians of every denomination, were the laymen G. K. Chesterton (1874–1936) and C. S. Lewis (1898–1963). Although they differed in significant ways, they also had much in common, including the fact that both were converts to Christianity; in fact, Chesterton's *The Everlasting Man* (1925) influenced Lewis's conversion. Both were public intellectuals who had the capacity to speak and write in ways accessible to ordinary people.[27] Both wrote prolifically in a variety of

27. Chesterton was a well-known Fleet Street journalist who was a friend and de-

genres: Chesterton in short stories (Father Brown) and novels (*The Man Who Was Thursday* and *The Napoleon of Notting Hill*), poetry, biographies, essays, and full-length books; Lewis in scholarly studies in literature, novels (the space trilogy, *The Chronicles of Narnia*), popular books, and essays. Both wholeheartedly embraced the catholic tradition (Lewis as an Anglican and Chesterton eventually as a Roman Catholic). Both were well acquainted with modernity and fought against its negative manifestations.[28] Both were apologists who based themselves on the classic tradition and common-sense philosophy and, with a combination of rigorous logic and literary charm, made the case for Christian identity.[29]

Perhaps because they were converts from a kind of agnosticism, Lewis and Chesterton did not preoccupy themselves with the particularities of Christian doctrine and practice so much as with the vision of life itself that Christianity offered to those whose ability to see the truth had been diminished by the specious claims of modernity and had been twisted by the distortions of progressivism in any form. Such wideness of vision perhaps helps account for their continuing influence within a broadly ecumenical Christianity, above all among students who particularly need and desire clear thinking when academicism threatens to stifle thought altogether and seeks to cancel any trace of Christian thinking or behavior.

---

bate partner of Hilaire Belloc and participated in public (and published) debates with the likes of H. G. Wells and George Bernard Shaw; Lewis was a longtime professor of medieval literature at Oxford and Cambridge universities, who was a close colleague of J. R. R. Tolkien.

28. See, for example, G. K. Chesterton's *Heretics* (New York: Lane, 1909) and *Eugenics and Other Evils* (New York: Dodd, Mead, 1927); C. S. Lewis's *The Abolition of Man* (London: Bles, 1946) and *The Screwtape Letters* (New York: Macmillan, 1953).

29. G. K. Chesterton above all in *Orthodoxy* (New York: Lane, 1909) and *The Everlasting Man* (New York: Dodd, Mead, 1925); C. S. Lewis above all in *Mere Christianity* (New York: Macmillan, 1952) and *Miracles: A Preliminary Study* (New York: Macmillan, 1947). It is their capacious and open spirit that distinguishes Chesterton and Lewis from the evangelical apologist Francis Schaeffer (1912–1984), whose call for engagement with the intellectual and political dimensions of modernity influenced many conservative teachers; in books like *The Great Evangelical Disaster* (Westchester, IL: Crossway, 1984), however, his defense of a conservative/fundamentalist version of Christianity sometimes carries an angry edge. For a spirited tribute to Schaeffer, see John Piper, *A Hunger for God: Desiring God through Fasting and Prayer* (Wheaton, IL: Crossway, 1997), 155–72.

But what other resources can contemporary American Christians make use of if they seek guidance in the traditional mode of discipleship? In my effort to identify some of these, I distinguish for the sake of efficiency between Catholic and Protestant resources, acknowledging that in this more ecumenical age (and among those seriously seeking sanctity), less attention is paid to differences than to points of common wisdom.

Catholic Resources

Two great advantages on the Catholic side are the uniform teaching of the magisterium (pope and bishops) and the way that formation is embodied in practices. The lengthy and conservative papacy of John Paul II (1978–2005) followed by the equally conservative Benedict XVI (2005–2013) stabilized central authority within the church after the Vatican Council and tilted it in a traditional direction; emblematic was the publication of the monumental *Catechism of the Catholic Church* in 1992. Among many Catholics, every statement of the bishop of Rome is eagerly read and studied.

The post–Vatican Council restoration of the ancient catechumenate is also significant for the way in which it moves adult converts (each with a sponsor) through a sustained period of ritual, doctrinal, and moral initiation. The Rite of Christian Initiation for Adults (RCIA) provides a uniform and responsible start to formation according to the mind of Christ.[30] Baptism, confirmation, confession, and participation in the Eucharist draws converts into sacramental life of the community and the imitation of Christ. Regular participation in the liturgy, in turn, exposes believers to the practices of reading Scripture, singing psalms and other hymns, and patterns of formal prayer. Congregants are not, alas, exposed very often to effective homiletics; truly powerful preaching is rarely a positive aspect of Catholic liturgy.

Distinctive paraliturgical practices continuous with medieval piety offer reinforcement of the classic model of discipleship: praying the Rosary invites meditation on the central moments in the gospel story; following the

30. The common and popular designation has been officially corrected to OCIA (Order of Christian Initiation for Adults).

stations of the cross during Lent stimulates contemplation of Christ's passion; adoration of the Blessed Sacrament invites meditation on Christ's gift of himself to humans, and on his continuing resurrection presence among his people. In most parishes, a balance is sought among providing Catholic education for the young (parochial schools), continuing adult education, and social engagement for the unborn and the poor (soup kitchens, shelters, clothing drives, and the like).[31] Seriously committed Catholics frequently seek further formation through silent retreats at Jesuit or Benedictine or Franciscan centers that lead them through the *Spiritual Exercises* of Ignatius of Loyola, or the *Rule of Saint Benedict*, or the teachings of Saint Francis of Assisi. Some join third-order associations linked to such spiritualities and apply the respective teachings and practices to their lay existence.[32]

What about literature? Pious Catholics have continued to read on their own Ignatius of Loyola, Francis of Assisi, Teresa of Ávila, Francis de Sales, Lorenzo Scupoli (*The Spiritual Combat*), and Thérèse of Lisieux. These are regularly available at Catholic bookstores. Access to a wider range of classics became easier. The valuable but cumbersome nineteenth-century translations of patristic literature in the *Ante-Nicene Fathers* and *Nicene and Post-Nicene Fathers of the Church* have largely been supplanted by more contemporary translations in the series Ancient Christian Writers, as well as Fathers of the Church.[33] Even more accessible are the richly annotated volumes in the Classics of Western Spirituality, a series that includes patristic, medieval, reformation, and early modern devotional works, as well as many volumes from the Jewish and Muslim mystical traditions.[34] But are there contemporary voices shaping the classic understanding of discipleship within Catholicism?

31. The Saint Vincent de Paul Society is an organization in virtually every parish and provides hands-on assistance to an astonishing number of marginalized people.

32. See, for example, Kathleen Norris, *Dakota: A Spiritual Geography* (New York: Houghton Mifflin, 1992) and *The Cloister Walk* (New York: Riverhead Books, 1997).

33. *The Ante-Nicene Fathers*, 10 vols., ed. Alexander Roberts and James Donaldson (1885–1887; repr., Peabody, MA: Hendrickson, 1994); *A Select Library of Nicene and Post-Nicene Fathers of the Christian Church*, 28 vols. in 2 series, ed. Philip Schaff and Henry Wace (1886–1889; repr., Peabody, MA: Hendrickson, 1994); Ancient Christian Writers (New York: Paulist, 1946–); Fathers of the Church (New York: Fathers of the Church; Washington, DC: Catholic University of America Press, 1947–).

34. The series Classics of Western Spirituality (New York: Paulist, 1978–) has more than three hundred volumes.

Pride of place among more recent and contemporary Catholic writers who speak out of the traditional understanding of discipleship and continue to regard the transformation of the self (becoming a saint) as the point of discipleship must be given to Thomas Merton (1915–1968), a Trappist monk whose 1948 autobiography, *Seven Storey Mountain*, became a bestseller and whose many subsequent books on spirituality were (and are) avidly read. Merton uniquely combines a wide and deep learning in the tradition, an inquiring spirit, an openness to the implications of experience, and a prophetic edge.[35] His most systematic exposition of discipleship and the mystical path is *The Ascent to Truth*.[36] Despite its great learning, it was probably his least successful book, because it lacked the personal element that so animated his other writings. I will consider Merton at greater length in the next chapter.

Similarly offering a combination of personal experience and reflection on the demands of committed discipleship is the Dutch priest Henri Nouwen (1932–1996). Although an admirer of Merton and attracted to the monastic life,[37] Nouwen was a restless pilgrim who moved almost constantly from one social setting to another, lecturing all over the world, and ending in a lengthy commitment to the L'Arche Daybreak Community in Toronto, one of the intentional communities founded by Jean Vanier in which people with and without intellectual disabilities live and pray together.[38] Lacking Merton's deep knowledge of patristic and medieval spirituality, Nouwen brought his own training in psychology to bear on the struggles of real people, writing in a clear and accessible way and showing remarkable insight into Scripture.[39] The continuing influence of Merton and Nouwen is indicated by the societies dedicated

35. A small sample: *The Sign of Jonah* (New York: Harcourt Brace, 1953); *Bread in the Wilderness* (New York: New Directions, 1953); *Seeds of Contemplation* (New York: New Directions, 1949); *No Man Is an Island* (New York: Harcourt Brace, 1955); *Thoughts in Solitude* (New York: Farrar, Straus & Cudahy, 1958).

36. *The Ascent to Truth* (New York: Harcourt Brace, 1951).

37. See his fine study, *Thomas Merton: Contemplative Critic* (Notre Dame: Fides, 1972) and *Genesee Diary: Report from a Trappist Monastery* (Garden City, NY: Doubleday, 1976).

38. For Nouwen's constant peregrinations, see Michael Ford, *Wounded Prophet: A Portrait of Henri J. M. Nouwen* (New York: Doubleday, 1999).

39. Among Nouwen's thirty-nine books, see *The Wounded Healer: Ministry in Contemporary Society* (Garden City, NY: Doubleday, 1972); *Reaching Out: Three Moments of the Spiritual Life* (Garden City, NY: Doubleday, 1975); *The Way of the Heart: Desert*

to the study of their work.[40] And Catholic religious orders continue to produce writers of spirituality aimed at the laity. Among them are Joan Chittister, OSB; Richard Rohr, OFM; Ronald Rolheiser, OMI; Benedict Groeschel, CFR; Timothy Gallagher, OMV; Jacques Philippe; and James Martin, SJ.[41] I will defer comment on such prolific production until after I have reviewed some Protestant efforts, with this exception: perhaps reliant on Catholicism's strong structural elements (noted above), these works generally (not entirely) focus much more on soul-grooming spirituality than on the transformation of character through obedience to the workings of the Holy Spirit.

Protestant Resources

American Protestantism is a ridiculously capacious tent under which a bewildering variety of Christian expressions can be found, ranging from major denominations within which distinct forms of tradition are maintained to storefront ministries that are essentially new inventions. The uniformity that characterizes Roman Catholicism can be found only partially in the Episcopal, Lutheran, Presbyterian, and Methodist denom-

---

Spirituality and Contemporary Ministry (New York: Seabury, 1981); and *Return of the Prodigal Son: A Story of Homecoming* (New York: Image Books, 1994).

40. The International Thomas Merton Society and the Henri Nouwen Society.

41. See Joan Chittister, *The Radical Christian Life* (Collegeville, MN: Liturgical Press, 2011); Chittister, *In God's Holy Light* (Cincinnati: Franciscan, 2015); Chittister, *The Way of the Cross* (Maryknoll, NY: Orbis Books, 2013); Richard Rohr, *Immortal Diamond: The Search for Our True Self* (San Francisco: Jossey-Bass, 2013); Rohr, *Quest for the Grail: Soul Work and the Sacred Journey* (New York: Crossroad, 1994); Rohr, *The Naked Now: Learning to See as the Mystics See* (New York: Crossroad, 2009); Ronald Rolheiser, *The Shattered Lantern: Rediscovering the Felt Presence of God* (New York: Crossroad, 1993); Rolheiser, *The Holy Longing: Guidelines for a Christian Spirituality* (New York: Doubleday, 1999); Benedict J. Groeschel, *Listening at Prayer* (New York: Paulist, 1984); Groeschel, *Spiritual Passages: The Psychology of Spiritual Development for "Those Who Seek"* (New York: Crossroad, 1984); Timothy M. Gallagher, *The Discernment of Spirits: An Ignatian Guide to Everyday Life* (New York: Crossroad, 2005); Gallagher, *Meditation and Contemplation: An Ignatian Guide to Prayer* (New York: Crossroad, 2008); Jacques Philippe, *Time for God* (Strongsville, OH: Scepter, 2008); Philippe, *Interior Freedom* (Strongsville, OH: Scepter, 2007); James Martin, *A Jesuit Guide to (Almost) Everything: A Spirituality for Real Life* (New York: HarperOne, 2010); Martin, *Between Heaven and Mirth: Why Joy, Humor, and Laughter Are at the Heart of the Spiritual Life* (New York: HarperOne, 2011).

inations. Free Church and evangelical congregations, in turn, may call themselves Baptist or Congregationalist, but each draws eclectically—depending on the education and tendency of the pastor—from multiple Reformed, Anabaptist, Holiness, or Pentecostal strands. It is certainly a lively mix (even when we have excluded many of the most marginal versions) and one that is difficult for an outsider—like me—to grasp.[42]

In this discussion of resources, then, I refrain from any attempt to characterize the presence or coherence of ecclesial formation practices (preaching, Bible study, faith sharing, counseling, conferences, revivals) and focus instead on hortatory literature that can legitimately be called "traditional" in the best sense of the term, that is, teaching on discipleship that is authentically based in the vision of discipleship as the transformation of the self in imitation of Christ. And even as I organize such resources according to denomination/tradition, I remind my reader that serious seekers cross such boundaries; Henri Nouwen is as widely read among Protestants as among Catholics.

Believers within the Anglican/Episcopal traditions have readily available to them the classic hortatory works of Jeremy Taylor and William Law—not forgetting C. S. Lewis—as well as the finely crafted collections of sermons by William Temple and Austin Farrer.[43] The sermonic form is a feature as well in the more recent published works of Rowan Williams, Fleming Rutledge, and Barbara Brown Taylor.[44] Not unexpectedly, such

42. My knowledge of Roman Catholicism comes from a lifetime immersion and commitment. My knowledge of American Protestantism is based mainly on engagement with several thousand Protestant ministry students—and faculty—at Yale and Emory over some forty years, and conversations with several hundred Protestant congregations and clergy conferences to whom I made presentations.

43. For example, William Temple, *The Nature of Personality* (Suffolk: Clary & Sons, 1911); Temple, *Fellowship with God* (London: Macmillan, 1920); Temple, *Christian Faith and Life* (New York: Macmillan, 1931); Austin Farrer, *The End of Man*, ed. Charles C. Conti (London: SPCK, 1973); Farrer, *The Brink of Mystery*, ed. Charles C. Conti (London: SPCK, 1976).

44. For example, Rowan Williams, *A Ray of Darkness: Sermons and Reflections* (Cambridge: Cowley, 1995); Williams, *Being Christian: Baptism, Bible, Eucharist, Prayer* (Grand Rapids: Eerdmans, 2014); Williams, *Being Disciples: Essentials of the Christian Life* (London: SPCK, 2016); Williams, *Holy Living: The Christian Tradition for Today* (New York: Bloomsbury, 2017); Fleming Rutledge, *The Bible and the New York Times* (Grand Rapids: Eerdmans, 1998); Rutledge, *Not Ashamed of the Gospel: Sermons from Saint*

reflections are firmly situated within canon and creed and combine a highly literate mode of delivery with an acute social awareness. Similarly, Lutherans seeking a deeper sense of discipleship have available to them the complete works of Luther in English, as well as the edifying works of Søren Kierkegaard from the nineteenth century, and, from the twentieth century, the writings of Dietrich Bonhoeffer, whom I will consider again in the next chapter.[45] Likewise, twentieth-century Methodists—and the broader Wesleyan tradition—experienced a renewed appreciation for the wonderfully accessible writings of John Wesley (above all his sermons) and were led by theologians like Albert Outler to understand that Wesley brought experience and tradition together in distinctive ways,[46] which led in turn to the sort of conversation with the classic sources of spirituality that so animated his own compositions.[47] Thomas Oden, for example, exerted great effort to move the Wesleyan tradition of theology and pastoral care closer to the classic tradition and a scriptural interpretation informed by ancient commentary.[48] Similarly, the prolific

---

Paul's Letter to the Romans (Grand Rapids: Eerdmans, 2007); Barbara Brown Taylor, *God in Pain* (Nashville: Abingdon, 1998); Taylor, *Learning to Walk in the Dark* (New York: HarperOne, 2014).

45. See Martin Luther, *Luther's Works*, 55 vols., ed. Jaroslav Pelikan et al. (Saint Louis: Concordia; Minneapolis: Fortress, 1955–1986); S. Kierkegaard, *Eighteen Edifying Discourses* (1843–1844); Kierkegaard, *Works of Love* (1847); Kierkegaard, *Practice of Christianity* (1850); Dietrich Bonhoeffer, *The Cost of Discipleship* (New York: Macmillan, 1961); Bonhoeffer, *Letters and Papers from Prison* (London: Collins, 1965); Bonhoeffer, *Life Together* (London: Collins, 1965). One can add more contemporary works, such as those by John W. Kleinig, *Grace upon Grace: Spirituality for Today* (Saint Louis: Concordia, 2008); Adolf Köberle, *The Quest for Holiness: A Biblical, Historical, and Systematic Investigation*, trans. John C. Mattes (Eugene, OR: Wipf & Stock, 2004); and Gene Edward Veith, *Spirituality of the Cross: The Way of the First Evangelicals* (Saint Louis: Concordia, 1999).

46. See Albert C. Outler, *Theology in the Wesleyan Spirit* (Nashville: Tidings, 1975); Outler, *The Wesleyan Theological Heritage: Essays of Albert C. Outler*, ed. Thomas C. Oden and Leicester R. Longden (Grand Rapids: Zondervan, 1991).

47. See the discussion of Wesley in chapter 4.

48. See, for example, Thomas C. Oden, *After Modernity . . . What? A Guide for Theology* (Grand Rapids: Zondervan, 1992); Oden, *Care of Souls in the Classic Tradition* (Philadelphia: Fortress, 1984); Oden, *The Transforming Power of Grace* (Nashville: Abingdon, 1993). Oden edited *The Ancient Christian Commentary on Scripture*, 29 vols. (Downers Grove, IL: InterVarsity Press, 1993).

preacher and writer William Willimon emphasized equally the traditional base and the social posture of Methodism.[49]

It is perhaps among writers in the Free Church traditions, among whom I include all those who do not fit within the mainline denominations—the broadly evangelical, Baptist, Congregationalist, Quaker, Pentecostal, Holiness, Christian—that the most surprising recovery of the longer tradition is to be found. A renewed sense of the seriousness of discipleship, of the importance of disciplines or practices, of the riches to be found in the classic tradition, together with a deep sense of frustration at a Christianity concerned only with being saved by faith and not works and with getting to heaven, and with enjoying membership in the church as a badge of social respectability, has driven prophetic voices to challenge readers with the severe demands of authentic discipleship.

Two names from the twentieth century that command wide respect, even reverence, are those of Oswald Chambers (1874–1917) and A. W. Tozer (1897–1963). Born a Baptist, Chambers became associated with the Holiness movement and worked with the Pentecostal League of Prayer, serving as a traveling preacher and as teacher in London's Bible Training College, before serving as a YMCA chaplain to soldiers of the British Commonwealth in Egypt, where he met a sudden death at the age of forty-three. His devotional work, *My Utmost for His Highest*, is a collection of daily reflections on scriptural texts; it has stayed in print continuously for over seventy-five years, has been translated into thirty-nine languages, and has sold over thirteen million copies.[50]

Although he published only three books in his lifetime, his wife Gertrude Hobbs was an expert amanuensis, who transcribed all his lectures and published them piecemeal until her death in 1966, and Chambers's complete works (running to almost fifteen hundred pages) are now available.[51] Reading through them brings several realizations. First, Chambers had an extraordinarily well-furnished mind; his essays and lectures are

49. See William Willimon and Stanley Hauerwas, *Resident Aliens: Life in the Christian Colony* (Nashville: Abingdon, 1989); Willimon and Hauerwas, *Where Resident Aliens Live: Exercises for Christian Practice* (Nashville: Abingdon, 1996); Willimon, *This We Believe: The Core of Wesleyan Faith and Practice* (Nashville: Abingdon, 2010).

50. The classic edition comes from Grand Rapids: Discovery House, 2017.

51. *The Complete Works of Oswald Chambers*, with notes by David Macasland (Grand

studded with long citations from poets—with Browning and Milton be-
ing particular favorites—and references to theologians (Augustine, John
Tauler, Erasmus, Luther, Law, Edwards, Wesley, and many others), philosophers (Socrates, Aristotle, Epicurus, Nietzsche), scientists (William James,
Thomas Huxley, Adam Smith), and assorted writers and thinkers (G. K.
Chesterton, George Eliot, Henrik Ibsen, Francis Thompson). Second, he
truly inhabited a scriptural imagination, finding everything needful for
Christian formation within the texts of the Bible. Third, he was deeply and
authentically infused with the Holy Spirit of which he spoke. Fourth, his
teaching on discipleship was consistently rigorous, demanding formation
through disciplined practices. Fifth, he recognized that discipleship involved suffering, not as an accidental dimension but as an essential one.

In some respects, A. W. Tozer is an even more remarkable figure,
not least because his witness was so entirely uncredentialed in human
terms. He was raised on a farm and never attended college or seminary.
But when he felt called by God, he entered a lifelong process of self-
education, becoming a speaker and writer of unusual directness and
clarity. Five years after his conversion, he became an evangelical minister associated with the Christian and Missionary Alliance, serving as
a pastor for over forty-four years. He became a writer for the *Weekly
Alliance* and then its editor. Most of his books (some forty have been
published, many of them posthumously) are drawn from his columns
in this magazine. He led a life of great simplicity and donated much of
his income to others.

In 1948, the publication of *The Pursuit of God* was instantly recognized as a classic and made his reputation among evangelical readers, for
whom his many subsequent books became mandatory reading.[52] Part of
Tozer's power is that, like Chambers, he so clearly inhabits the reality of
which he speaks. When he speaks of the presence of God behind the veil
of appearance, he speaks with the authority of one who has discerned
that presence. Even more than Chambers, I think, he communicates

---

Rapids: Discovery House, 2000), consists of over forty distinct works, many of them
combining sets of lectures or essays.

52. I am using an updated version, *The Pursuit of God* (Abbotsford, WI: Aneko,
2015). Tozer's other universally recognized masterpiece is *The Knowledge of the Holy:
The Attributes of God; Their Meaning in Christian Life* (New York: HarperOne, 2009).

the essence of that reality with both clarity and subtlety. Writing about the reading of the Bible, for example, he states, "The Bible will never be a living book to us until we are convinced that God is articulate in His universe. . . . The facts are that God is not silent, has never been silent. It is the nature of God to speak. . . . The Bible is the inevitable outcome of God's continuous speech" (*Pursuit*, 64–65).

Tozer's self-education in the classics of Christian spirituality is everywhere obvious. It is not simply that he refers to Augustine and Bernard and Nicolas of Cusa and Wesley; he clearly had studied them, as he had also *The Cloud of Unknowing* and Julian of Norwich. For Tozer, the entire point of life is the pursuit of the God who first pursued us, and he honors those who have engaged in that pursuit: "Come near to the holy men and women of the past and you will soon feel the heat of their desire after God" (*Pursuit*, 5). Indeed, in his book on the Holy Spirit, he argues that the Spirit has never been absent from God's people, by listing a litany of saints that includes Augustine, Bernard of Cluny, Bernard of Clairvaux, Richard Rolle, Brother Lawrence, Thomas à Kempis, Martin Luther, Zinzendorff, Tersteegen, John Newton, Charles and John Wesley, William Booth, Frederick Faber, Charles Finney, and other near contemporaries.[53] His "examples from history" are eclectic, or, to use another term, catholic in the proper sense of the term.

Tozer was unrelenting in his insistence on genuine (and not merely nominal) discipleship, which inevitably demands not only personal transformation but also the endurance of suffering. With characteristic directness, he states,

> When all is said, it may easily be that the great difference between professing Christians (the *important* difference in this day) is not between modernists and evangelicals but between those who have reduced Christianity to an intellectual formula and those who believe that the true essence of our faith lies in the supernatural workings of the Spirit in a region of the soul not accessible to mere reason.[54]

53. See *Life in the Spirit* (Peabody, MA: Hendrickson, 2009), 126–30.
54. *We Travel an Appointed Way*, ed. Harry Verploegh (Camp Hill, PA: Christian, 1988), 90.

The recovery of tradition among broadly evangelical writers became more explicit in the work of Richard J. Foster (b. 1942). An evangelical Quaker, Foster founded Renovare, a Christian renewal parachurch organization. In his *Celebration of Discipline: The Path to Spiritual Growth*,[55] he argued for the practice of prayer, meditation, fasting, and solitude/silence as means to a discipleship that had some depth,[56] and he extended his embrace of the tradition to the reading of spiritual classics through the ages.[57] A similar range is displayed by the remarkable Dallas Willard, a professor of philosophy at University of Southern California whose specialty was Husserl, he was also a Southern Baptist minister whose wide learning and rigorous reasoning make his devotional works distinctive; one is reminded when reading him of C. S. Lewis. Like Foster, Willard makes the case for the spiritual disciplines as the way through which God can transform believers into genuine disciples.[58] His acknowledged masterwork is *The Divine Conspiracy*,[59] a closely reasoned exposition of how the kingdom of God already envelops humans and how they might more explicitly bring it to realization in their own lives.

As in my survey of Catholic resources, I conclude with a short list of other worthy authors within the broadly evangelical tradition whose writings command respect both for the vigor and point of their writing, for their reasoned rejection of the negative aspects of modernity, for their immersion in biblical imagination, and for their openness to the wisdom offered by the past. R. C. Sproul (1939–2017) combines all these elements, despite his rather rigid view of biblical authority. A Presbyterian pastor who founded Ligonier Ministries, Sproul (like the others considered in this paragraph) published prolifically. A fair amount is worth reading.[60] John Piper (b. 1946) is a Baptist who was a New Tes-

55. 3rd ed. (New York: HarperCollins, 1998).

56. See also his *Prayer: Finding the Heart's True Home* (New York: HarperOne, 1992).

57. Richard J. Foster and James Bryan Smith, *Devotional Classics: Selected Readings for Individuals and Groups*, rev. and exp. ed. (New York: HarperOne, 1990).

58. See *The Spirit of the Disciplines: Understanding How God Changes Lives* (San Francisco: Harper & Row, 1988) and *Hearing God: Developing a Conversational Relationship with God* (Downers Grove, IL: InterVarsity Press, 1999).

59. *The Divine Conspiracy: Rediscovering Our Hidden Life with God* (San Francisco: Harper, 1998).

60. See, for example, *Pleasing God* (Wheaton, IL: Tyndale House, 1988); *Following*

tament professor before serving as a pastor for some thirty-three years. He combines wide learning with pastoral conviction and innovative approaches to the devotional life.[61] Eugene H. Peterson (1932–2018) was a Presbyterian pastor who also served as a seminary professor for twenty-nine years. A poet as well as a scholar, Peterson's collected essays and sermons (often brilliant in execution) reward careful reading.[62] Another Presbyterian pastor who writes explicitly in the tradition of C. S. Lewis is Timothy Keller (b. 1950), whose work, like that of Lewis, is as much apologetic as it is devotional.[63] Finally, the works of Howard Thurman, who so greatly influenced Martin Luther King, deserve careful reading.[64]

CONCLUSION

I called the evidences of authentic discipleship in recent Christian literature "sparks of light," but the darkness around them is great indeed. When compared to the great volume of noise produced by counterfeit Christianity, they represent but a still small voice. They are, nevertheless, the more valuable for their fidelity to a vision of discipleship that is more demanding, and more beautiful, than that peddled by Christ-

---

Christ (Wheaton, IL: Tyndale House, 1991); *In the Presence of God: Devotional Readings on the Attributes of God* (Nashville: Word, 1999); *The Prayer of the Lord* (Ann Arbor: Reformation Trust, 2009).

61. See, for example, *Desiring God: Meditations of a Christian Hedonist*, 4th ed. (Colorado Springs: Multnomah, 2011); *Future Grace: The Purifying Power of Living by Faith in Future Grace* (Colorado Springs: Multnomah, 1995); *A Hunger for God: Desiring God through Fasting and Prayer* (Wheaton, IL: Crossway, 1997).

62. See, for example, *Where Your Treasure Is: Psalms That Summon You from Self to Community* (Grand Rapids: Eerdmans, 1993); *The Contemplative Pastor: Returning to the Art of Spiritual Direction* (Grand Rapids: Eerdmans, 1993); *Subversive Spirituality* (Grand Rapids: Eerdmans, 1994); *As Kingfishers Catch Fire: A Conversation on the Ways of God Formed by the Words of God* (New York: Waterbook, 2017).

63. See, for example, *The Reason for God: Belief in an Age of Skepticism* (New York: Dutton, 2008); *The Prodigal God: Recovering the Heart of the Christian Faith* (New York: Dutton, 2008); *Counterfeit Gods: The Empty Promises of Money, Sex, and Power, and the Only Hope That Matters* (New York: Dutton, 2009).

64. I have in mind especially *Disciplines of the Spirit* (New York: Harper & Row, 1963), as well as *Jesus and the Disinherited* (Nashville: Abingdon, 1970), and *Meditations of the Heart* (New York: Harper & Row, 1953); see also Luther E. Smith Jr., *Howard Thurman: The Mystic as Prophet* (Washington, DC: University Press of America, 1981).

huskers and timeservers. In the best of these witnesses, a reader has the sense that discipleship is not simply a goal about which they speak but a living process out of which they testify. In some of them, indeed, talk about the presence of God and sanctification bears the marks of lived experience.

Still, taken as a whole—and acknowledging the important exceptions—even these faithful witnesses deviate in significant ways from the longer tradition they seek to represent.[65] I take note of four elements whose relative absence strikes me as significant, especially among writers whose commitment to Scripture is overt:

(1) Scriptural eschatology is diminished. One could argue that the avoidance of language about heaven and hell, the resurrection of the just, eternal life with God, and the coming judgment is so exaggerated in millenarian preaching that some discreet avoidance is necessary. Likewise, one understands among Protestant writers why a "how am I saved so as to get to heaven" attitude is regarded as a trivializing distraction. But the reality of God's judgment—not just in the future but at every moment—and the truth that this life is a preparatory pilgrimage toward life with God are so central to the world Scripture imagines, that speaking of discipleship without reference to these truths seems itself to be an accommodation to the world imagined by modernity.

(2) In line with a this-worldly emphasis, talk about spirituality and the disciplines—however welcome as topics introduced at all—at times appears as closer to psychic pluming (it's good for you) than to an engagement with God's Holy Spirit and the effort to discern the work of the Holy Spirit in human lives.[66]

(3) That suffering in imitation of Jesus Christ is an essential element of discipleship is a truth that appears only in the margins. Meditation on the passion of Christ—such an important aspect of traditional piety—is seldom mentioned. When suffering is discussed, it tends to be as something accidental to be endured rather than as something to be embraced as God's favored way of transforming human freedom.

---

65. Even while recognizing that the tradition itself is not entirely uniform or consistent.

66. See Luke Timothy Johnson, "Theology and the Spiritual Life," in *The Living Gospel* (New York: Continuum, 2004), 3–10.

(4) Most importantly, it is shocking to find how little of the serious talk about discipleship or spirituality focuses on the love of neighbor. The intrinsic bond between these two loves in the tradition is weakened and at times disappears. In this, as with the other points, there are exceptions. But the overwhelming impression gained by a fresh reading of these authors is that discipleship is an individual rather than a communal reality and that it does not demand, at its very heart, the self-sacrificial love of others. It is here that prayer, fasting, and almsgiving gain their point, in the way they fuse love of God and neighbor. It is here that the imitation of the obedient faith of Jesus finds embodied expression—in the moment-by-moment self-emptying of self in service to others.

The odd lack of emphasis on the service of others provides an edge to the social gospel/liberation critique of the older tradition as passive, self-preoccupied, and solipsistic. I have already identified the ways in which that alternative is inadequate; indeed, it betrays Scripture and the truth of the gospel. But its utterly deficient and distorted option gains whatever credibility it has from the way in which writers representing the older tradition themselves betray the most critical element of that tradition, which is that the love of God must find expression in every circumstance through the practical, embodied care for others.

In the end, though, we must ask whether any literature suffices for the shaping of authentic discipleship. Are not saints formed through the imitation of other saints? Is not the living example of obedient faith and self-sacrificing love more compelling, more convincing, and more attractive than even the most impressive prose? In the next chapter, I argue that God makes disciples of Christ precisely through the imitation of authentic disciples, that God shows how to become a saint by offering for imitation the example of saints.

8

IMITATING SAINTS

Learning to be a disciple of Jesus Christ does not come from reading a devotional book, or from attending a powerful service, or from undergoing a process of catechesis—however fine and helpful any of these expressions of faith may be.[1] Discipleship is best learned through the imitation of other disciples. Learning to be a saint—the goal of the classic understanding of discipleship—is learned first and best through imitation of the saints. Both terms, "saints" and "imitation," require some preliminary discussion.

I use the language of sanctity quite deliberately, even though I am aware of the difficulty such language presents to some (not all) Christians in Reformed traditions.[2] I use it not simply because it is the language used by the New Testament for the telos of discipleship—being transformed by the Holy Spirit into the image of Christ[3]—but also

---

1. Even the exclusive pondering of Scripture, absent other influences, can lead to a distorted conception of discipleship.

2. Sanctification is a central conviction animating the Roman Catholic and Orthodox traditions, the Anglican/Episcopal and Methodist traditions, and Holiness/Pentecostal traditions. The reality of sanctification is also celebrated by such authors as Tozer and Sproul, among others.

3. For "sanctify"/"make holy" (*hagiazō*), see, for example, Rom 15:16; 1 Cor 1:2; 6:11; 7:14; Eph 5:26; 1 Thess 5:23; 2 Tim 2:21; Heb 2:11; 10:10, 14, 29; 13:12; 1 Pet 3:15; for "sanctification" (*hagiasmos*), see Rom 6:19, 22; 1 Cor 1:30; 1 Thess 4:3 ("this is the will of God, your sanctification"), 4, 7; 2 Thess 2:13; 1 Tim 2:15; Heb 12:14; 1 Pet 1:2; for "holy one"/"saint" (*hagios*) applied to humans, see Rom 1:7; 8:27; 15:25, 26, 31; 16:2, 15; 1 Cor 1:2; 3:17; 6:1, 2; 14:33; 16:1, 15; 2 Cor 1:1; 8:4; 9:1, 12; 13:12; Eph 1:1, 4, 15; 2:19; 3:5, 8; 4:12; 5:3, 27; Phil 1:1; 4:21, 22; Col 1:2, 4, 12, 22, 26; 3:12; 1 Thess 3:13; 4:8; 5:27; 2 Thess 1:10; 1 Tim 5:10; Phlm 5, 7; Heb 3:1; 6:10; 10:19; 13:24; 1 Pet 1:15, 16; Jude 3; Rev 5:8; 8:3, 4; 11:18; 13:10; 18:24; 22:21.

because it belongs to that longer tradition of Christian discipleship to which all Christians today are indebted (for their very existence) and to which they owe attention. It can be argued, indeed, that the most genuine history of Christianity is to be found in the lives of the saints, for it is through such witnesses that the faith has been transmitted from age to age.

When I speak of saints, then, I mean precisely those Christians in whom the marks of authentic discipleship are sufficiently realized as to provide a light to the world, whose manner of life leads others to "glorify your Father in heaven" (Matt 5:14–16). The term "saint" is, for my purposes, the functional equivalent to "authentic disciple." I clearly do not mean only those figures officially designated as saints by the church but those in whom God has brought about a life transformed (or at least in the process of being transformed) according to the mind of Christ. If we believe in the power of God to transform lives (our own as well as others), then the language of sanctification is both legitimate and necessary, for that names the transformation that God accomplishes. If we cannot so speak, then it is time to close shop.

Likewise, some readers may cavil at my use of "imitation," since somewhere in their memory of theology classes, they remember what furious energy was expended by some German Lutheran exegete or another on the essential distinction between following Christ and imitating Christ, the point being that Protestants followed (and were correct) while Catholics imitated (and were wrong). Furious energy was required because it is a distinction without a real difference, since in the ancient culture within which the New Testament was written, following a leader or teacher meant, in fact, learning through imitation the character of the teacher in order to translate that character into the circumstances of their own lives.

Transformation through Imitation

Ancient moral philosophy and the New Testament agree that virtue is learned through the imitation of models, preferably living models.[4] In

---

4. Providing an example of the paraenetical (advising) letter, Pseudo-Libanius states, "Always be an emulator, dear friend, of virtuous men. For it is better to be well

the *Demonicus* of Pseudo-Isocrates, for example, a classic Greco-Roman paraenetical composition,[5] the author presents himself as the uncle of a young man who has taken up the responsibility of instructing him in the good life in the place of his deceased father (2). He begins by reminding Demonicus of the living representative of the virtuous life he had in his father and exhorting him to imitate that example (9–11). He then offers a series of maxims by way of amplifying and specifying various virtuous dispositions and actions (12–38), before returning in the end to a further set of examples (this time from literature) that the young man might emulate (50–51). The ancient sages understood that mere verbal instruction is not enough; one needs to see how virtue actually looks in action. Such mimesis does not call for the mechanical duplication of the model but rather for the translation of the thought and dispositions of the exemplar into the changed life circumstances of the disciple. Epictetus does not expect his students to be as poor or as celibate as himself but to cultivate similar simplicity and courage in their lives as diplomats.[6] Mental and moral excellence can be learned through observation and practical application.[7] The imitation of moral exemplars is therefore a staple of ancient moral philosophy.[8]

When the apostle Paul exhorts the Corinthians, "Be imitators of me, as I am of Christ" (1 Cor 11:1), then, he shows himself to be one who shares such convictions. His statement concludes an argument concerning the legitimacy or nonlegitimacy of eating food that had been offered to idols

---

spoken of when imitating good men than to be reproached by all for following evil men." See Rudolf Hercher, *Epistolographi Graeci*, Bibliotheca Scriptorum Graecorum (Paris: Didot, 1873), 8.

5. For a discussion of paraenesis as a form of hortatory writing, see Luke Timothy Johnson, *The Letter of James: A New Translation with Introduction and Commentary*, Anchor Yale Bible 37A (Garden City, NY: Doubleday, 1995), 16–25.

6. See, in particular, *Discourse* 3.23 and the full discussion of Epictetus's program of *askēsis* in Luke Timothy Johnson, *Among the Gentiles: Greco-Roman Religion and Christianity*, Anchor (Yale) Bible Reference Library (New Haven: Yale University Press, 2009), 71–78.

7. The same conviction, to be sure, animates all apprenticeship programs. Book learning only goes so far in matters requiring expertise; excellence in any trade means observing, imitating, and practicing that trade in association with master craftsmen.

8. See also Lucian of Samosata, *Demonax* and *Nigrinus*, as well as Dio Chrysostom, *Oration* 77/78.

(8:1–10:33), a case that he uses to illustrate the truth that "knowledge puffs up, but love builds up" (8:1). Paul acknowledges the right of individuals to follow their own conscience (their knowledge) but insists that their right is relativized by consideration for others who do not have the same knowledge: "if food is a cause of my brother's falling, I will never eat meat, lest I cause my brother to fall" (8:13). Before continuing his exposition concerning the eating of food, Paul moves into a personal account that is not a deviation from his point but a sharpening of it. In 9:1–27, he applies to his own circumstances the dispositions he desires among his readers. He has the right to be supported financially by the church, a right established by nature, Scripture, and the command of the Lord (9:7–14), but he makes no use of those rights for the sake of the gospel (9:15–22). It is this practice of "becoming all things to all men," making himself a "slave to all," that requires of Paul a constant discipline like that of athletes (9:19–27). At the conclusion of his discussion of food and conscience in 10:1–30, therefore, Paul returns to the moral dispositions that ought to animate all their behavior if they are truly to live according to "the mind of Christ" (1 Cor 2:16):

> So, whether you eat or drink, or *whatever you do*, do all to the glory of God. Give no offense to Jews or to Greeks or to the church of God, just as I try to please all men in *everything* I do, *not seeking my own advantage but that of many*, that they may be saved. Be imitators of me as I am of Christ. (1 Cor 10:31–11:1)

I have underscored the phrases in this statement that show how the argument (and example) Paul has provided is to be generalized: these dispositions are to govern "whatever" and "everything" that they do, always with the desire to build up others rather than inflate the self (see 8:1). Two important principles thus emerge: first, imitating Christ is above all a matter of living according to "the mind of Christ," that seeks the good of others more than the self; second, the mind of Christ can be learned by seeing it at work in those who already live according to that measure and power. The imitation of Christ, in sum, can be mediated through the imitation of those displaying Christlike qualities—the saints.

An even more impressive example is provided by Paul's Letter to the Philippians. Writing to a community in which rivalry and competition exist (Phil 1:15; 4:2–3), Paul emphasizes a unity in the Spirit that expresses itself in self-donative service (2:1–4): "Do nothing from selfishness or conceit, but in humility count others over yourselves. Let each of you look not only to his own interests, but also to the interests of others. Have this mind among yourselves, which is yours in Christ Jesus" (2:3–4 RSV, adapted). Paul then offers a series of examples of this mind of Christ, beginning with Jesus himself, who did not count equality with God a thing to be grasped but emptied himself out as a servant who died in obedience to God (2:6–11). But this same pattern of self-giving is found, Paul says, in his delegate Timothy, who is anxious for their welfare and is unlike those who "look after their own interests, not those of Jesus Christ" (2:19–24). It is found likewise in their own delegate Epaphroditus, who "nearly died for the work of Christ, risking his life to complete your service to me" (2:25–30). Finally, he offers his own example (3:2–16). As in 1 Corinthians 9, his declaration of how he gave up all his privileges as a Jew in order to "know Christ Jesus" (3:8) may appear as a distraction if we do not recognize that Paul is presenting himself as another example of the mind of Christ:[9]

> Whatever gain I had, I counted as loss for the sake of Christ. Indeed I count everything as loss for the surpassing worth of knowing Christ Jesus my Lord. For his sake I have suffered the loss of all things, and count them as refuse, in order that I may gain Christ and be found in him.[10]

That Paul intends to present Timothy, Epaphroditus, and himself as living exemplars of imitating the pattern established by Jesus is made perfectly clear by his conclusion: "Brethren, join in imitating me, and mark those who so live as you have an example in us" (3:17).

Paul again presents himself as example to be imitated—together with his delegates Timothy and Silvanus—to the church at Thessalonica, once more with reference to giving up rights for the sake of others:

---

9. The rhetorical transition in 3:1 is sufficiently sharp to have given rise to fragment hypotheses, which miss the point of the overall argument in this section of the letter; see, for example, Helmut Koester, "The Purpose of the Polemic of a Pauline Fragment (Phil III)," *New Testament Studies* 8 (1962): 317–32.

10. The best treatment of Paul's argument is by William S. Kurz, "Kenotic Imitation of Paul and Christ in Phil 2 and 3," in *Discipleship in the New Testament*, ed. Fernando Segovia (Minneapolis: Fortress, 1985), 103–26.

For you yourselves know how you ought to imitate us; we were not idle when we were with you, we did not eat anyone's bread without paying, but with toil and labor we worked night and day, that we might not burden any of you. It was not because we had not that right, but to give you in our conduct an example to imitate. (2 Thess 3:7–9)[11]

Paul likewise wants his delegate Timothy, who represents him in the Ephesian church, to "set the believers an example in speech and conduct, in love, in faith, in purity" (1 Tim 4:12). Timothy is able to be an example, because he has imitated the example of Paul, who tells him, "Follow the pattern of the sound words that you have heard from me, in the faith and love that are in Christ Jesus" (2 Tim 1:13), and, "you have observed my teaching, my conduct, my aim in life, my faith, my patience, my love, my steadfastness, my persecutions, my sufferings" (2 Tim 3:10).[12] Similarly, Paul expects his delegate Titus, whom he has left in Crete, to "show yourself in all respects a model of good deeds, and in your teaching show integrity, gravity, and sound speech that cannot be censured" (Tit 2:7–8).[13] It is important to note that Paul wants his delegates to be examples of a certain kind of character; what is learned through the imitation of a living model is not a set of facts but a revelation of character.

The Character of Saints

If we can speak, then, of learning authentic discipleship through imitating saints—who themselves have imitated Christ—it is appropriate to ask, first, where we find the saints whom we can imitate and, sec-

11. For discussion, see Ronald F. Hock, *The Social Context of Paul's Ministry: Tentmaking and Apostleship* (Philadelphia: Fortress, 1980).

12. Both in 1 Cor 9:24–27 and in Phil 3:12–16, Paul makes clear that his own transformation into the mind of Christ is not yet fully achieved but is in process, which requires disciplined effort. The "renewal of the mind" (Rom 12:1–2) does not happen automatically with the gift of the Spirit but demands the application of the human will (see Rom 6:12–23; 12:3–21). See also Luke Timothy Johnson, "Transformation of the Mind and Moral Discernment in Romans," in *Interpreting Paul*, vol. 2 of *The Canonical Paul* (Grand Rapids: Eerdmans, 2021), 48–68.

13. In Heb 13:7, we also read, "Remember your leaders, those who spoke to you the word of God; consider the outcome of their life and imitate their faith."

ond, what sort of character is it that we seek to learn. I take them up in reverse order.

We seek to find, over the long arc of individuals' lives, those salient traits that the Gospels ascribe to Jesus: a radical faith in God and a love of neighbor that is expressed through self-donative service.[14] Their faith in God is radical in that they refuse to be defined by the idolatries that attend ordinary human existence: they seek not their own pleasure, wealth, power, or their reputation before other humans but persistently (within all the flaws of their humanity) seek the face of God. Their faith is radical because it is not exhausted by conformity to creed or custom but responds with obedient hearing to God's summons as they discern it in the circumstances of their lives. Their faith is radical because it loyally persists in the face of scorn and rejection.

Their love of neighbor is neither notional nor momentary but is embodied and consistent, with the neighbor being whomever God places in their path through life. They do not confuse such love with the emotions associated with *erōs* or the good fellowship associated with *philia*. Rather, they will the good of the other in all circumstances and seek to enact that benevolent will through dispositions and practices that respond to the actual needs of the neighbor rather than their own fantasy concerning what might be the neighbor's good. Rather than desiring to be "puffed up" through conceit or vainglory, they seek to "build up" their neighbor and the community (1 Cor 8:1–2). They consistently seek to apply Paul's characterization of love in 1 Corinthians 13 in their own responses to the neighbors they encounter.

Such characterological traits represent what Paul in 1 Corinthians 2:16 calls "the mind of Christ." They are not to be confused with personality or temperament. They are compatible with a variety of personalities and temperaments. They represent the self that stands under God's judgment, for which the individual is responsible before God, because it is a self that is freely chosen and consciously embraced moment by moment through life. Indeed, a paradox of sanctity is that the more one

14. See Luke Timothy Johnson, *Faith's Freedom: A Classic Spirituality for Contemporary Christians* (Minneapolis: Fortress, 1990), 78–96, 174–85; *Living Jesus: Learning the Heart of the Gospel* (San Francisco: HarperSanFrancisco, 1999), 38–55, 195–203.

is inhabited and led by the Spirit of God—the more one is transformed into the image of Christ—the more one's own distinctive temperament and personality are revealed.

The saints thus paradoxically appear to us as at once the most remarkably diverse humans at the level of temperament and personality and the most alike in their fundamental character—which is an image of the image of God in Christ. Throughout the ages, they provide contemporary readers examples of how Christ might be imitated in contexts utterly unlike his (or our own). They resolved in their own lives the sad separation of love of God and love of neighbor that we have seen in the survey of recent literature. They took up the cross daily (Luke 9:23) not by constructing wooden beams to carry around but by practicing self-denial and selfless service within the cultures of twelfth-century England, sixteenth-century Spain, and seventeenth-century Brazil.

SEEKING SAINTS

If, then, this is the character of Christ that is replicated by the Holy Spirit in the lives of those believers who have committed themselves to serious discipleship, where are the saints from whose character we ourselves might learn, whose devotion to God and love of neighbor we might imitate? The short answer is that they are all around us. As with the evidence for the presence and power of God in creation through miracles, what is needed are "eyes to see and ears to hear" (Matt 13:16).[15] Once we know what we are looking for—the character of Jesus enacted in humans like us—and once we seriously start looking, we shall find what we seek (Matt 7:7). The obvious starting point is the study of those Christians of the past that the church has recognized as saints.[16] Hagiography has progressed since the days of *The Golden Legend* and *Foxe's Book of Martyrs*, and it is now possible to read critically responsible treatments of the saints' lives (and deaths). Pondering how God worked the

15. See Luke Timothy Johnson, *Miracles: God's Presence and Power in Creation*, Resources for the Use of Scripture in the Church (Louisville: Westminster John Knox, 2018).

16. I have noted earlier how John Wesley and A. W. Tozer generously recognized and celebrated the saints of the past.

transformation of the self in those figures of the past—for saints are not born but made—can be a valuable step toward the discernment of such transformation in one's own life.[17]

Such study, in turn, can enlarge our imagination to the point that we can perceive, all around us, the ways in which God is transforming lives and teaching us precisely through such evidences of God's presence and power: "for Christ plays in ten thousand places, lovely in limbs, and lovely in eyes not his to the Father through the features of men's faces."[18] The saints are not long ago and far away; they are among us, quietly bearing witness as nurses and teachers and mothers and soldiers and cooks and waiters and busboys. They are, like Brother Lawrence, attending to the needs of others with unobtrusive devotion, bringing the presence of God in the world to expression through simple (but not easy) service.[19]

There are also men and women of our own time whose devotion to God and service to neighbor have provided examples of intense and sustained discipleship. I will consider two males at greater length below, but I begin by reminding the reader of a number of holy women whose love of God was expressed through an embodied love of the poor and needy—not long ago and far away but within the world shaped by modernity.

The name "Mother Teresa" (1910–1997) commands instant recognition, for her dedication to the poorest among the poor in India was widely publicized and made her,[20] like Mahatma Gandhi or Nelson Mandela, a figure of international renown—and controversy—in the twen-

---

17. James Martin, *My Life with the Saints* (Chicago: Loyola, 2018).

18. Gerard Manley Hopkins (1844–1889), "As Kingfishers Catch Fire."

19. As an experiment, I once asked a group of Presbyterians—for whom I was leading a small retreat based on my book *Living Jesus*—to share with each other their answer to this question: from what saint did I learn Jesus? Once these Reformed Christians accepted the terminology of "saints," they shared with each other and with me the most remarkable narratives of learning Jesus (and being led to Jesus) by significant people in their lives—grandparents and teachers dominant among them. It was consistently the way such figures conducted themselves rather than the words they spoke that was convicting.

20. In 1969, Malcolm Muggeridge produced a documentary called *Something Beautiful for God* that began decades of unrelenting public attention, including her receiving the 1979 Nobel Peace Prize, whose financial award she donated to the work for the poor. Her life and ministry figured centrally in at least three subsequent films.

tieth century.[21] It is all too easy amid the honors and publicity showered on the elderly Teresa to forget that this tiny Rumanian woman dedicated herself to God as a nun at the age of eighteen and in 1929, at the age of nineteen, went to Calcutta where, having learned Bengali and worked as a teacher, felt called in 1948 to hands-on ministry to the poor, against all odds establishing orphanages, clinics, soup kitchens, and above all hospices (open to people of all faiths) for those wretchedly ill from leprosy, HIV/AIDS, and tuberculosis. She formed her female helpers and associates into a religious order—the Missionaries of Charity—that now numbers some 4,500 nuns and continues the same work among the poor in 133 countries.[22]

Female disciples have also made their witness to God in the United States. Frances Xavier Cabrini (1850–1917), for example, was born a sickly child in Italy but with seven other women formed the Missionary Sisters of the Sacred Heart of Jesus (1880). She was sent by the pope to the United States to care for Italian immigrants. Despite her poor health, she managed to found schools, orphanages, and hospitals, some sixty-seven of them all across the country. Elizabeth Ann Seton (1774–1821), in contrast, was born to socially prominent parents in New York and was raised as an Episcopalian. She married a wealthy businessman and, while raising five children and six stepchildren, continued the kind of social ministry she had learned from her own stepmother. She lost her husband and her wealth in 1803. She became a Catholic in 1805 and started an academy for women. In 1809, she founded the Sisters of Charity, an order that established orphanages and schools as far west as Saint Louis by 1830. Seton herself died in 1821 at the age of forty-six. Katherine Drexel (1858–1955) was similarly born to a very wealthy banking family in Philadelphia but took a vow of poverty and founded the Sisters of the Blessed Sacrament in 1891. She used her inherited wealth to address the needs of Native Americans and Blacks in the southern and southwestern

21. Charges against her tend to be based on her (thoroughly Catholic) stances on contraception and abortion, on the careless use of donations, on the failure of her clinics and hospices to have state-of-the-art technology, and on the conviction that in some fashion she and her work must be fraudulent.

22. It is worth noting that while—like her namesake Teresa of Ávila—Teresa experienced severe periods of spiritual dryness (or alienation) for much of her life, she never wavered from her commitment to prayer and the care of the needy.

United States, financing over sixty missions and schools, including the historically Black (and Catholic) Xavier University in New Orleans.

Such examples remind us of the powerful and effective witness to God made by religious orders of women. These founders of orders are exceptional in their ability and in their devotion to God, it is true, but it must be remembered that their witness was amplified by the thousands of women who joined their communities and (often in great need themselves) spent their lives in service to the dispossessed of the earth. As such religious orders diminish in size, and as so much of their mission has been taken over by state and corporate agencies, it is easy to forget the extraordinary work they did—and often still do—for the little ones in the name of Christ.[23]

Nuns did not own a patent on radical discipleship. Dorothy Day (1897–1980) was a thoroughly secular version of sanctity. Raised Episcopalian, her early life was decidedly bohemian in character.[24] Working as a journalist, she had a number of love affairs (and an abortion) before being married. Rather than abort another child—as her husband desired—she left her marriage and raised a daughter by herself. She became Catholic (and an oblate of the Order of Saint Benedict) and began writing essays and articles for the lay Catholic journal, *Commonweal*. She found focus for her anarchic, pacifist, and socialist tendencies when she met and began working with Peter Maurin in 1932, founding with him the radical journal, *The Catholic Worker* in 1933—which is still published.[25] She spent the rest of her life in the Catholic Worker movement, feeding the poor and homeless of the Bowery in New York City every day at her hospitality house and establishing communal farms in upstate New York. She never ceased agitating for racial justice and protesting war. Arrested many times for her civil disobedience (the last time in her late seventies), she remained faithful to her radical dedication to God's kingdom to the end.[26]

23. See especially Mary Jo Weaver, *New Catholic Women: A Contemporary Challenge to Traditional Religious Authority* (Bloomington: Indiana University Press, 1995).

24. See her autobiography, *The Long Loneliness* (New York: Harper & Brothers, 1952), and the short biography by Patrick Jordan, *Dorothy Day: Love in Action* (Collegeville, MN: Liturgical Press, 2015).

25. The name of the paper set it in explicit opposition to the Communist publication, *The Daily Worker*, which began publication in 1924 and advanced the party positions.

26. Like Mother Teresa, she received much positive recognition late in life—which

Less celebrated but no less radical in her discipleship was Catherine de Hueck Doherty (1896–1985).[27] Born to great wealth as a baroness in pre-revolutionary Russia, she was a decorated nurse in the front lines of World War I. She fled the revolution with her first husband in 1917 and emigrated to Canada. Having been married at the age of fifteen to a first cousin who was spectacularly unfaithful, she had her marriage annulled. In 1934, she sold her possessions and began Friendship House as a ministry of communal living with the poor of Toronto. A second house was established in Harlem to serve the impoverished among the Black community. She was an ardent activist on behalf of racial justice. Before deciding to be a Trappist monk, Thomas Merton was a frequent participant in this radical service and was seriously tempted to join that work permanently. In 1947, with her second husband, the journalist Eddie Doherty, she began the Madonna House Apostolate in Ontario, Canada, which offered a vision of communally living out the gospel in daily life. Lay men and women as well as priests took vows of celibacy and poverty as they joined the apostolate, which eventually spread to other locations. Catherine Doherty was a profoundly charismatic woman—as all witnesses attest—who sought to merge Eastern (Orthodox) and Catholic spiritualities in some thirty books, advocating in particular the practice of periodic contemplative prayer in a *postinia*—a small hut that serves as a hermitage.

This list of holy women can be extended almost indefinitely. But I want to offer a slightly longer consideration of two men whose lives present themselves as examples of radical discipleship, Dietrich Bonhoeffer and Thomas Merton. I choose them because they are already well known, because their published writings are extensive, widely available, and remarkably self-revealing, and because their (brief) lives demonstrate how an authentic imitation of Christ demands personal transformation as well as—or even as the basis of—social engagement. In both figures, we see how personal piety and radical social witness are not contrary but complementary.

---

did not deter her from her commitment to a radical life—and was the subject posthumously of several admiring films.

27. See Donald Alfred Guglielmi, *Staritsa: The Spiritual Maternity of Catherine de Hueck Doherty* (Rome: Pontifical University of Saint Thomas, 2003); Lorene Hanley Duquin, *They Call Her the Baroness* (New York: Alba House, 1995).

Dietrich Bonhoeffer (1906–1945)

No great argument is needed for the social commitment of Dietrich Bonhoeffer.[28] Even those totally unaware of his theological works know that he was a leader in the Confessing Church during the Nazi regime in Germany (1932–1945), that he engaged in extensive ecumenical conversations on the Continent and in England, that he publicly preached against the Nazi usurpation of power with its programs of eugenics and persecution of the Jews, that he was a participant in the conspiracy to assassinate Hitler, that he spent his last years in prison, and that at the age of thirty-nine he was executed by the Nazis. What is perhaps less known and appreciated is that his active engagement with the world was supported by a deep dedication to the person of Jesus Christ, in whose name he spoke and acted.

With his twin sister Sabine, he grew up in a privileged German family with extensive social connections and with high standards of achievement; his father was an eminent academic psychologist. His family was Christian and exercised domestic forms of piety but did not attend church. A brilliant student and gifted musician, Bonhoeffer surprisingly chose theology as his academic field of endeavor, embracing the rigorous historical-critical perspectives of teachers like Adolf von Harnack but showing his independence—a constant character trait—by writing a dissertation in 1927 on the church called *Communio Sanctorum* ("Communion of Saints"), an unusual title and topic for a German theologian at that time. He argued for a social understanding of the church. Only twenty-one when he completed his dissertation, he was too young to be ordained as a pastor. At this point, it would be fair to say that Bonhoeffer saw theology primarily as an intellectual exercise, as a professional career that would be carried out in the university, in the same way his brothers were scientists or lawyers.

To fill the time until he could be ordained, Bonhoeffer sailed to the United States in 1930 to study at Union Theological Seminary in New

28. For a (very) full treatment of Bonhoeffer's life and thought, see above all Eberhard Bethge, *Dietrich Bonhoeffer: A Biography*, trans. Eric Mosbacher et al., rev. and ed. Victoria J. Barnett (Minneapolis: Fortress, 2000). A much-criticized shorter treatment by Eric Metaxas, *Bonhoeffer: Pastor, Martyr, Prophet, Spy* (Nashville: Nelson, 2011), nevertheless provides a more accessible overview of his life.

York, where the social gospel of Rauschenbusch still exercised a strong influence. Bonhoeffer was not impressed by the theological depth of American students. But through a friend, he went to Harlem to hear the preaching of Adam Clayton Powell and learned about the struggle for civil rights. He also traveled to the segregated South and to Mexico. He learned how the struggle for civil rights among African Americans drew its inspiration and power from the deep piety of the Black church. He began to understand that his more academic, theoretical approach to theology needed to be grounded in the actual experience of the oppressed.

When Bonhoeffer returned to Germany in 1931 to be ordained and to take up a position as a lecturer at the University of Berlin, he found that the option of being simply a scientific theologian was no longer open. Hitler came to power in 1932 and imposed the totalitarian rule of Nazism, which included control of the church as a manifestation of Aryan ideology. The German National Church quickly aligned itself with the Nazi regime. In the face of these circumstances, Bonhoeffer saw that he had to turn from phraseology to reality and underwent an intense conversion experience that turned him from a nominal to a committed disciple of Jesus Christ.

He was an author of the Bethel Confession, which was one of the cornerstones of the Confessing Church that set itself in direct opposition to the idolatrous claims of National Socialism. And with others in the Lutheran, Reformed, and United churches, he signed the Barmen Declaration composed by theologian Karl Barth—a declaration of unswerving obedience to the word of God and the Lord Jesus rather than dictates of state rule. During this period, Bonhoeffer represented the Confessing Church at ecumenical meetings and served for a year at a German Lutheran church in London. His lectures at the University of Berlin in 1932–1933 became the book *Creation and Fall*, which revealed his willingness—in contrast to all the scientific biblical scholarship of the day—to reflect directly and theologically on Scripture, in this case the first three chapters of Genesis.

Between 1935 and 1937, Bonhoeffer had his teaching license at the university revoked and served the Confessing Church as the head of its seminary at Finkenwalde, while continuing to represent it at sharply contentious ecumenical meetings. It was during this period that he used

Matthew's Gospel (especially the Sermon on the Mount) to reflect more deeply on the true meaning of discipleship. The fruit of these reflections is his 1937 book *The Cost of Discipleship*, which is widely and rightly regarded as a contemporary spiritual classic that eschews the easy construal of Christianity as the friend of any and all cultures and embraces the costly following of Jesus that demands resistance to every form of idolatrous claims in any and all cultures.[29]

The seminary had to become truly underground when Finkenwalde was closed by the Nazis in 1937, and in 1940, the seminary was raided by the gestapo and its students arrested. While serving as the director and spiritual guide of theology students under duress, Bonhoeffer's experience of a diaspora church encouraged him to think more deeply on the experience of the early church and specifically on the monastic model of discipleship. He structured the seminarians' life around a common life of prayer, study, music, meals, and relaxation, and he showed himself to be a true pastor, willing to sacrifice his own time, energy, and attention on his students. After his death, his formulation of the common life as witness was published as *Life Together*, which repristinates the ascetical practices of the earlier tradition for mid-twentieth-century German Protestants. Similarly, his lovely small work *The Psalms: The Prayer-Book of the Church* could have been written, or read with profit, by Thomas à Kempis—whom he quotes several times in *Life Together*. Bonhoeffer's favorite psalm, on which he meditated and spoke frequently, was Psalm 119, a meditation on God's law as the path to true wisdom and life.

After his students were scattered by the Nazis, in 1938, Bonhoeffer returned to the United States for a very short period but quickly returned to Germany to share the fate of his people. Forbidden to teach, to print, or to publish, he nevertheless maintained contact with his students and continued writing. His *Ethics*—written in large part at the Benedictine monastery at Ettal, where the monks provided sanctuary—was a major project that was published only after his death. The topic of what God wants of us was much on his mind, because from 1943 on, while un-

---

29. The German title was simply *Nachfolge* ("following"), but the English title captures the central theme of rejecting "cheap grace" in favor of the "costly grace" of the gospel. Reading the book in light of Bonhoeffer's circumstances, the looming threat of the Nazi ideology is everywhere apparent even when not directly stated.

der the cover of being an intelligence agent for the *Abwehr*, he took the deeply ambiguous step of joining the conspiracy against Hitler, serving as a courier between members of the conspiracy.

For him, such a drastic move was part of the cost of authentic discipleship and the riskiest form of love for his neighbors. It was this role that led to his arrest and incarceration in Tegel prison for one and a half years—where he wrote the materials that were published posthumously as *Letters and Papers from Prison*. In a fit of rage eleven days before his own suicide, Hitler ordered Bonhoeffer's execution, and he was hanged at Flossenburg concentration camp on April 9, 1945. His fellow prisoners bore witness to the way he lived out his discipleship to the end, serving as friend, counselor, and patron both to them and to the prison guards.

Bonhoeffer's radical challenge to the Nazi regime and to the culturally accommodating National Church was not based on a sociological theory or even in a theological proposition but in the profound conviction that the living God alone was to be worshiped and that Jesus Christ is Lord, a conviction that cannot be derived from social analysis but only from a deep immersion in the prayerful reading of Scripture and in the practice of prayer itself. Bonhoeffer's is an example of a discipleship that is at once totally oriented to the love of God and totally expressed through love of neighbor.

THOMAS MERTON (1915–1968)

At first blush, Thomas Merton's seems to be the perfect example of a world-rejecting discipleship.[30] Born in France of artistic parents who died young, he was nevertheless supported by wealthy relatives and grew up as a brilliant, entitled, and intemperate rebel (completely scornful of anything religious) who made a hash of his schooling in British public schools and Cambridge University, before coming to the United States—

30. For Merton's life in great detail, see Michael Mott, *The Seven Mountains of Thomas Merton* (Boston: Houghton Mifflin, 1984); for a crisper treatment, see Jim Forest, *Living with Wisdom: A Life of Thomas Merton*, rev. ed. (Maryknoll, NY: Orbis Books, 2008). For my own reflections on the man who was an exemplar for me and other monks of my generation, see "The Myth, the Monk, the Man: Reading and Rereading Thomas Merton," *Commonweal* 142 (2015): 22–24, and "How a Monk Learns Mercy: Thomas Merton and the Rule of Benedict," *Commonweal* 145 (2018): 21–24.

having been cut off by his godparent patron in England—and gaining some traction as a student at Columbia University. In New York, he lived a bohemian life with his intellectual friends but found himself drawn by a series of encounters (the reading of *The Imitation of Christ* among them) to the Catholic faith and the growing desire to become—as proposed by his friend Robert Lax—a saint.

Failing in his attempt to become a Franciscan and failing repeatedly to get his poetry or fiction published—he was first and last a writer— he was attracted while teaching at Saint Bonaventure University to the social radicalism of Baroness Catherine de Hueck Doherty, and he spent time working at the Friendship House, thinking perhaps that this was God's call to him. But a retreat at the monastery of Gethsemani in Kentucky led to his seeking admittance there in 1941 as a member of this strictest of all monastic orders, the Cistercians of Strict Observance (Trappists).

Merton began as a monk with a strong sense of *fuga mundi* ("flight from the world") and sought in the strict observance of the *Rule of Saint Benedict* the discipline he both craved and resented. He was, and remained, however, a good monk, avid in his pursuit of prayer and contemplation, and (in addition to his writing) serving his fellow monks as forester and then as novice master—a position that, like Bonhoeffer's directing of Finkenwalde, demanded both the regular teaching and spiritual direction of other monks. With the permission of his abbot, he wrote an account of his conversion called *The Seven Storey Mountain*, which became an international bestseller in 1948, making Merton the most famous monk in the world and drawing hundreds of others into the monastic life. For his next twenty years, Merton had to deal with the ambiguous fact of celebrity and with the reputation of being a preeminent authority on traditional, specifically monastic, spirituality. His early writings such as *Sign of Jonas*, *Seeds of Contemplation*, and *No Man Is an Island* met the expectations of readers seeking to combine in their own lives what Jean LeClercq calls "the love of learning and the desire for God."[31]

Merton's own quest of sanctity was simple in nature but was made complex due to the complicated personality of a brilliant and funda-

---

31. Jean LeClercq, *The Love of Learning and the Desire for God: A Study of Monastic Culture* (New York: Fordham University Press, 1961).

mentally restless man. His journey as a disciple is vividly depicted in the seven volumes of his *Journals*, which show him constantly pulled in two directions. One impulse led him to an ever-deeper experience of the contemplative life, manifested in his desire to live as a hermit—eventually securing a hermitage on the monastic grounds of Gethsemani—and in his correspondence with other contemplatives, including those from other religious traditions. (He was attracted to Zen Buddhism and Sufism in particular.)

The other impulse was stimulated by an epiphanic moment while in Louisville (the city nearest to Gethsemani) for a doctor's appointment: he was stunned by a profound sense of empathy for all of God's creatures. Increasingly, then, Merton began to engage from his monastic post the great social issues of his time, meeting and corresponding with radical activists like Dorothy Day, Jim Forest, John Howard Griffin, Daniel Berrigan, and others, and writing passionately against racial segregation, war, and the economic distortions of contemporary life. In works like *Raids on the Unspeakable* (1962), *Seeds of Destruction* (1964), *Conjectures of a Guilty Bystander* (1966), and *Faith and Violence* (1968), Merton was outspoken in his opposition to the idolatries of the age. His prophetic stance met with considerable opposition among ecclesiastical authorities and among readers who wanted him to remain the pious monk of his early works, but Merton was convinced that the contemplative life gave a unique view of the secular world that must be given articulation.

Merton died suddenly and by accident while at a monastic conference in Thailand in 1968. He was only fifty-three. His remarkable body of writings continued to be published after his death and continued inspiring both those who find in them guidance to contemplation and those who find in them the basis for a life of Christian activism. There can be little question, though, that the convincing character of Merton's turn to the world was grounded in the authenticity of his search for God in prayer.

CONCLUSION

Why are Bonhoeffer and Merton good examples of discipleship in today's world? It is certainly not because of their personalities: each had more than a share of human quirks and faults; neither was—on the evidence—a particularly comforting presence; stimulating and challenging, yes, comfortable, not so much. Bonhoeffer was demanding of himself and of others; Merton could swing between the antic and the morose.

Nor is imitating them a matter of duplicating the specifics of their lives: we are not called to conspire against totalitarian rule or to enter a Cistercian monastery. Rather, we look to them for the character marks of the disciple, or saint, which is to say, we look for the marks of the image of Christ shown in their manner of life. They are of interest to the biographer for all the ways in which their historical existence was distinctive in the past; they are of interest to those seeking sanctity for the ways in which their character revealed the character of Christ and continues to reveal it to those desiring to be disciples today.

Three things in particular strike me as reasons why these two men of the past century are of particular importance for those pondering the meaning of discipleship today.

A first is that both were radicals rather than progressives. I mean by this that neither aligned himself with a particular scheme for the improvement of society but resisted evil within society in the name of the gospel. They did not propose replacing one political party with another, one economic system for another, or one social organization for another. Rather, they identified and challenged the idolatrous impulses within all such proposals. In the sense that both Merton and Bonhoeffer were *evangelical*, that is, based themselves on the sovereignty of God revealed in Jesus Christ, they were also profoundly countercultural.

A second is that, although they were both intellectuals, deeply cultured and broadly learned, they did not for a moment submit their minds to the epistemological hegemony of modernity. Instead, they allowed their minds to imagine the world that Scripture imagines—for both, the Psalms were particularly pertinent—and on the basis of *that* epistemological standpoint, they were able to discern, define, and defy the idolatrous claims of other ideologies. Because they practiced the ancient asceticism of spiritual attentiveness—checking their own consciences for the ways vice and self-deception might be at work—they were able to challenge the self-delusionary pretenses of what Merton calls "the behavior of Titans." Because Bonhoeffer believed in God's love for all humans, he stood against the racist and genocidal policies of the Nazis; because Merton was persuaded that all humans bore the image of God, he opposed the racist policies of the segregated United States.

A third reason is that each of them read Scripture passionately as a word of God directed to their own lives and the state of the world. Consistent with their refusal to view reality through the lens of the Enlightenment—much less the pseudoscientific reductions of religion advanced by Christianity's cultured despisers in the nineteenth century—they showed no interest in the academic dissection of the Bible in the name of history. The notion that a scholarly construct called the historical Jesus should replace the Gospels as a model of discipleship would have struck both Bonhoeffer and Merton as ludicrous. They read all of Scripture in the manner that the tradition before them had read it, as the source of a wisdom that disclosed God's vision for the world and therefore as the source of all genuine human wisdom as well, and thus the basis for prayerful and engaged witness to the world.

We can regard Bonhoeffer and Merton as twentieth-century saints. In traditional terms, one is a martyr, and the other a confessor. If the language of sanctity is difficult for us, we can at least recognize in them genuine discipleship. Because we know so much about each of them— they wrote so much in such a short life!—we can tell that they were flawed human beings, who experienced uncertainty, doubt, temptations and failings, fear and humiliation. Like us, in fact. But in their lives, we can also see how the Holy Spirit can transform an intellectualizing Lutheran theologian and an aestheticizing Catholic monk into the image of Christ.

In them, we see that discipleship means imitating Jesus's absolute obedience to the Father. Neither Bonhoeffer nor Merton was a careerist, time server, people pleaser who sought to secure himself by going along with the crowd. Instead, they risked everything to follow what they perceived as God's call to them, no matter that this following meant the cost of home, loved ones, possessions, honor, and life itself.

In them, we also see that discipleship means imitating the self-donative and self-emptying service of Jesus—"who did not please himself" (Rom 15:3)—to others. The martyr Bonhoeffer risked and at the end gave his life so that others might live free of a murderous ideology that corrupted all human exchanges. The confessor Merton gave his life teaspoon by teaspoon in the service of his brothers in the monastery, in his hospitality to visitors of every kind, and in the countless hours he spent writing in witness to the wisdom of the Christian past and of other cultures, so that his readers might catch a glimpse of what love of God and love of neighbor might mean.

It is certainly the case that the mind of Christ is best learned by observing those who live by that mind and imitating them. The living Christ shows his presence and power through the authentic disciples we call saints. May it not also be the case that the greatest motivation for seeking to be a saint, to live as an authentic disciple, is so that others might praise and imitate the work of the living Christ that dimly shines through our flawed and failed humanity?

Suggested Reading

Especially in chapters 2, 3, and 7, I discuss or refer to many writings that, through the history of Christianity, express what I have called the classic vision of discipleship. Such works are available and accessible to contemporary believers. They are resources to nourish and support true discipleship. This list is selective and suggestive, containing works I mention in the text, but leaving out such wonderful hortatory writings as Origen's *On Prayer*, or Augustine's *Commentary on the First Letter of John*. It goes without saying, I hope, that genuine discipleship is best formed through the reading of Scripture, above all the letters of Saint Paul, who first and definitively taught us what it means to live with the mind of Christ.

Collections and Series

Ancient Christian Commentary on Scripture, ed. Thomas C. Oden (Inter-
 Varsity Press)
Ancient Christian Writers (Paulist Press)
Ante-Nicene Fathers (reprinted by Hendrickson)
Classics of Western Spirituality (Paulist Press)
Devotional Classics: Selected Readings for Individuals and Groups, ed. Richard J.
 Foster and James Bryan Smith (HarperSanFrancisco, 1993)
Fathers of the Church (Catholic University of America Press)
Nicene and Post-Nicene Fathers, Series 1 and 2 (reprinted by Hendrickson)

100–1000

Athanasius. *The Life of Anthony*. Translated by Robert C. Gregg. Classics of
 Western Spirituality. New York: Paulist, 1980.

Augustine. *Commentary on the Lord's Sermon on the Mount*. Fathers of the
    Church 11. Lanham, MD: Catholic University of America Press, 1951.

Benedict of Nursia. *The Rule of St. Benedict*. Edited by Timothy Fry, OSB. New
    York: Vintage, 1998.

Evagrius of Pontus. *Chapters on Prayer*. In *The Praktikos and Chapters on
    Prayer*. Translated by John Eudes Bamberger, OCSO. Collegeville, MN:
    Cistercian Publications, 1970.

Gregory the Great. *Moralia on Job*. 6 volumes. Translated by Brian Kerns,
    OCSO. Collegeville, MN: Cistercian Publications, 2014–2017.

Ignatius of Antioch: The Letters. Translated by Alistair Stewart. Yonkers, NY:
    St. Vladimir's Seminary Press, 2013.

John Cassian. *Conferences*. Translated by Colm Luibheid. Rev. ed. New York:
    Paulist Press, 1985.

John Cassian. *The Institutes*. Translated by Boniface Ramsey, OP. New York:
    Paulist Press, 2000.

John Climacus. *The Ladder of Divine Ascent*. Translated by Colm Luibheid
    and Norman Russell. New York: Paulist Press, 1982.

Origen. *Exhortation to Martyrdom*. In *Prayer; Exhortation to Martyrdom*.
    Translated by John J. O'Meara. Westminster, MD: Newman, 1954.

The Sayings of the Desert Fathers. Translated by Benedicta Ward, SLG. Col-
    legeville, MN: Cistercian Publications, 1984.

1000–1600

Anonymous. *Cloud of Unknowing*. In *The Cloud of Unknowing and Other
    Works*. Translated by Clifton Wolters. New York: Penguin, 1978.

Bernard of Clairvaux. *Sermons on the Song of Songs*. In *Saint Bernard on
    the Song of Songs; Sermones in Cantica canticorum*. Translated by a
    religious of C.S.M.V. London: A. R. Mowbray, 1952.

Julian of Norwich. *Showings*. Edited by Denise N. Baker. New York: Norton,
    2005.

Rolle, Richard. *The Fire of Love*. Translated by Clifton Wolters. Harmond-
    sworth: Penguin, 1972.

Thomas à Kempis. *The Imitation of Christ*. Translated by Joseph N. Tylenda.
    New York: Vintage, 1998.

1600–1900

Arndt, Johann. *True Christianity*. Translated by Peter Erb. New York: Paulist, 1979.

Brother Lawrence. *The Practice of the Presence of God*. Translated by John J. Delaney. Garden City, NY: Image, 1977.

Calvin, John. *Institutes of the Christian Religion*. Edited by John T. McNeill. Translated by Ford Lewis Battles. Philadelphia: Westminster, 1960.

Edwards, Jonathan. *Charity and Its Fruits: Christian Love as Manifested in the Heart and Life*. Edited by Tryon Edwards. Edinburgh: Banner of Truth Trust, 2000.

Francis de Sales. *An Introduction to the Devout Life*. Translated by Allan Ross. London: Burns, Oates, and Washbourne, 1924.

Gerhardt, Johann. *Sacred Meditations*. Translated by C. W. Heisler. Philadelphia: Lutheran Publication Society, 1896.

Ignatius of Loyola. *Spiritual Exercises*. In *The Spiritual Exercises and Selected Works*. Edited by George E. Ganss et al. New York: Paulist, 1991.

Kierkegaard, Søren. *Works of Love*. Translated by Howard Hong and Edna Hong. New York: Harper, 1962.

Law, William. *A Serious Call to a Devout and Holy Life; The Spirit of Love*. Edited by Paul G. Stanwood. Classics of Western Spirituality. New York: Paulist, 1978.

Luther, Martin. *The Freedom of a Christian*. Translated by Mark D. Tranvik. Minneapolis: Fortress, 2008.

Scupoli, Lorenzo. *The Spiritual Combat*. In *The Spiritual Combat, and a Treatise on Peace of the Soul*. Translated by William Lester and Robert Mohan. New York: Paulist, 1978.

Taylor, Jeremy. *Rule and Exercises for Holy Living and Holy Dying*. London: William Pickering, 1847.

Teresa of Ávila. *The Way of Perfection*. Edited by Henry L. Carrigan Jr. Brewster, MA: Paraclete, 2000.

Wesley, John. *A Plain Account of Genuine Christianity*. London: Paramore, 1795.

1900–2000

Bonhoeffer, Dietrich. *The Cost of Discipleship*. Translated by R. H. Fuller. London: SCM Press, 1948.

Chambers, Oswald. *My Utmost for His Highest*. Grand Rapids: Discovery House, 2017.

Chesterton, G. K. *Orthodoxy*. New York: Lane, 1911.

Foster, Richard J. *Celebration of Discipline: The Path to Spiritual Growth*. 3rd ed. New York: HarperCollins, 1998.

Lewis, C. S. *Mere Christianity*. New York: Macmillan, 1952.

Merton, Thomas. *Seeds of Contemplation*. New York: New Directions, 1949.

Nouwen, Henri. *Reaching Out: Three Moments of the Spiritual Life*. Garden City, NY: Doubleday, 1975.

Oden, Thomas. *The Transforming Power of Grace*. Nashville: Abingdon, 1993.

Peterson, Eugene H. *As Kingfishers Catch Fire: A Conversation on the Ways of God Formed by the Words of God*. New York: Waterbook, 2017.

Piper, John. *A Hunger for God: Desiring God through Fasting and Prayer*. Wheaton, IL: Crossway, 1997.

Rutledge, Fleming. *The Bible and the New York Times*. Grand Rapids: Eerdmans, 1998.

Sproul, R. C. *Pleasing God*. Wheaton, IL: Tyndale House, 1988.

Thurman, Howard. *Meditations of the Heart*. New York: Harper & Row, 1953.

Tozer, A. W. *The Pursuit of God*. Abbotsford, WI: Aneko, 2015.

Willard, Dallas. *The Divine Conspiracy: Rediscovering Our Hidden Life with God*. San Francisco: HarperSanFrancisco, 1998.

Williams, Rowan. *Being Disciples: Essentials of the Christian Life*. London: SPCK, 2016.

Index